RAMBLE ON

Also by Sinclair McKay

The Secret Life of Bletchley Park
The Man With The Golden Touch: How the Bond Films
Conquered The World

SINCLAIR McKAY

Ramble On

The Story of our Love
for Walking Britain

FOURTH ESTATE • *London*

1

The right of Sinclair McKay to be identified as the author
of this work has been asserted by him in accordance
with the Copyright, Designs and Patents Act 1988

A catalogue record for this book is
available from the British Library

ISBN 978-0-00-742864-9

Typeset in Minion by G&M Designs Limited,
Raunds, Northamptonshire
Printed and bound in Great Britain by
Clays Ltd, St Ives plc

MIX
Paper from
responsible sources
FSC
www.fsc.org   **FSC C007454**

FSC™ is a non-profit international organisation established to promote
the responsible management of the world's forests. Products carrying the
FSC label are independently certified to assure consumers that they come
from forests that are managed to meet the social, economic and
ecological needs of present and future generations,
and other controlled sources.

Find out more about HarperCollins and the environment at
www.harpercollins.co.uk/green

To my mother Helen and father Peter

CONTENTS

INTRODUCTION

You are not long out of the railway station before you catch the desired view: the enchanting old windmills – one white, one black – on the crest of the hill, like odd little boats with bright wooden sails riding a giant green wave. A map is scarcely necessary, your destination can be in no doubt. The authorities have fallen over themselves to pepper the road with brown signs that point insistently. They gesture to the 'South Downs', as if to say: 'Well – why else would you be here?'

The initial stretch of railway-hugging concrete pathway is slightly urinous in smell, but bordered on the other side by delicate woodlands, throbbing with bluebells on this sunny spring day. It is a trifling nuisance, this blistered tarmac cut-through that discreetly ushers you out of the Sussex town of Hassocks; a tiny price to pay for the goal that lies ahead. A mile later, you look right up again, at the green hill with its white skeleton of chalk beneath. You rejoin the 'South Downs' path, with more of those signs urging you on; you gaze up at that distant ridge, and the sky above that with all its pale blue promise. No one who considers themselves to be any kind of a walker could conceivably hold back.

The old children's story formulation 'over the hills and far away' is one of the most evocative phrases in the English language. It expresses that impossibly ancient curiosity and yearning for adventure; there is also, somehow, the possibility of transformation. Any rambler will also know that the phrase has a physical truth; that when one is walking across a great plain towards hills, the urge to see beyond them becomes magnetic, instinctive. To stop, to turn, to go back requires a powerful exertion of will. So here I am, after a short, rigorous climb, by those old windmills called Jack and Jill, but gazing at yet more green ridges above. This is the South Downs Way, in the South Downs National Park. It is the most recent of such Parks, having attained this special status in 2009. This path is a superb and beautiful tribute to a movement that has been campaigning not merely for decades – but centuries.

On a day such as this, with a refreshing but subtle breeze, and the sun dazzling down, the obvious weekend destination for urban fugitives is not here. It is about five miles to the south: the huge majority of the people crammed – standing room only – on to the train out of London were heading for the beach at Brighton. But we who are up on this ridge – and there are a good many of us – have a purer purpose in mind. And as we pass one another, on that path that is now snaking around towards Ditchling Beacon, we recognise each other through clothing conventions.

There are the big beige sunhats, with a hint of floppy foppishness; the baggy shorts of indeterminable synthetic fibre; the sturdy boots, laces wrapped around like thick spaghetti. For some, there is also a map, worn around the neck on a lanyard. And having made the effort of getting up this hill – as we will see, there is always this Calvinist question of effort – we happy few are richly rewarded. This is a ridge of cattle-nibbled grassland – the grass is crew-cut, military neat – spotted with cakes of sun-dried dung. For those with the eyes and the experience to see, here is ribwort plantain, squinancywort and Devil's bit scabious. Meanwhile, dancing and being hurled in random directions by puffs of breeze, are rare butterflies such as the Adonis blue and the Chalkhill blue. Come the summer, there will be the shy, secretive magenta of retiring pyramidal orchids.

This path – bright with white chalk – is on a gentler upward gradient now, and sweeping across the ridge to Ditchling Beacon. As you walk along this handsome escarpment some 800 feet up, the woods and green fields of Sussex are laid out beneath you, sharp and neat and crisply three-dimensional in the bright sunshine. There are churches and old windmills and manor houses and playing fields; there are also intimations of distant post-industrial warehousing and offices. You are looking at the past and the present simultaneously. Meanwhile, small birds compete in the blowy skies above. The attentive might see linnets, or yellowhammers, or skylarks. There is one elderly couple here with binoculars, lurking by the bushes of bitter-yellow gorse. One assumes they are here for avian reasons, as opposed to human surveillance. You always think the best of your fellow walkers. When seen from a great distance – in our walking gear, on hillsides, or marching along the edges of fields – we ramblers ourselves look like tiny colourful butterflies milling around on green plant-life. There we go: processing up slopes, in lines, like fluorescent ants. We are the very image of unabashed enthusiasm. Sometimes, the more adverse the conditions, the better. Such dedicated walkers will look out upon stinging rain whipping across bare moorland, take a deep breath of pleasure, then stride forwards – and upwards, into the raging storm.

Daniel Defoe, who made a tour of the nation in the 1700s, would have regarded such walkers with some mystification. In the eighteenth century, the only people to be seen tramping across such a landscape either worked it, owned it, or were trespassing on it. The idea that ordinary men and women would simply walk upon it for pleasure and recreation would have struck him as insane. As it was, he was already quite rude enough about those before him who had professed to have seen the beauty in landscapes such as this.

But fashions changed – quite soon after Defoe passed away, in fact. In the 1700s, the stern mountains and valleys began to draw poets and painters who were freshly alive to the more sublime aspects of nature. The echoes of their enthusiasm are still heard now. Whether we know it or not, we continue to be influenced by their passions, even if we consider our own regular rambles to be happily quotidian. These days, for a huge number of people, any satisfactory weekend should ideally include a drive out into the country, a loading up of the knapsack with refreshments ready for a good few hours of walking. The ostensible reasons all overlap: the need for some exercise and fresh air after a week sitting in an office, staring at a computer; the desire to see a wider horizon, one not interrupted by houses, tower blocks, or out-of-town supermarkets; and then perhaps the slightly more spiritual sense that it is important to keep in touch with the land itself – that by planting our feet on grass and soil, we are reasserting our true, organic natures. Yes, those reasons are certainly part of it. But it goes rather deeper than that.

It is estimated that some 18 million Britons enjoy regular country walks. Less casually, the Ramblers' Association has over half a million members. Think of all these people, taking off on Sunday mornings, eager to stride across meadows, and to survey grand views. Think how, just a few generations ago, so many of these people would have been spending Sunday morning in church. Walking is sometimes a form of religious practice in itself; a meditation or even prayer, but at a steady pace. The very idea that there should be an official association for those who enjoy walking is in itself telling. We spend colossal quantities of money on our desire to get mud on our boots. Mud that our forebears would have strenuously tried to keep off theirs.

Despite the peaceful, even meditative nature of the pursuit, the story of rambling, as we shall see, is actually a story of constant bitter conflict. It is grand country aristocrats pitted against town-dwelling working class men and women. It is farmers with spring-guns and bone-shattering man-traps dedicating themselves to thwarting those who wish to tread ancient rights of way. It is municipal water boards, hysterically convinced that walkers could infect reservoirs with TB, and doing everything in their power to close off all the land around. It is gamekeepers in tweed with heavy sticks neurotically certain that the slightest suggestion of footsteps on the moor would disturb the partridges and plovers. The story of rambling is, in one sense, a prism through which we can view the ebbs and flows of social conflict in Britain, from the Reformation right up to the present day.

Nor is the story entirely about the pursuit of innocent, wholesome pleasure. There are darker reasons for walking, too. Again, reaching back through history, we find that walking has sometimes been a symptom of depression, even madness. The compulsion that leads the hearty rambler on to the hills is not too far away from the compulsion that has led poets onto long, long walks on which they lost their minds. Sometimes the walker is a tired fugitive; often they are outsiders. These figures move around at the very edge of popular imagination and they are always there.

So it is unsurprising that walking is also threaded through British literature, like a network of well-trodden paths. Celebrated trampers include Wordsworth and Coleridge, the countryman poet John Clare; Jonathan Swift and Jane Austen; Charles Dickens and W. G. Sebald. In many cases, walking is integral to their poetry and their fictions. It brings to the fore far wider truths about human nature. In James Joyce's *Ulysses*, in the space of a single day in Dublin in 1904, Leopold Bloom seems to be constantly walking – from Dignam's funeral to the newspaper office; from pub to beach to brothel. Yet although he is at the centre of the narrative, Bloom is also the novel's great, profoundly moving outsider: it is the others who watch him, as he walks alone.

Walking also carries an element of enlightenment. For instance, many weavers and mill-workers in the nineteenth century educated themselves through their rambles across the land. They became greatly knowledgeable about geology and botany, to the extent that some went on to attain academic posts. Walking, for these men and women, provided intellectual liberation from the grim fetters of urban or domestic life. In the twentieth century, one of the rambling movement's most influential figures was an entirely self-taught man who had left school at thirteen to become a calico printer.

The other curious thing about the story of rambling is that this struggle over forbidden land, the furious conflict over incursion, is an almost uniquely British struggle, certainly in the European context. By contrast, walking throughout Continental Europe – from the experiences of Jean Jacques Rousseau to the film director Werner Herzog – has always been, and still is, relatively free and easy. Over here, the phrase 'Trespassers Will Be Prosecuted' is practically stamped upon the national psyche. Or it was. In the last decade or so, though, there has been a quiet revolution in Britain. The balance has invisibly, miraculously, shifted. And now, the sheer acreage of land that we can stroll across with impunity is one that would have surprised our grandparents.

Stretching even further back, there is an interesting sense of philosophical similarity between today's walking campaigners and the Diggers – the radical seventeenth-century movement, led by Gerrard Winstanley – which aimed to take over tracts of common or vacant land for cultivation. Winstanley's stand, a religious one, was to do with the iniquity of huge expanses of open, fertile land being owned by a few rich individuals. The

Diggers, working in tiny communities, began moving onto patches of common land from Northamptonshire to Surrey, and distributing crops to local villagers. Grand landowners took fright at this apparent anarchy and sent in hired thugs to expel the Diggers – with violence. Winstanley's pleas to the authorities for help met with silence. Yet somehow the essence of Winstanley's short-lived crusade finds a much more fruitful echo in today's Ramblers' Association, which believes that cherished English landscapes – even the most secluded – should not merely be at the disposal of a few property owners, but open for all to roam upon.

The shade of Winstanley might look upon the South Downs Way with pleasure. This trail is ministered to by the National Trust, a charity. This path – and countless thousands others around the country – is the result of a burst of idealism that found its fullest flowering during and after the Second World War. But in effect, be it National Trust, Woodland Trust, National Park or just simple privately-owned land, the fact is that there is now remarkably little hindrance anywhere for the dedicated walker. Certain recent Parliamentary Acts have had a bearing, but the momentum has somehow been more philosophical than political.

Whether they know it or not, walkers have, over the decades and centuries, changed our entire national approach to ideas of property and ownership. Boundaries, both physical and mental, have shifted greatly. The relationship between landowner and walker – very often a source of rancour – has changed like the colours of a kaleidoscope. Perhaps the only constant factor between the two is a sense of wariness. In some cases, today's landowners are warier of walkers than walkers are of them. It wasn't so long ago that some landowners were still illegally employing steel-jawed traps to deter trespassers. It also wasn't so very long ago when local county magistrates could be counted on to favour the landowner's case over that of the walker. Such bias would be relatively unusual to come across now, not least because the relevant laws have changed dramatically even in the space of just the last fifty years or so.

We can drift where we like, within reason. But the other fascinating thing, of course, is why we would wish to do so. Why are we happy to spend so much time yomping across rugged heaths or muddy meadows? That's not as easily answered as you might think. For walking can be as much an unconscious, abstract activity as one involving concrete decisions and plans. My own walking patterns over the years have been quite random. In common with many other Londoners, for instance, I have been pacing different parts of the city by means of exploration for years. There were all those names on the A–Z map, so redolent of bucolic charm: Arnos Grove, Gospel Oak, Burnt Oak, Belvedere. Once you have walked around such places, the rather less than sylvan reality sinks in (no offence to the good people of Belvedere in south-east London, but can I just say – I was not expecting *that*).

Yet the urge to walk persists. Often quite randomly, with only the faintest sense of where you want to get to. Like William Blake, I've wandered through each chartered street. I have certainly marked many faces of woe. But none of that is the reason for walking. It goes deeper and deeper yet. Of late, that twitch, that desire, has taken me with greater frequency beyond the symbolic boundaries of the M25, that eight-laned border around London. Like many who live in the East End, I had some residual apprehension about the countryside; some sense that it was filled with malevolent cattle, barely rational farmers and tightly regulated footpaths from which one was never allowed to deviate. Then, almost from the start, I found that the freedom out there is rather greater than I had imagined. It is still not quite enough for the Ramblers' Association – there are still certain areas, both physical and mental, where the barriers are still in place and full access is not possible. In the time that I, a thoroughgoing townie, have been exploring this undiscovered country – this land of sharp hills and deep hidden valleys, of warm gritstone and bright, slightly vulgar foxgloves, of silent woodlands and windy, roaring coasts – my notions of the countryside formed by 1970s Ladybird books, beautifully painted pictures of dairies and deep red tractors, have changed rather sharply.

The only way to understand a land is to walk it. The only way to drink in its real meaning is to keep it firmly beneath one's feet. In all these years driving up and down motorways, I had no idea about the different sorts of emotional resonance that each individual area has, like a charge of electricity. Drivers can never know this. Only the walker can form the wider view. The question of how we walkers arrived at a position of such extraordinary luxury – the ability, finally, to explore the vast majority of the country, and the huge, almost unquantifiable effect that this has had upon the British landscape – are themes that we shall be exploring as the book progresses.

The story of walking – how the very nature of the activity has changed so much in the last 200 years or so – also happens to be the story of a population's evolving relationship with what we now term 'the countryside' – this single word implying that all forms of landscape are somehow one and the same thing, and that it can always be quite easily separated from urban land. It is a story that embraces all sorts of fads, fancies, intellectual and physical quirks – from the rise of the Romantic movement to the psychogeography of Alfred Watkins' ley lines; from the development of wet weather gear to the ever-shifting tectonic plates of class; from the first stirrings of the Green movement, to the highly furtive pursuit, favoured by a few, of outdoor lovemaking.

There are other forms of gravity at work too. When many of us walk in our leisure hours, we are not even walking *towards* things – rather, we are rambling in carefully plotted loops, traced on a map, in order to get back to where we started. The circular route is one that Defoe would have found particularly extraordinary – the walk without a destination other than where one started. Yet even this has its roots in something more ancient. The image that comes to mind is that of medieval labyrinths. The path through these labyrinths twists, winds, and ultimately folds back on itself. People would process through them and understand, through these loops and double-backs, the metaphor. The procession, or the walk, is more important than the destination. 'Above all,' wrote the philosopher Kierkegaard in a letter in 1847, 'do not lose your desire to walk; every day I walk myself into a state of well-being and walk away from every illness. I have walked myself into my best thoughts, and I know of no thought so burdensome that one cannot walk away from it.'

The South Downs Way, with its unending stream of walkers going in both directions, is the cheering confirmation that more of us than ever enjoy regenerating our weary town-bound selves by taking to paths and bridleways. But the genesis of this walking enthusiasm, the idea that rambling could be a mass pursuit, enjoyed by all classes, and all over the country, was actually sparked a few hundred miles north of here. In particular, there is one rather bleak, weather-ravaged spot in Derbyshire where, in 1932, the story of the modern walking movement began.

CHAPTER 1

Edale to Kinder Scout: The Peak District and the First Modern Rambling Battle

It is a prospect that can conceivably dampen the soul, as well as lift it. The round hills swooping up in a crest and rising away into the distance, promising mile after mile of austere pale grass; black, wet peat; and moist limestone. This is the skeleton of Britain, the nobbled spine protruding through the dark muddy flesh.

Catch a view of the high empty peat-lands near Edale in the Derbyshire Peak District, on a cold day when the iron-grey clouds are hanging oppressively low, and a darker curtain of rain is drawing in from the west, and you might find yourself turning away from it. Perhaps like Daniel Defoe, who travelled through these parts in 1715 with a mounting sense of dismay, you might observe that

> Upon the top of that mountain begins a vast extended Moor or Waste which … presents you with neither Hedge, nor House or Tree, but with a waste and howling wilderness, over which when Strangers travel, they are obliged to take Guides, or it would be next to impossible not to lose their way.[1]

For Defoe, this was a region where one would be confronted with 'frightful views' of 'black mountains'. Today, by contrast, such 'frightful views' – from the remote north-western tip of

Scotland, to the hearty Cheviots, to Cornwall's wind-scoured Bodmin Moor – are, of course, considered extremely attractive to walkers. No matter how lowering the weather, or inhospitable the terrain, or hedge-less or tree-less the perspective, a wide expanse of country on any day of the year will have a guaranteed number of rambling enthusiasts tramping around.

For those more accustomed to the dainty charms of rural southern England, Edale – and the raw Derbyshire hills around – might not sound immediately alluring. But maps and guide-books can only ever convey a fraction of the attraction. There are keen walkers I know – of a certain age – who have retired to Sheffield in order to have easy access to this exhilarating coun-tryside. But even for me, travelling up from London by train, it couldn't be simpler – one change at Sheffield, and a small local train bound for the valleys of the Pennines. It is here, on this line, that the sense of occasion begins. My fellow passengers are wearing big walking boots. I should imagine that we are all heading for the same destination. Of course we are. Thousands upon thousands do, every year. For some, it is a ritual. And like any ceremony, it carries with it a palpable charge of anticipation. You can feel it on that little train, a butterfly-flutter of mounting excitement. For this particular area – noted not only by Defoe, but also by the sixteenth-century traveller Lady Celia Fiennes, and by seventeenth-century 'Leviathan' author, Thomas Hobbes – has the greatest symbolic importance to walkers everywhere.

The small train passes through a very long tunnel, several miles in length. When it emerges, we are out in a different world of high green hills, and strong stone-built houses. Edale is such a tiny station that there isn't even a canopy, a white-painted wooden gate marks the exit. Yet here we are, geographically pretty much in the centre of Britain, and arguably at the beating heart of its countryside. Edale is a pleasant village of dark grey stone nestling in the shadow of a vast wide hill that dominates the horizon like a great tsunami; an arrested wave of severe grey rock and grass. It is about twenty miles outside Sheffield, and not that many years ago, when that city lay under a perpetual cloud of industrial smoke, it was widely known as a village in the deep countryside which steelworkers could cycle to and taste unadulterated air. Now the place bustles with walkers, of every variety: eager day-trippers, solemn, solitary long-distance hikers, big family parties and groups of friends, and figures like the poet Simon Armitage, who frequently comes to these parts to feel the pulse of the land.

The train has practically emptied, and I was right: we are all here for the same thing. The famous historical aspect of the place is the Mass Trespass of the nearby Kinder Scout moorland in 1932 – the symbolic moment when the needs and desires of ordinary working people clashed with aristocratic landowners' desire to keep their thousands of acres private. The present-day draw of this landscape is that it marks the beginning of the mighty 272-mile Pennine Way. This is not only one of the indirect fruits of that 1932 clash, but also represents a mighty triumph for the Ramblers' Association in 1965, the year of the path's inauguration.

The starting point of such an epic undertaking should, of course, have something of a celebratory atmosphere about it. Edale has this in quantities: that perky little railway station, self-consciously celebratory National Trust tearoom, and bluff, hearty pubs. Walking appears to be the village's chief *raison d'être* now. Edale – and countless other villages and towns all around the country, near moors or meadows, close to grassy plains, on the sea – has taken on new life as a sort of shrine for recreational walkers. As rural economies wither, hikers bring fresh opportunities. The passengers who had been on that little train from Sheffield now, almost as one, make unerringly for the small path that leads down to the tearoom (a chance to grab water and sandwiches, possibly a last mug of tea) and thence to the path beyond. Striding along the track ahead is a straggling row of ramblers, snaking into the far distance. We are on the floor of a tight, vertiginous valley. I am fixing my eyes on distant high crags, and trying to see this place as it would have been seen back in the early 1930s by young people whose weekday city lives consisted of sulphurous smogs, and of sweltering manual labour.

* * *

On the morning of Sunday 24 April 1932, in the brisk air of these moors – the wind soughing and rushing through the grass, making it shiver, and the tiny white bobbles of nascent heather, nodding and bowing – there was another increasingly insistent sound to be heard. It was the soft thrum of sturdy boots on grass, and on the moist black peat. The local bird population, including the much-prized red grouse, as well as plovers and ring ouzels, must have been astonished by the sheer number of people climbing the hill on that day. Human footsteps were rare on those moors then. A long, winding procession of approximately 500 enthusiastic men and women – some sensibly attired in jerseys and stout coats, others in more hearty shorts – were walking up to the summit of Kinder Scout, the highest point in Derbyshire's Peak District. The collective mood of this extraordinarily large group was determined; some of the party were singing 'The Red Flag'. Others were singing the 'Internationale'. These people were not just here to take in the wholesome air and the wide vistas; they were here to make a stand of a symbolic sort. For this wild, open landscape, stretching for mile after seemingly illimitable mile, was one that they had absolutely no right to be standing on.

Kinder Scout – and indeed almost every other site of natural beauty in Britain at that time – was fiercely guarded by private landowners. And so, this was a quite deliberate, premeditated act of mass trespass. Although the day would end extremely unhappily for some participants, this moment – which had been in the offing for the last 100 years – finally galvanised the group's aims into a campaign with mass appeal.

George Orwell, writing *The Road to Wigan Pier* in 1936, sarcastically parroted southern middle-class views about how the labouring classes had very little taste for the natural beauties of the countryside:

> The [industrial towns] go on being ugly largely because the Northerners have got used to that kind of thing and do not notice it … Many of the people in Sheffield or Manchester, if they smelled the air along the Cornish cliffs, would probably declare that it had no taste in it.

It was an extraordinary assertion for anyone to make, and one that those marching up Kinder Scout on that Sunday in 1932 would have had words about. Indeed, in a sense, one of the trespassers did.

> 'The only chance that a young person had of getting away from mucky Manchester and Salford,' said trespasser Dave Nesbitt, 'away from those slums full of smoke and grime, for about a shilling or one and six, was to come out here in the fresh air, and there used to be a mass exodus every Sunday morning.'[2]

By the early 1930s, Manchester had a population of around 750,000. Even though the vast cotton mills, which had powered the city's wealth in the nineteenth century, were now in decline, the city's industry had branched out into modern engineering works, chemical factories, and electrical plants. The nature of the work may have changed slightly, but it was no less intense. The concomitant need to escape from the remorseless production line, and the tightly packed streets and homes, was as strong as it ever had been. By the late 1920s, tension about access to the moors being denied to thousands of walkers had grown to the point where, in 1928, there was a large rally in nearby Winnat's Pass, to the south of Kinder Scout. Attended by various members of established walking groups, these rallies became an annual fixture. But the Kinder Scout trespass of 1932 was a rather more direct and more shrewd form of action.

Today, I am following in some of these footsteps (though perhaps foolishly without the aid of a map). By the time I have clumped up an almost perpendicular hill of grass and muddy footholds – a gradient like a climbing wall which leaves me puffing like a fairground steam novelty – I can see exactly why this area attracted the trespassers. The immediate vista across this plateau is that of dusty brown heather and deep black peat; shivering tarns and vast boulders like enigmatic modernist sculptures. I know I have somehow taken a wrong turning because I have this part of the moor to myself; where are all the other hundreds of walkers I know are around here somewhere?

Thanks to the collective sense given by authors ranging from Bram Stoker to the Gawain poet, I was somehow expecting the area to be a little bleaker than this. But when the sun suddenly flashes out from behind fast moving clouds, all sorts of new colours bleed through the land – the peat becomes richer, more chocolatey, and there is a dash of citrus lime in the grass. Doubtless like all those walkers who came before me, I feel a surging sense of reward.

This high moorland was, in 1932, owned by the Duke of Devonshire. Its primary purpose was as a tract where his guests could enjoy shooting game. The moors were strictly patrolled by the Duke's gamekeepers and in the recent past, there had been a number of skirmishes between young urban walkers and the keepers. There were natural rebels who would make evasion of the gamekeepers part of the fun of the walk. There were also many unemployed young men, for whom walks in this empty landscape were a simple and essential escape from an otherwise overwhelming sense of powerlessness and frustration. But for these men, it was also about the assertion of an ancient right. For had these not once been common lands, before the Enclosure Acts? Tony Gillet said of the 1932 trespass: 'This was serious political action I was taking.'

A chief figure behind this 'serious political action' was Communist Benny Rothman, of a group called the British Walkers Sports Federation. Such were this group's far-left politics that the well-established and rather more moderate Manchester and Sheffield Ramblers' groups of the time kept a cautious distance from it. It could be that some people sensed that this proposed Kinder Scout action was less about asserting the simple right of walkers, and more about making a rather more aggressive point about property and land ownership. Nevertheless, Rothman was a charismatic and thoroughly committed enthusiast – he remains a folk hero to a great many today – and he was adept at recruiting followers to the cause. The Kinder Scout protest had been sparked directly by the failure of another British Walkers Sports Federation venture. According to Rothman, the BWSF had arranged a weekend camp for young people just outside the village of Raworth. These young people went for a hike across the moorland, and were met with furious gamekeepers, who forced them off the land. 'It was decided then and there,' said Rothman, 'that we would do something about it, and we decided to organise a mass trespass over Kinder Scout.' They went about this by distributing leaflets at railway stations to those who looked as though they might be ramblers and hikers. There were also notices written on pavements in chalk, all proclaiming that there would be a meeting at Hayfield Recreation Ground on 24th April. Rothman didn't stop there, though. He also succeeded in getting an interview with the *Manchester Evening News*, which dutifully went to press, advertising, in big headlines, 'Claims to Free Access' and 'Sunday's Attack on Kinder.' The reporter wrote that 'working-class rambling clubs in Lancashire have decided upon direct action to enforce their claims for access to beauty spots.'[3]

This was only true to a certain degree, though. There were also a great many rambling clubs in Lancashire – some established since the 1820s – that felt deeply disinclined to take part; groups that might also perhaps have felt that their walking movement was being hijacked by a small number of agitprop figures. By 1932, there was already a Ramblers' Federation, and having observed this pre-publicity for the Kinder Scout trespass, the Federation felt moved to disassociate itself from this particular cause; although a few of its members were none the less among those who turned up on Sunday 24 April.

These advance notices were also acted on by the authorities, and even before the prospective walkers had had a chance to set foot on private property, the police were out in force to make it clear that a Hayfield council by-law forbad meetings on the recreation ground. Such were the numbers of people who assembled that morning that there was little the officers could do. The walkers, discouraged from assembling in the park, gathered instead in a disused quarry nearby. From this point, they were urged to start the march upwards. Faced with such a multitude, the police could hardly hold them back; all they could do instead was follow them.

*   *   *

There was, according to Rothman, a cheerful atmosphere that day. Bear in mind that all the young men and women who joined him habitually worked six-day weeks, and very long hours; this was their precious day off, and they were clearly determined to enjoy it. Rothman said that they 'all looked picturesque in rambling gear, khaki jackets and shirts, abbreviated shorts, colourful jerseys. Away we went in jubilant mood, determined to carry out the assault on Kinder Scout, which was planned, and determined that no authority would stop it. Some of our youngsters [previously] wanted to go up on to one of the tops here,' Rothman added, 'and they were turned back. And they came back very annoyed, and they talked it over, and we decided that they couldn't turn all of us back. We didn't want any violence, we didn't want any clashes – but we were going up.'

The marchers that day were joined by a journalist from the *Manchester Guardian*. The reporter wrote his account of how, on those slopes, the trespassers caught their first glimpse of the Duke of Devonshire's gamekeepers. They, like the police and the press, had clearly been informed in advance of what was going to happen that morning. 'In a few moments,' the journalist wrote,

> the advance guard – men only, the women were kept behind – dropped down to the stream and started to climb the other side. I followed. As soon as we came to the top of the first steep bit, we met the keepers. There followed a very brief parley, after which a fight started – nobody quite knew how. It was not even a struggle. There were only eight keepers, while from first to last, forty or more ramblers took part in the scuffle.
>
> The keepers had sticks, while the ramblers fought mostly with their hands, though two keepers were disarmed and their sticks turned against them. Other ramblers took belts off and used them, while one spectator was hit by a stone. There will be plenty of bruises carefully nursed in Gorton and other parts of Manchester tonight … though no one was seriously hurt except one keeper, Mr E. Beever, who was knocked unconscious and damaged his ankle.

It leaves you wondering what, if any, part the police took in the brawl. But in the aftermath of this strange, symbolic fight on the peaty moor, the police were to step in more assertively. Benny Rothman himself was so fixated on the notion of reaching the top of Kinder Scout that he was not aware of the punch-up at all, save for an awareness of some 'confused shouting' on his right, and also the sight of just one keeper 'launching an attack on ramblers'. Then, near the top, he recalled seeing a dense group of people – these were walkers from Sheffield, equally determined to join in with the trespass.

Ironically, as the walkers then made the journey back to Hayfield, they adhered to a perfectly legal footpath that wove across another part of this land, and had done so for the past thirty-five years. The reason for this, according to Rothman, was to outwit the police. It would be impossible to levy fines on the walkers if they saw that the walkers were in fact marching on perfectly legitimate territory. However, the police had other ideas. According to the journalist from the *Manchester Guardian*, 'Ramblers formed up into a column and marched into Hayfield ... singing triumphantly, the police car leading their procession.' It was their last happy moment. When they got properly into the village, they were halted by the police. Still they suspected no ill, and it was not until police officers, accompanied by a keeper, began to walk through their ranks, that they realised they had been caught:

> Five men were taken to the police station and detained. The rest of the now doleful procession was carefully shepherded through Hayfield while, as the church bells rang for evensong, the jubilant villagers crowded every door and window to watch the police triumph.

Rothman was among those arrested. In his account, he recalled how they were first taken to cells in Hayfield, but their fellow ramblers knocked so hard upon the doors in protest that they were transferred to the nearby town of New Mills, and held overnight in the police station there. One more arrest had been made that afternoon, so in total, six men were standing in the dock of New Mills police court the next day. Aside from Benny

Rothman, there was Julius Clyne, Harry Mendel, and nineteen-year-old David Nussbaum. There was also a student from Manchester University called Arthur Gillett, also nineteen; and up on a charge of grievous bodily harm committed against the gamekeeper Edward Beever was twenty-one-year-old John Thomas Anderson. The others were looking at charges of riot-ous assembly, assault, and incitement. According to the prosecu-tion, one of the walkers had in his possession documents with the heading 'Friends of the Soviet Union'. There was also BWSF literature that proclaimed 'It is a crime for working class feet to tread on sacred ground on which Lord Big Bug and Lady Little Flea do their shooting.' Rothman conducted his own defence. It did not impress the judge, or indeed, the jury. Incidentally, the jury was apparently made up of 'two brigadier-generals, three colonels, two majors, three captains and two aldermen.'[4]

As a result of the fracas, five of the Kinder Scout trespassers were sent to jail. John Thomas Anderson was found guilty of bodily harm against keeper Beever, and he received six months. The others, guilty of incitement to riotous assembly, were sentenced to four months. The nineteen-year-old student, Arthur Gillett, might just have been spared, were it not for his reply when the judge asked him if he was ashamed of his behav-iour. Gillett replied 'No sir. I would do it again tomorrow.'

It is now an episode of what might be termed folk history, and one that still stirs powerful emotions. The folk singer Ewan MacColl, also there on that day, at the tender age of seventeen, set the events to music in his song 'The Manchester Rambler'. And just ten years ago, on the seventieth anniversary, the Duke of Devonshire attended a special anniversary event on Kinder Scout, and issued an unreserved apology on behalf of his father. It was perfectly sincere and in its way rather touching. It also helped to draw attention to the real injustice of that day in 1932, which was not merely an aristocratic landowner behaving heavy-handedly, but the authorities then colluding disgracefully in an over-reaction to a largely imaginary trangression. For the fact was that the actual physical trespass on that day was a curiously insubstantial thing. As some in the Ramblers' Federation noted, the forbidden land on which the walkers had strode amounted to no more than a few yards. On top of this, we might also see that some of this land was only strictly 'forbidden' for a small part of the year – the grouse-shooting season. 'In some ways,' says ninety-three-year-old rambling campaign veteran John Bunting, 'the Kinder Scout trespass was a publicity stunt. The real action over paths was happening on the other side of the Pennines.'

In other words, Rothman and his BWSF colleagues had found a cause of ideological, as opposed to practical, importance. The actual portion of land under dispute was not in itself of the greatest significance. For the BWSF, was this not really more about class? In the early 1930s, this was certainly the view of the *Daily Mail* (before it began to see the value in suggesting walks and hiking tips to its readers). In one feature, the *Mail* stated:

Our hikers by the ten thousand shoulder their packs and fare forth to discover the beauties of Nature. But the Communists are determined that they shall tramp our footpaths careless of rural charm, musing only on the iniquities of the capitalist system.

Theses views aside, there were also, in national terms, many in the walking movement who felt some unease about Benny Rothman's enthusiasm for direct action. Those moderates who gathered from around the country annually at Winnat's Pass (just a few miles from Kinder Scout) to make their demands for greater access did not think that taking the fight to the gamekeepers was the way forward. But what we see in this story now is one of those pivotal little episodes that throws a light on years, sometimes centuries, of traditions and rights being challenged. It came at a time when cheap motorised public transport – in the form of charabancs – was making access to Britain's wilder regions easier for prospective walkers. It also came during a time of uncertainty for Britain's upper classes, once so wealthy and impregnable, but now starting to seem a little vulnerable, particularly in terms of political influence, and with the rise of a growing, articulate middle class. Two centuries beforehand – by way of contrast – reluctant traveller Daniel Defoe had found that the then Duke of Devonshire was a force for extreme good in this landscape. Defoe wrote:

> Nothing can be more surprising … than for a Stranger coming from the North … and wandering or labouring to pass this difficult Desert Country, and seeing no End of it, and almost discouraged and beaten out with the fatigue of it (just such was our case) on a sudden, the Guide brings him to this Precipice, where he looks down from a Frightful height and a comfortless, barren and, as he thought, endless Moor, into the most delightful Valley, with the most pleasant Garden, and the most beautiful Palace in the World.

This 'Palace' with its 'pleasant garden' was Chatsworth. The land had belonged to the Cavendish family since 1549, when Sir William and his wife Bess of Hardwick bought it from the Leche family. By 1932, the estate was not in a healthy financial position; the death of the eighth Duke in 1908, with the heavy death duties incurred, had greatly increased the debt levels. Nonetheless, when the Kinder Scout trespassers mounted their incursion, the Duke of Devonshire was maintaining his lands in the old style, with a full retinue of gamekeepers. So, for the walkers, it was not so much the land itself, as what its ownership represented. How could there be any natural justice in the idea of a region of such great beauty being the exclusive preserve of one man and his family?

*   *   *

The Peak District was, and is, attractive for many reasons. There are some places that have a distinct, idiosyncratic feel, a presence, all of their own. The area has a quirkiness that piques curiosity. In contrast to the stolid images we all have of such places as the Yorkshire Dales or the Lakes, there is something slightly less easy to grasp in this landscape. It is neither homely, nor wild – unless you happen to stop by in one of the notoriously boisterous rural pubs dotted about this region, in which case the term 'wild' wins out. When you walk along the heights of Kinder Scout – even if there are bustling, rustling cagoule-wearing crowds all around you – you still get a sharp sense of otherness, which has the effect of transfixing the senses. The effect on the original Manchester walkers, escaping from uniformly drab streets and factories, must have been more powerful still. I have a moment of that pleasurable sense of dislocation while exploring the deep hollows between the vast, Easter Island-like boulders near the Kinder summit. Stand in certain spots – where the boulders form a slender passage, your hand against that rough gritstone weathered into undulating curves and holes – and the wind comes through with a sort of high sighing. Such aural effects are not what you automatically expect from English countryside. Round the other side of Kinder Scout lies Kinder Downfall – a dramatic waterfall which sometimes displays a curious phenomenon. If the wind is blowing hard in a certain direction, then the water appears to flow upwards. Ancient local folklore has it that the pools far below were the haunts of mermaids. Some have suggested that the medieval alliterative poem 'Sir Gawain and the Green Knight' was partly set in this region; Sir Gawain must travel across this eerie bog-land on his way to where the elemental Green Knight is said to have had his chapel, a little further north. Given that the Peaks are fretted through with mazes of natural tunnels, caves, and cathedral-like caverns, it is easy to envisage some of the possible chthonic inspiration for the poem. Meanwhile, in the Edwardian era,

Dracula author Bram Stoker set his supernatural novel *The Lair of the White Worm* in the Peak District, drawing on both the subterranean element and strange northern folk tales of local heroes slaying giant snakes.

As I walk back the way I came, striding across the peat, about to descend into the deep valley, back to the dinky railway station, a burst of sunlight falls on the dark path and makes it twinkle and glitter strangely. On the surface of the black mulch, as far as you can see, there are countless tiny fragments of quartz, scattered around like stage diamonds, flashing prism colours; these seem momentarily inexplicable. Have they been here as long as the hills themselves? There are those who don't react at all positively to the Peaks. Perhaps this is because the region looks familiar at first glance but feels odd on closer examination. For the otherwise enthusiastic seventeenth-century aristocratic traveller Lady Celia Fiennes, the area held very little charm. 'All Derbyshire is full of steep hills,' she wrote, 'and nothing but the peakes of hills.'[5] Nothing?

To climb Kinder Scout now is to experience some of the exultation, but also some of the paradoxes thrown up by the rambling movement. Any sense of solitude in this place, especially in the summer months, is illusory; you will never be more than a few yards from another rambler. And any sense of genuine wildness is dispelled by the views of Manchester. Yet for some, it is not the views, but simply the walk itself, that is the thing. In the 1848 novel *Mary Barton* by Elizabeth Gaskell, there is a small scene when a group of Manchester factory workers take to the paths, not so far from the Peak District, on a day off:

> Groups of merry and somewhat loud talking girls, whose ages might range from twelve to twenty, came by with a buoyant step. They were most of them factory girls, and wore the usual out-of-doors dress of that particular class of maidens; namely a shawl which at midday or in fine weather was allowed to be

merely a shawl, but towards evening, if the day was chilly, became a sort of Spanish mantilla or Scotch plaid, and was brought over the head or hung loosely down ... There were also numbers of boys, or rather young men, rambling among these fields, ready to bandy jokes with anyone, and particularly ready to enter into conversations with the girls.

So, almost a hundred years prior to the Kinder Scout trespass, we see that – despite what George Orwell's southerners may say – recreational walking in the north was already a strong tradition, certainly in Manchester, but in other industrialised cities too, such as Leeds, York and Glasgow. In fact, the forming of so many local walking groups was one of the first organised social responses to the depredations of the Industrial Revolution, and its fierce local conflicts percolated through to a nascent popular press. The way that rambling so swiftly evolved holds a mirror up to some of the greatest social changes that convulsed the nation.

CHAPTER 2

Rannoch to Corrour Shooting Lodge in a Howling storm: An investigation of the Lure of Wilderness, and the Earliest Days of Organised Rambling

There are times when open countryside by itself is not quite enough. Walkers – especially city-dwelling ramblers – instead feel the need to seek out raw, authentic wilderness; areas that are remote, untouched and bare. This compulsion to shake free from oppressive urban life seems relatively modern, yet has its antecedents in the earliest days of the Industrial Revolution, and the first stirrings of an organised walking movement in the nineteenth century.

These days, many hardy ramblers are drawn to Rannoch Moor, in the north-west of Scotland; a stark landscape that can make you feel that you have swirled back in time to the very beginning of the earth. The wide empty prospect of echoing hills can evoke an odd mix of leaping euphoria and quiet unease. The term 'prehistoric' does not quite cover it: this is an elemental realm of sparse grass, wet mud, freezing clear water, and lonely peaks. For a walker stepping, slightly dazed, off the Caledonian Sleeper train at 8.40 a.m. and standing taking cold breaths on the platform of tiny Rannoch station, it is rather disorientating. It is one thing to yearn for such prospects while sitting at home, to arrive at them always feels just a little different.

The question of whether Rannoch – or many other parts of the Highlands – can be strictly termed 'authentic' wilderness is one that we shall return to. This plateau seems in some ways the perfect distillation of what the modern rambler is looking for: the implacable, unbeautified face of nature: a plain upon which one would struggle to survive a winter's night in the open; yet also a sanctuary for rare plant species that one would never find anywhere else. It is the sort of terrain that the enthusiastic walker cannot wait to test him or herself against. It promises the deep pleasure of heavy exertion, with the corresponding sense of wide open freedom. In the nineteenth century, as molten furnaces billowed blackening ash over darkened cities such as Glasgow – just 60 miles or so to the south – healthful, open hills and glens became places that men would dream of.

It is partly through Glaswegians that we see the organised walking movement first coalescing. In 1854, Hugh MacDonald published *Rambles Around Glasgow*, which described in detail long walks out of the city, along with examples of flora and history. In 1892, it was a group of working-class Glaswegians who formed Britain's first ever rambling federation: the West of Scotland Ramblers Alliance. It should also be borne in mind that for a few of the manual workers, trapped by economics in Clydeside's squalor in the earlier years of the nineteenth century, the wilds of the Highlands and Loch Lomond were just a few miles away. This represented a treasure that had been stolen from them, this is where some of their families had once lived and farmed before the notorious Clearances.

On Rannoch railway station platform, you drink in the silence after the train moves away. Look up at the low-pressing clouds, and you think: surely this land of hills and water and heather has always been like this. It cannot have changed in over 100,000 years. Yet can this be true? James Hutton, an eighteenth-century Scottish farmer who was also a pioneer in the science of geology, was among the first to grasp the vast yet infinitesimally slow processes that are wrought across the millennia. In 1785, Hutton wrote wrily:

> As there is not in human observation proper means for measuring the waste of land upon the globe, it is hence inferred, that we cannot estimate the duration of what we see at present, nor calculate the period at which it had begun; so that, with respect to human observation, this world has neither a beginning nor an end.

That is, human observation as it stood; yet Hutton was to bring his own human deductions to the subject and, in doing so, spark a religious uproar akin, if on a smaller scale, to that of Galileo. For Hutton was among the first to understand, and assert, that the earth is very, very much older than the Bible seems to say. He was among the first to see that the earth has been here rather longer than humanity itself. This sense of an unfathomably ancient landscape is certainly what pulls walkers here.

In this age of ubiquitous car travel and GPS orienteering, Rannoch Moor remains a formidably inhospitable prospect. It covers a vast area, with very few signs of habitation for miles around. There is only one road in and out, the rest is rough track, often leading nowhere. The nearest big town is Fort William, and Fort William is not a big town. Rannoch itself comprises two or three private houses, and a larger house which is now a popular hotel among keen walkers. Nor is this easy territory, by any means. Even though the Scottish authorities have been assiduously laying down paths and cycle routes all over the country, Rannoch remains one of those ancient regions that should always be hard-going.

Before the twentieth century, the remoter regions such as Rannoch were regarded by many travellers as utterly deadly. It was impossible to live upon, and difficult to cross. The forests were thought to be filled with lurking wolves with a taste for warm flesh. There was no perceived beauty here, just harshness, and silence, and everything inimical to human comfort. In the winter months, the vast black tarns that mark this watery plateau freeze over. The lochs quiver with tiny ice-cold waves. The earth sparkles with frost. In the nineteenth century, Robert Louis Stevenson's historical adventure *Kidnapped* features a lengthy passage in which Alan Breck and Davey Balfour cross the treacherous ground of Rannoch Moor. They attempt to conceal themselves from troops and nearly perish in the process. More harrowing was the real-life construction of the West Highland railway line across the moor. Not only were the workmen fighting against the most savage weather conditions, they were also pulling off the unthinkably complex engineering feat of laying heavy steel lines across bog-land.

Even the doughtiest of poet-walkers William Wordsworth, weathered and wind-beaten after years tramping his beloved Lake District, could not find it within himself to recommend Scottish wildernesses to his readers. 'In Scotland and Wales are found, undoubtedly, individual scenes, which, in their several kinds, cannot be excelled,' wrote Wordsworth, 'but in Scotland, particularly, what long tracts of desolate country intervene! So that the traveller, when he reaches a spot deservedly of great celebrity, would find it difficult to determine how much of his pleasure is owing to excellence inherent in the landscape itself: and how much to an instantaneous recovery from an oppression left upon his spirits by the barrenness and desolation through which he has passed.'[1]

Surprisingly, Wordsworth failed to see what many other walkers could: that the 'barrenness and desolation' could actually be powerful attractions in their own right. It is the perpetual draw of these places that takes us right back to the paradoxical roots of walking for pleasure.

* * *

In a centrally-heated, fleece-swaddled age, it is often difficult for us to imagine just how harsh some British landscapes can be. One dark December a few years ago, I was visiting family in Scotland. Fancying a brief taste of wilderness, I took a train to Kingussie, not too far away from Rannoch Moor, and from there followed a path directly up to the great shouldering hills that encompassed the little Highland town. There had already been snow that day, and more was falling; the air was so cold that I could feel it sharp in my lungs. Good though my boots were, the road I was walking up was glassy with impacted ice. The going was slow, but it was so intensely enjoyable that there was no question of cutting the walk short.

On this particular road – private, though without any of the big, irritable signs that remind you so – the gradient was acute and it was not long before I was above the tree-line, looking upwards at shimmering hills of white, luminous against a sky of solemn dark grey. Save for my boots croaking and crushing the snow beneath, there was not even the riffle of any wind in my ears; the falling snow was sound-proofing the entire world.

But then came the reminder of just how indifferent to life this beautiful world was. There was a small iced hummock on the left of the road, on it sat a small, shivering hare. I wondered why it did not leap away at the very sight of me and as I drew closer to it, I saw the snow dappled with the brightest red, and one of the hare's legs seemed to be hanging half off. The hare watched me as its tiny muscles shook, and its entire body rippled with convulsive shudders. I drew closer, a weight of dismay in my stomach. Then I walked on. To this day, I still feel a pang of remorse about this. Could I not have put the small animal out of its pain? Or perhaps – on the wilder shores of compassion, and utterly absurd, but it did flit through my mind – have tucked it inside my coat and taken it to a local vet? The notion of killing it did fleetingly occur to me: perhaps stove in its small skull with a big stone? But I also knew, almost without having to think

about it, that I would bodge the job through urban squeamish-
ness and incompetence. I wouldn't hit hard enough, or would
hit the wrong spot, or the hare would try to escape and the leg
would become even more mangled. I would somehow end up
adding to its pain a hundredfold.

In that one moment, the winter wonderland feel of this land
had been exposed for what it is: a perfectly impervious, blank
wilderness. The snow was still falling, big fat chunky flakes. I
walked on, higher and higher up this road, which now, in its
dazzling whiteness under that dark iron sky, was snaking up
between two glacial hills.

It never occurred to me on that mid-December afternoon –
with the temperature falling still further – that I was vulnerable
too. I was stupidly oblivious to the never-ending snow, and the
distance that I was covering. I didn't have a hat, or gloves. I was,
quite simply, not dressed properly. There came a point, after
about two hours of walking, that I was still not at the peak, nor
within sight of any pleasing views of lochs or forests. There was
now just the whiteness that seemed to throb and pulse. And the
sun was very low; looking eastwards, the clouds had shades of
both pink and green in them. It was time to turn back.

The road down was slippery, and after two tumbles, which
left me winded, I felt a flutter of apprehension. My hands were
numb and my fingertips were stinging and pulsating with icy
pain, but I couldn't jam them into my pockets for warmth
because I needed to balance properly on that hazardous snow.
Then the idiocy of what I had done began to dawn on me. I was
just another inadequately dressed townie, the sort which
Highland rescue teams despair of. I had completely failed to
appreciate the true nature of the landscape that I was walking
into. It was a mixture of ignorance and urban arrogance, at the
root of which lay the simple misguided conviction that, here in
modern Britain, we have tamed the land and no harm can come
to us when we are walking on it.

Perhaps I am overstating the case, especially since, after ninety minutes of sliding, shuffling and crawling, I eventually made it back down. The sun had set behind me and the rich blue snow-capped peaks of the Cairngorms in the far distance seemed to hover in that indistinct twilight, with the stars out above, and the lights of Kingussie beneath me, looking like an old-fashioned illustration on a Christmas biscuit tin. The sheer physical discomfort of that journey back rather outweighed the earlier pleasure of walking and climbing without care. Yet I would do exactly the same walk again without hesitation. One crucial element of the rambling movement in Britain is the paradoxical belief that old wildernesses are disappearing, but that we can preserve them in all their purity by walking on them. Rannoch Moor stands as the most perfect example of this strange, nostalgic, in many ways completely counter-intuitive yearning.

* * *

The idea of preserving wild landscapes is older than we would perhaps think. The year 1824 saw the formation of the Association for the Protection of Ancient Footpaths In The Vicinity of York. This was followed two years later by the Manchester Association for the Preservation of Ancient Footpaths. Despite the formality of these titles, the groups were more to do with a sense that working people needed a sanctuary, a guaranteed place of escape.

As nineteenth-century journalist Archibald Prentice wrote of the environs of Manchester at that time: 'There are so many pleasant footpaths, that a pedestrian might walk completely round the town in a circle which would seldom exceed a radius of two miles from the Exchange.' He also noted that other northern towns were similarly close to excellent country, and that 'thousands … whose avocations render fresh air and exercise an absolute necessity of life, avail themselves of the rights of footway through the meadows and cornfields and parks of the immediate neighbourhood.'

The closure of many footpaths at a time when urban populations were beginning to increase dramatically also started to attract attention. A petition was drawn up in 1831 to protest against the 'stopping up' of such paths. Then, in 1833, a Select Committee on Public Walks was formed. It found that there were no common lands around Blackburn and that the inhabitants had nowhere that they could walk. Meanwhile, in Bury, there was some 'uninclosed heath' – but it was over two miles away from the town. In the same period, this idea of walking and escape percolated into popular literature. In 1842, John Critchley Prince wrote an essay, 'Rambles of a Rhymester', which was published in 'Bradshaw's Journal.' In one passage, he declares: 'What relief it was for me, after vegetating for twelve months amid the gloom, the filth, the squalid poverty ... to find myself surrounded by green fields, luxuriant hedgerows, and trees just opening to the breath of Spring!'[2] Similarly, local newspapers in towns such as Burnley would often publish readers' verse to do with the beauty of the countryside. They were appealing, not merely because of the conditions in the towns, but also because each family would have in its antecedents all sorts of memories of the rural life that had not long passed away. The preservation and protection of footpaths was also a metaphor for the preservation of treasured family memories.

These rights of way had a political dimension as well, though. From the eighteenth century, Parliamentary Acts of enclosure had been parcelling up the land: areas that had once been common land were acquired by landowners, and the result had been countless bitter disputes, not just about rights of way, but also about wood and berry gathering, and the trapping of rabbits and hares. By the late eighteenth century, poaching was, in some cases, a capital offence. Enclosures had been going on rather longer; common grounds had been encroached upon heavily in the wake of the Reformation, when new landlords made grabs for former monastery lands. Hedges – which these days stand as one of the beloved metonyms for the English countryside – were once extremely unpopular. They marked the boundaries of seized land. Asserting the right to walk on what had been regarded as an ancient footpath was a symbolic way of redressing the balance a little. It seems that this in turn had the effect of making rural landlords rather more hostile to the old Rights of Way that bisected their lands. There was further fencing, and hedging, and stone walls were built. Although this was partly to do with new agricultural techniques – in essence, not allowing cattle to roam as far as they used to – there was also an undeniable effort to keep labourers off private land.

On the banks of the Clyde in the 1830s, there was the case of one landowner who decided to prevent walkers – usually working men from closer to the centre of Glasgow – using the river path. The case grew so heated that it was put before the local authorities, who ordered that the path be opened again. But for every such victory, there were countless cases up and down the country of the Enclosure Acts making landowners consolidate their rights of ownership.

Nevertheless, this nascent walking movement very swiftly spread to other industrial cities such as Liverpool and Leeds. These were all cities where the rivers reeked with effluent, and where the unsanitary nature of the accommodation made terrible diseases inevitable. The vast manufactories were monolithic, the opposite to anything that anyone would find in the openness of country. The desire to walk was to do with space, physical as well as mental. Home and work darkly mirrored one another. In 'miasmatic courts and alleys', an entire family would be crammed into one room; here they would eat, sleep and live. Then at work, men and women were hemmed in tight, in occupations that required them either to stay in one place to carry out repetitious mechanical tasks, or move through intensely claustrophobic tunnels, unable to stand up or stretch out.

* * *

The Scots, with their even greater abundance of wild country-side, had their keenness for walking made even sharper by recent memories of the Clearances. What once had been the wide open common land, upon which whole communities had thrived, was seized in a series of brutal land-grabs perpetrated by Scottish aristocrats, intent upon maximising the profitablity of their land by turning thousands of acres over to sheep grazing, and later to game and to forestry. We might timorously say – for the sake of some kind of balance – that the landowners in turn were not always acting out of malice, but were sometimes simply respond-ing to different sorts of economic pressure. One of these pres-sures was the rate of emigration among the young in rural communities – even before the Clearances. Before such journeys were enforced, increasing numbers of young labourers had been beginning to set sail for Canada, to lay claim to their part of a New World, in search of greater prosperity.

The crofting communities these young people left behind were part of a way of life that simply, inevitably, was going to go – much in the way that, two centuries later, the remote island of St Kilda had to be evacuated. The point about any period of economic turbulence – regardless of cruelty, intentional or otherwise – is that it is always those at the bottom who find that their security and stability have been ruthlessly stripped away. So it was during those decades that, for the sake of landowners grazing their sheep or turning their estates into hunting grounds, men, women and children were herded out of villages; some were sent to the western ports, from which they were expected to emigrate. Others went to the towns. Villages were burnt to the ground and old traditions destroyed in a matter of hours. And perhaps for this reason above any other, in Scotland the very notion of private land continues to this day to be of the most fantastic political sensitivity. There are those who still want revenge for the Clearances.

After this came a Scottish version of enclosure, or empark-ation: rich Victorians who gazed upon these vast glens and moors and who closed them off as far as possible for the purposes of hunting. For example, much of the south of the Cairngorms came to be owned by the Atholl Estate, having been seized in the early nineteenth century. In the 1840s, the Duke of Atholl became involved in a much-publicised skirmish with ramblers. These men – a professor of botany from Edinburgh University called John Balfour, and seven of his students – were trying to walk up Glen Tilt via the old drover's road. The party was stopped by the Duke of Atholl's ghillies. The result: Professor Balfour brought a lawsuit, the aim of which was to establish firmly the public's right to use the route. The Duke of Atholl was having none of it. A couple of years later, it was students from Cambridge – botanists again – who took up the Glen Tilt chal-lenge, resulting in yet another skirmish with ghillies. This led to even more court action, to seek the protection of this and other routes throughout the Highlands. The Duke of Atholl remained stoutly unrepentant, and the practice of establishing gates across old roads was subsequently picked up by neighbouring land-owners. It took an Edinburgh lawyer called Thomas Gillies to come up with an idea that even the most recaltricant landowner would find it difficult to argue with: calling for shepherds and drovers to attest in court that these roads had an established history of public use.[3]

The Royal Family must shoulder some more of the blame for the increasing inaccessiblity of the Highlands during this era. Thanks to Queen Victoria's sojourns at Balmoral, the craze for hunting, shooting and fishing – not merely among landowners, but also wealthy mercantile figures – took hold. It was not just old Scottish aristocratic families eating up the land, thousands of acres were also being bought up by American millionaires who fancied that somewhere down the line, they had some form of Scottish ancestry.

Indeed, in 1884, it took a Scotsman to present the first effort in Westminster to allow walkers full access to moor and mountain. James Bryce – an MP with an extremely colourful hinterland – made valiant efforts to push through an Access to Mountains Bill. What made this striking was that at that time, Bryce was the Liberal Member of Parliament for Tower Hamlets – one of the very poorest districts in London, encompassing St Katharine's Docks, Limehouse and Whitechapel. His constituents – from the stevedores to the prostitutes – were extremely unlikely to catch any views of any sort of countryside. Despite this, his concern was for them, and all men and women who lived in conditions of horrific urban poverty. Bryce understood the restorative power of wilderness.

He also was a keen climber and, on one occasion, he had scrambled up Mount Ararat. When, at the summit, he found a fragment of old timber, this was a source of huge excitement to him. He was convinced that it was a tiny part of Noah's Ark. Back in London's East End, he was instrumental in setting up the charitable foundation Toynbee Hall.

His Access to Mountains Bill failed to get a second reading. But he and his brother, Annan, fought on, though. They tried to push the Bill through the Commons repeatedly. And there were also attempts – not merely through Parliamentary means, but also through speeches and articles – to establish the idea that the open Highlands should be available to all, and not just the very rich.

Even as Bryce's political career rocketed ever higher, and he was sent to the US as ambassador, he never lost sight of the walking movement. And now, in the twenty-first century, Bryce's view that every man should have unhindered access to all parts of the Highlands has prevailed.

* * *

Over the last few years, Scotland has become increasingly adept at turning its landscape into a sort of commodity, not just for hard-core walkers (incredibly lucrative and important though this is) but also more casual visitors. In the 1996 film adaptation of Irvine Welsh's *Trainspotting*, Renton, Begbie and Sickboy very briefly leave their squalid needle-filled Edinburgh lives and come to Rannoch Moor for a 'healthy hike'. The images are now replicated on specialised walking websites recommending Rannoch to visitors from around the world.

Meanwhile, simple wilderness is nominated as a 'Site of Scientific Interest' and vast tranches of land are signposted as 'Nature Reserves'. It is one of the ways a nation feels good about itself. Walkers are invited to discover a pre-lapsarian organic purity. But then, for many ramblers, Scotland has always carried that lofty sense of somehow being a purer, less spoilt place than England. Even in John Buchan's 1915 thriller *The Thirty Nine Steps*, gung-ho hero Richard Hannay, on the run for a murder he did not commit, finds the time to have a quick revel in its beauty. Despite the desperation of his circumstances, Hannay acquires a sort of exultation as he makes his way out into Scottish open country:

> Over a long ridge of moorland I took my road, skirting the side of a high hill which the herd had called Cairnsmore of Fleet. Nesting curlews and plovers were crying everywhere, and the links of green pasture by the streams were dotted with young lambs. All the slackness of the past months was slipping from my bones, and I stepped out like a four-year-old.

When it comes to igniting that sense of child-like delight, sometimes a cheesy touristy label actually does do the trick. About a mile from Rannoch station is the start of a simple track heading northwards called 'The Road to the Isles'. One can almost imagine this road name being set to music and sung by Sir Kenneth

McKellar, dressed in shortbread-tin tartan. But even if that is the lure, 'The Road to the Isles' really is rather gratifying, especially if, like me, you are fortunate enough to find yourself caught on it in the middle of a howling tempest. The track makes a steady climb into the quietly forbidding hills, northwards, towards Corrour. With me on this walk – deceptively blue-skied in its opening stages – are Richard, a land management expert who lives in the Orkneys, and his dog Bramble. Our various mutual friends (we are all based at the Rannoch Station Hotel) have turned back quite early on in the expedition at a swollen river. They did not wish to face the delicate tip-toeing across slippery rocks that could end in soaking disaster. Richard and I are a little more insouciant about it, however, and Bramble the labrador – after some thought – seems happy to swim across.

Having negotiated the river, we rise higher and higher. Before us, the stern aspect of brown hills; behind us, the great peaks that shoulder Glencoe. The most striking thing, this many miles into the wilderness, is the depth of the silence. There is not an animal to be heard anywhere. No rabbits, no hares, nothing. There are large buzzards wheeling and floating, tasting the air, but they too are soundless. Apart from the strengthening wind in our ears, and the sound of our conversation, there is nothing else out here at all in this world of dark brown land and blue sky. Richard is a keen, experienced walker, who has travelled all over Scotland in search of beauty like this. At one point, we see the blackened wood that is often found buried in the peat around here. Some argue that such submerged wood proves that, centuries ago, this land was once covered with great forests which were gradually cut down and destroyed by man. However, a different view is taken by the eminent natural historian Professor Oliver Rackham; that such fragments of wood on Rannoch Moor have blackened naturally as a result of their contact with the peat. My companion Richard goes with the first theory. In an extension of his line of thought, there are very few vistas, at least in Britain, that have not been affected in some way by man's influence. So in some ways, there are very few genuinely natural landcapes left in the British Isles; the rest are the results of tinkering, whether intentional or not. From this angle, Rannoch is not an authentic wilderness.

It is local landowner Lord Pearson's belief – now shared by some other conservationists all over Scotland – that countless years of sheep and deer grazing in the area of Rannoch inflicted a grievous wound on the landscape, and in effect reduced it to acidic peat bog, whereas once it had flourished with a variety of different species. In short, they believe, this was a landscape created as a direct result of the Clearances. 'Rannoch Moor is dotted with derelict crofts,' said Lord Pearson in an interview. 'Around these would have been fields for wintering the cattle.' Added to this, he said, 'in a three year spell from 1837, an adjacent estate listed the killing of 246 pine martens, 15 golden eagles, 27 sea eagles, 18 ospreys, 98 peregrines, 275 kites, 63 goshawks, 83 hen harriers, and hundreds of stoats, weasels, otters, badgers and crows – all in the name of increasing grouse numbers.'[4] Where once were trees and a wide variety of flora, man's activities left us with the desolation we see now. It might be attractive desolation, but it was not strictly nature's intention.

Experienced walker or not, Richard has somehow failed entirely to notice what is coming towards us. So have I. Some 10 miles to the west, there is silvery cloud obscuring the hills, and what looks like a mist. It sweeps over quickly and the first heavy drops tell us that this is rather more than a little light rolling fog. The ensuing storm is so spectacular that it made all the newspapers the next day. In the area of Rannoch, it brought trees down across the railway line, and across the one driveable road leading out of the place. For a few hours, Rannoch was literally cut off from the rest of the modern world.

As for Richard, myself and Bramble, we spent the next ninety minutes picking our way back across the moor in the midst of a tempest so violent that even King Lear would have had difficulty shouting in it. The world blurred into grey, silver and black: all colours were washed away. My glasses were near impossible to see through. The marshy puddles on the path became mires. The large stones on that same path became slippery. The wind – screaming horizontally from the west – was so strong that the rain on bare skin actually hurt. Bramble quite often tried to find shelter behind my legs. It blew on, relentlessly. The hood of my waterproof was repeatedly blown back and soon filled with icy rainwater. A small area near my throat that was insufficiently covered admitted yet more icy water. Soon the front of my shirt was sopping beneath the coat. Even the *pockets* of my waterproof were inundated. A spare fiver I had in one pocket was reduced to a blue-white mush.

Throughout it all, Richard and I were yelping with laughter, and failing to hear each other's enthusiastic shouts. Even as we came down from the hills, the wind, which was tearing at distant trees and shrieking through the heather, was freezingly ineluctable. Our faces, by the time we got back on to the road and along to the hotel, were puce with windburn.

The fact of it is that this is the sort of place, and even the sort of wild weather, that urban dwellers yearn for in their imaginations, as runners thirst for cold water. We think ourselves like Richard Hannay, children of nature who have simply been denied the countryside that we desire. But this is also a countryside that we can take refuge from. Even if the hotel is miles away, you still know that it is there. The knowledge of comfort enables us to sentimentalise desolation. Imagine if there was no such shelter to be found anywhere, within several days of walking. However much you may yearn for those hills and that peat, the landscape has no use whatsoever for us. You will never really be a welcome part of it.

* * *

The romance of an empty land is a pre-conditioned, learned thing; there is no particular reason why it should be inherently natural for us to seek out that which so many of our antecedents would have flinched from. In some generations past, the idea of drawing spirtual succour from the country would have been seen as eccentric. In the eighteenth century, Dr Johnson, for instance, was baffled by the contemporary passion for pastoral poetry. He wrote: 'though nature itself, philosophically considered, be inexhaustible, yet its general effects on the eye and ear are uniform, and incapable of much variety of description.'

During that period, there were those who were more concerned with wrangling with nature's effects, and contriving their own landscapes artificially, rather than leaving the land as it was. Before then, in the Middle Ages, observes Timothy Brownlow, 'nature in the medieval world existed as a decorative backdrop or as a narrative or moral device. Indeed,' he added, 'the word "landscape" did not emerge until the late sixteenth century.'[5] In Milton's poetry, it is rendered as 'lantskip'.

After the Restoration, there was still very little appetite for seeing wilderness as an attractive, unspoiled ideal; instead, many of the grander landowners of the seventeenth and eighteenth centuries sought harder than ever to bend nature to their own will. This period saw the rise in enthusiasm among the gentry for landscaped gardens. The earlier highly-mannered, geometrical style inspired by French gardening began to give way to a new sort of landscape, as championed by Capability Brown and Humphry Repton among others. This new sort of English garden was in the 'picturesque' style and had features such as follies, grottoes, or ornamental ruins, blended with artfully sloped lawns, carefully placed trees, running streams and waterfalls. In this milieu, even walking took on a measure of artifice. There were specially constructed 'lovers walks', along which wooing couples would be framed with fragrant pergolas. One such eighteenth-century effort in the Borders was praised highly in the *Edinburgh Review*.

This sort of artifice was not to last. By the late eighteenth century the emphasis would be placed on the virtue of the natural, and untouched. This was a direct result of the rise of the Romantic movement, with its emphasis on unschooled innocence. The movement was trailed in the mid-eighteenth century by essayist and philosopher Jean Jacques Rousseau – himself an enthusiastic walker, and observer of nature. For a coming generation of poets and philosophers, walking would be central to their understanding of the world; the untamed wildness of nature had both a primal innocence and an awful majesty. The philosopher Edmund Burke wrote an influential treatise in 1756 concerning 'the sublime' and 'the beautiful':

The passion caused by the great and sublime in nature is astonishment, and astonishment is that state of the soul in which all its motions are suspended, with some degree of horror. The mind is so entirely filled with its object that it cannot entertain any other, nor reason on that object which fills it … No passion so effectually robs the mind of all its powers of acting and reasoning as terror; and whatever is terrible with regard to sight, is sublime.

A little earlier, poet Thomas Gray was so thrilled by the 'terrible' spectacles he saw of the Alps on his Grand Tour with Sir Horace Walpole that he later toured the Lake District in 1769 and, in an extended account, ascribed to this region similar turbulent natural scenes. With the writers that followed – who were responding, however unconsciously, to the Industrial Revolution – there came the sense that nature had to be freed from mankind's manipulations. They felt that in authentic landscapes were to be found atmospheres, a sense, a feeling, that would have an answering chime within every soul, like Coleridge's Aeolian Harp.

Over 200 years later, the modern walker in a region such as Rannoch clearly has similar desires. Here, as the sun is setting its final fiery orange rays across these hills and tussochs, you see a perfect example of the sublime: the prospect that can at once unsettle you and yet leave you marvelling at its gaudy beauty. Such a sunset is not that far removed from J. M. W. Turner's depiction of an erupting Vesuvius; the sky raging and glowing, the people below just dim, phantom-like silhouettes.

We can balance romanticism against the implacable rationality of eighteenth-century proto-geologist James Hutton, and his revolutionary observations of the cycles of nature. His understanding of the rocks and soil being washed into the sea, forming bedrock, forced volcanically to the surface and then being worn away over infinite years back into sediment. Even then we might feel an odd poetic link between local legends of the ageless faerie folk who 'dwell in the hollow hills' and Hutton's awe at the eternity-old land. 'The result, therefore, of this physical enquiry,' Hutton told the Royal Society of Edinburgh in 1788, 'is that we find no vestige of a beginning, no prospect of an end.'

The new learning was teaching men that the ground beneath their feet had been there long before Eden. Some of the walkers who were to take up the pursuit with such vigour in the Victorian age did so in part as a challenge to the church, and to the hold that it had on society. But even before them, the idea of walking as a genteel pursuit, a subtle pleasure that could reveal much about personal character, and which could even be enjoyed by refined women, was to be immortalised in English literature.

CHAPTER 3

Dorking to Box Hill: Introducing Jane Austen, and the Subsequent Rise of the Victorian Walking Club

My grandmother was a keen walker all of her life. But she had a freezing disdain for the landscape of south-east England: it was too flat, too undramatic, too safe, too cosy. What on earth would be the point of walking anywhere within easy reach of London? Only the Highlands would do, or perhaps parts of Northumberland at a pinch. It is a prejudice shared by veteran rambling campaigner John Bunting, who spent so many of his formative years being chased by gamekeepers in the Peak District. Would he ever fancy a walking tour, say, of the South Downs? 'When I get a bit older,' replies the ninety-three-year-old.

For a long time, I shared my grandmother's dismissive attitude towards the southern Home Counties, which in my case was shaped by many very dull train journeys from London to Brighton. Is it insane to judge a landscape from a railway line? Apart from anything else, many better people than me have been drawn to walking in this gentle area. Throughout the nineteenth century, this part of Surrey not only formed the backdrop to some immortal literature, but also captured the imaginations of a generation's finest thinkers, who strode across these sleepy fields, hopped over these stiles and bounded up these silent hills with all the enthusiasm and vigour that the Victorian age could summon.

I find myself wandering through silvery mist at the top of a wooded hill, admiring the thickness of the silence, and the darkness of the cover of the oaks, and the mysterious low shapes of the old sprawling yews. I have to take all my own shallow prejudices back. After all, I am only a mile and a half outside Dorking and just a few miles from Gatwick – yet there is a subtle splendour in the quietness of this country. As for gentler walks, in the early nineteenth century, before Victoria reached the throne, Jane Austen practically turned southern counties roaming into a sub-genre of literature.

In all of Austen's novels, characters walk, and each walk always carries its own significance. Sometimes it will be triggered by a banal reason – a carriage is not available at a particular moment, say; but the walk that follows either carries emotional or symbolic resonance. Be it an act of social defiance, or a response to a moment of romantic crisis, the gentle paths and fields and hills are as delicately and closely suggested as the figures that move across them. And it is broadly the pastures and meadows of the southern counties that Austen's characters walk about in. In *Emma*, we often find Mr Knightley striding from his house; even Mr Darcy, in *Pride and Prejudice*, sometimes ventures out on foot, as opposed to horseback. Walking is frequently indicative of mood; there are times of upset when an Austen heroine wishes to walk alone and refuses a companion. For these heroines, the very act of walking itself can be taken as an assertion of independence: the exercise is sometimes cathartic. At other times, as in *Emma*, it is distinctly pleasurable and the company stimulating:

As a walking companion, Emma had very early foreseen how useful she might find [Harriet Smith] … Her father never went beyond the shrubbery, where two divisions of the ground sufficed him for his long walk, or his short, as the year varied; and since Mrs Weston's marriage, her exercise too had been too much confined. She had ventured once alone to Randalls, but it was not pleasant; and a Harriet Smith, therefore, one whom she could summon at any time to a walk, would be a valuable addition to her privileges.

These days, walkers are enticed into sampling 'Jane Austen country', following trails that wind around Chawton in the county of Hampshire, where she lived so long. A little more vigorous is the walk up to the scene of one of Austen's most famous passages from *Emma*. A party ascends Box Hill for a picnic. Emma Woodhouse humiliates Miss Bates and is roundly picked up on this by Mr Knightley. Distress and embarrassment are signalled by members of the party detaching and going for their own small walks atop the Downs. For Emma herself, she ends up wanting to be 'sitting almost alone, and quite unattended to, in observation of the tranquil views beneath her.'

There are other walking crises to be found in Austen. In *Pride and Prejudice*, Elizabeth Bennet is accused of 'conceited independence' when she undertakes a mighty 3-mile crosscountry walk to visit her ill sister.

That she should have walked three miles so early in the day, in such dirty weather, and by herself, was almost incredible to Mrs Hurst and Miss Bingley; and Elizabeth was convinced that they held her in contempt for it.

The accuser, Miss Bingley, also wonders what effect such an expedition might have upon Mr Darcy. It is clear that one unspoken source of her discomfort with the idea is that Elizabeth has done something quite improper; that there is a forwardness about a young women walking such a distance out in the open all on her own. In fact, Miss Bennet is such a keen walker that when, at one stage in the novel, a proposed tour to the Lake District is altered to a journey to Derbyshire instead, she vents her irritation loudly. The pursuit of recreational walking seemed to have become part of genteel 'English culture and comfort' about a century before Austen's fiction. In 1710, Jonathan Swift wrote, in *Journal To Stella*:

> I have always been plying you to walk and read. The young fellows have begun a kind of fashion to walk, and many of them have got swinging strong shoes on purpose; it has got as far as several young lords; if it hold, it would be a very good thing.

* * *

Young lords and gentlewomen were obviously not alone in their sensibilities; by the middle years of the nineteenth century, pleasant prospects were sought out by increasing numbers of highly organised rambling groups from a wide array of social and professional backgrounds. There was an element, for ordinary working people, rather lower on the social scale than Austen's heroines, of raising themselves up. Walking became not just about fresh air; there was also an element of virtue, and sober fellowship, and education. In the industrial towns at this time, there had been a huge rise in entertainments such as the music hall and the public house. Walking groups were being founded to stand deliberately apart from the noise and vulgarity of such pursuits.

Many of these walking clubs had a distinctly Methodist or Non-Conformist flavour; some were organised directly by churches. For instance, in the Lancashire mill towns, a Saturday half-day holiday was established in the mid-nineteenth century so that workers now had that afternoon for leisure. A great number of churches – many of them congregationalist – leapt in to try and ensure that this time would not be 'wasted' on drink or other such 'worthless' recreations. Rambling expeditions were proposed instead. A number of temperance associations also encouraged group walks out into the country.

There were other associations such as the Ancoats Brotherhood, based in Lancashire and formed by Charles Rowley, the founder of the Sunday Recreation Movement. In part, the group was about 'rambling with a bevy of chums' in places as far away as Wales. The group would also attract impressive guest speakers, such as William Morris and Ford Madox Brown.[1] The act of walking in such organised groups was a very different thing to the solitary, dreamy rambles of the Romantic movement. This was about urban dwellers roaming about the crags and the moors and the coniferous woodlands as a deliberate means of breaking out of the work–recreation patterns that were being laid down for them.

There was a strong element of self-improvement; the working man who took a lively interest in the world around him, in the paths beneath his feet, had a greater claim towards shaping that world. Such walking groups were keenly interested in ideas to do with the spread of democracy. Early industrialisation, with its remorseless demands of time and energy of its workers, could also have the side effect of infantalising them. Walking out on to the Cheshire Plains, or into the vales of North Wales, on the other hand, gave those workers the sense of a certain independence of movement and of thought.

One of the most inspirational and pivotal figures in the walking movement, G. H. B. Ward, formed the Sheffield Clarion Rambling Club at the turn of the twentieth century. He was an engineer at the Hecla works, and an active Labour Party man. Indeed, as the years went on, he would rise to become a senior Labour figure. But it is his passion for walking that is remembered today. The explicit aim of the Clarion Club was the mental and physical improvement of the working man. Interestingly, the Club also posed an explicit challenge to the church; and that was over the use of the Sabbath. According to G. H. B. Ward, Sundays would be more satisfyingly spent out in the refreshing air. On this point, the Sheffield ramblers, and a small club of middle-class intellectuals down south, intriguingly mirrored one another. For as the walking movement grew – and despite the best efforts of the churches to get involved – it was also clear that it had a certain cerebral and secular appeal to many. There were also those who went out rambling on Sunday mornings precisely in order to get away from the church and its influence.

This corner of Jane Austen-land – that is, the countryside clustered around Box Hill and Leith Hill – was also deeply favoured by key members of the Victorian rambling group the Sunday Tramps. The 'Tramps' were a small and perhaps rather self-conscious assembly of intellectuals, scientists, writers and naturalists. They started meeting in 1879, led by Sir Leslie Stephen, a formidable Cambridge intellectual, editor of *The Dictionary of National Biography*, and enthusiastic mountaineer, among other things.

In this club, the men – there were no women – got out of London on Sunday to go for rather austere, brisk 25-mile walks. The fact that they missed church was all part of it. These men wanted to escape the 'dreary Sabbath' in London. Sir Leslie Stephen revelled in his 'flock of cranium tramps' and wrote that 'tramping with them, one has the world under review, as well as pretty scenery.'[2]

The Sunday Tramps were by no means unique in finding the Sabbath dreary. Though our image of Victorians is that of respectable, upright families, occupying the church pews without fail, the truth was more complex, especially towards the end of that century. In rural parishes, and certain parts of Scotland, there was practically no escape from the Sunday service, simply because in a small community, any absence from the rituals of any particular day would be extremely noticeable. By contrast, in the vast sprawling towns, parish priests had a far more difficult job. In the poorer districts, the community was transient – families moving in or moving out according to the fluctuations in their economic circumstances. Among a number of the intellectual middle-classes – mostly educated men, who had read Charles Darwin and Charles Lyell's *Principles of Geology* – the church no longer had any real grip.

According to historian A. N. Wilson, had the Victorian middle classes thought to seek out the opinions of the urban working classes on the subject of the church and its teachings, 'they would have found religious practice (except among Irish immigrants) all but unknown, and indifference to religious ideas all but total.' One contemporary observer noted that in 'the alleys of London … the Gospel is as unknown as in Tibet.'[3]

It is not quite as if the Sunday Tramps were dedicated atheists; they simply looked at the dull city, which was sullen and silent apart from church bells. The shops were all shut, the factories were still, and the Tramps took that opportunity to worship the beauty of Home Counties countryside instead. They charged across those small green fields, pointed themselves towards the startlingly abrupt hills of the South Downs, and took in the neatly proportioned prospects of downland and meadow. In *In Praise of Walking*, Leslie Stephen is especially clear on the pleasure of temporarily shaking off the capital, escaping its 'vast octopus arms' and mapping a course 'between the great lines of railway'. The benefits were almost instantaneous; in counties such as Surrey and Kent, the old rural ways still held hard, and there was great hospitality to be found in even the most humble cottages. In many ways, Stephen was as great a romantic as Wordsworth, though he laid claims to being rather less sentimental. When once writing about the Lake District, he declared: 'Much as I respect Wordsworth, I don't care to see the cottage in which he lived.'

Another of the prominent Sunday Tramps, the novelist George Meredith, lived in a house on the side of Box Hill, and his enthusiasm for exploring the surrounding countryside was undinted. His 1885 novel *Diana of the Crossways* contained evocative hymns of praise to the downland: 'Yews, junipers, radiant beeches, and gleams of service-tree or the white-beam, spotted the semi-circle of swelling green down, black and silver.'

Stephen and his assorted followers were not dreamers; this was walking as a highly masculine – and, in some curious way, acutely Victorian – activity; they marched across the land as though they claimed it for their own, in the true Imperial manner. In his obituary of Stephen, George Meredith paid this tribute, recalling the boisterous energy and enthusiasm of these Sunday Home Counties hikes:

A pause ... came at the examination of the leader's watch and Ordnance map under the western sun, and void was given for the strike across country to catch the tail of a train offering dinner in London, at the cost of a run through hedges, over ditches and fellows, past proclamation against trespassers, under suspicion of being taken for more serious depredators in flight.

The chief of the Tramps had a wonderful calculating eye in the observation of distances and the nature of the land as he proved by his discovery of untried passes in the higher Alps, and he had no mercy for pursy followers. I have often said of this life-long student and philosophical head that he had in him the making of a great military captain.

The mere fact of a 'no trespassing' sign had always been enough to pique Stephen, and goad him into doing that very thing. He wrote:

I looked out for signs saying trespassers will be prosecuted ... That gave a strong presumption that the trespass must have some attraction. Cyclists could only reflect that trespassing for them is not only forbidden but impossible. To me it was a reminder of the many delicious bits of walking which, even in the neighbourhood of London, await the man who has no superstitious reverence for legal rights.

There speaks the true vigorous Victorian. Although his near contemporary A. H. Sidgwick, who published his *Walking Essays* in 1912, had this to say on the subject:

> There is a definite type of walker who loves trespassing for its own sake, and exults, as he climbs a fence or turns up a path marked 'private', in a vision of the landed aristocracy of England defied and impotent … There is much excuse for this attitude: as we review the history of English commons and rights of way, of the organised piracy of the body politic and the organised perjury which supported it, it is difficult to stifle an impulse to throw at least one pebble … at the head of Goliath.

He added with a semi-humorous shake of his head, 'To indulge the love of trespassing involves ultimately making trespassing an end rather than a means, and this – like the twin passion for short-cuts as an end in themselves – is disastrous to walking.'[4] Sidgwick's view was that no matter how unjust the circumstances of its creation, the fact was that the enclosed English countryside was also, paradoxically, the thing of beauty that the walker admired so, and that fulminating against the landed aristocracy could only leach pleasure away from any walk. Added to this, it has always been rather easier for the patrician middle classes to trespass simply because, if confronted, they could sound eminently reasonable in perfectly modulated tones of Received Pronunciation.

Over 100 years on, the territory of these Sunday Tramps would now give Stephen little of that 'delicious' sense, though. Box Hill and Leith Hill are now firmly National Trust territory. What would either Leslie Stephen or indeed Emma Woodhouse make of it now? And so off I stride, out of Dorking station – and thanks to my airy dismissal of maps, I inevitably, immediately, take a wrong turning. As a result of my mistake, the next rather stressful thirty minutes involve following a busy road running along the base of Box Hill, heading towards Reigate. Walking along, I look yearningly up at those thick woods on the steep slopes – but without seeing any hint of public footpaths or indeed any particularly promising field I can simply trot across. In the meantime, my attempted Jane Austen-esque promenade has suddenly narrowed into a flinching, shrinking-back-from-vast-delivery-lorries ordeal. If I resemble any Austen figure at this moment, it is probably the oleaginous, cringing vicar Mr Elton.

What might have ended with a frustrated about turn – is there anything worse than having to go back the same way, over unlovely territory? – thankfully culminates in a side road, marked as a dead end. Following this a little way, past the eerie howling of a combined kennel-cattery, and just a quarter of a mile on, you are in business. I find a right hand turn, with a lane leading directly up the hill. When you are directly beneath it, the hill looks absurdly steep.

The lane soon gives way to some discreet National Trust signage. What previously looked steep, actually becomes steep. This lovely wooded path, slightly wet with the spring mist, moist flint-stone and mud, angles upwards through a tunnel of old trees. The cover is so dense that there is no possibility of looking out at the view – just a fairly solid climb. It doesn't last long, you are at the top surprisingly quickly. Now you can see the prospect before you. Except, that is, on the day I have chosen to climb. I can't see anything. There is a delicate yet impenetrable mist all around, and the Mole Valley beneath is a gauzy haze. It is not that disappointing; any views at all – from anywhere – offer at best a certain amount of limited novelty. This one, down to the river, over to the trees on the other side of the valley, would have been pretty enough, yet I know it would not have detained me for long. With hills and country such as this, there are other things. There are breathtakingly beautiful trees to be seen on this plateau. Oaks so nobbled that the trunks look as though they contain a multitude of faces. Box Hill, incidentally, is so called because of its profusion of box trees on its slopes and summit.

Thence to Emma Woodhouse's picnic site. Back then, parties would have been taken up the hill by carriage via a zigzagging road. Much the same thing seems to be the case now. Indeed, these are the very roads used for the 2012 Olympic cycle races. On a day like this, when the mist drifts like the spray in a vast greenhouse, there is a magic to the glistening barks, and the squelchy dark mud underfoot. What is most impressive, though, is that this place – nestled between the M25, Gatwick Airport, and countless main roads – is so extraordinarily quiet. And in this, I see Leslie Stephen's point about wriggling free from the octopus arms of London. Even in an ancient woodland like Epping in Essex, there is always, somewhere, the noise of traffic, or overhead aeroplanes. Here, you really do feel that you are somewhere slightly more remote than a London dormitory town.

The mist, however, prevents me from assessing the other thing I came here for; and that is how much the landscape below has changed over the years. The walker might, as an initial point of reference, turn to one of the earliest examples of British landscape painting, 'A View To Box Hill', by George Lambert, painted in 1733. This was one of the first works focusing on the land itself, and not some castle or tower or other similarly imposing man-made structure. In Lambert's work, the focus is the hill, which is starkly delineated, but the air is thick with a honeyed light. In the foreground, there are labourers reaping corn. Today, that same field in the foreground is instead a vineyard. The other difference is that in the painting, there are very few trees on the hill. Either all these trees have grown since then; or Lambert simply left the trees out, for his own artistic reasons. Not that such paintings could ever be taken as accurate, but it does raise that perenially interesting question of how much tree cover we have lost over the centuries – and how much, quietly, we have gained.

For a more recent point of reference about the look and the feel of Home Counties countryside, we might turn to films and documentaries made in the 1930s and 1940s. There we see, in the countryside of Kent and Surrey, an agricultural landscape still composed of small fields and horse-drawn carts; working blacksmiths and dusty lanes – a world that simply isn't there now. All it has taken is seventy years. There is the difficult-to-shake sense that the great 'octopus arms' of London now stretch all the way down to Brighton and the south coast. That apart from the odd Down or the occasional woodland trail, it is a region composed purely of uniform dormitory towns with joyless shopping precincts. One would never expect any hint of wilderness. One would scarcely even anticipate getting lost.

But wildness is not everything, and we return to the miniature artistry of Jane Austen. Just as she captured with funny and searing vividness the everyday vanities, anxieties and turbulence of small social groups, so the country that she moved in has a counterpointed sense of understated, though perfectly apparent beauty. On Box Hill and Leith Hill are to be found old beeches, oaks and yews. Rare species include silver-wash fritillary butterflies, bee orchids and orange butterflies. In the summer months, wild basil grows. Just several miles to the south, Leith Hill is one of the highest points in southern England; on clear days you might catch a glimpse of the south coast.

Leslie Stephen, who clearly had a great deal of affection for this part of the world, felt that through walking, he was maintaining a very grand literary tradition. In one essay, he cited the great walker-writers of history: Shakespeare, Ben Jonson, Jonathan Swift, Samuel Richardson, Byron, among many others. He saw the act of walking as being, in its own way, as creative as 'scribbling'. 'The memories of walks,' Stephen wrote,

Are all localised and dated; they are hitched on to particular times and places; they spontaneously form a kind of calendar or connecting thread upon which other memories may be strung … the labour of scribbling books happily leaves no distinct impression, and I would forget that it had ever been undergone; but the picture of some delightful ramble includes incidentally a reference to the nightmare of literary toil from which it relieved me. The author is but the accidental appendage of the tramp.

He went on to discuss how past walker-writers have somehow blocked out the sheer physicality, the corporeal realism of walking. They

have inclined to ignore the true source of their impulse. Even when they speak of the beauties of nature, they would give us to understand that they might have been disembodied spirits, taking aerial flights among mountain solitudes, and independent of the physical machinery of legs and stomachs.

Now, gazing up at the startlingly abrupt Box Hill, it is extremely easy to envisage Stephen, with his own 'physical machinery of legs and stomachs', leading his followers with cries of enthusiasm up those vertiginous paths. In the late Victorian era, Stephen's emphasis on the physicality of walking found an answering echo elsewhere in the country. In Lancashire, one Dr James Johnston gathered a rambling group together dedicated to the works of American poet Walt Whitman. The poet's work was filled with the exultation of nature, and the sense of man engaging fully with the wildness around him. The Lancashire walkers who devoured Whitman's poetry even inaugurated a Bolton 'Whitman Day'.[5] There was the sense here of a Victorian middle-class association celebrating the virtue of vigour, but also to a degree intellectualising it. Not merely was it necessary for gentlemen to explore their physical limits, they had to do so while engaged in serious discussions to do with philosophy and religious belief. As A. H. Sidgwick wrote:

> Leave the intimate character of your surroundings to penetrate slowly into your higher faculties, aided by the consciousness of physical effort, the subtle rhythm of your walk, the feel of the earth beneath your feet, and the thousand intangible influences of sense.

Lovely though the Surrey countryside is – a porcelain miniature, compared to Derbyshire's ceramic vase – one cannot entirely abandon oneself to the thousand intangible influences of sense. It is interesting how many hardcore walkers still view Surrey as something not quite worth bothering with. As I emerge from the National Trust woodland and plod happily back to the railway station, I realise that I have had a good, vigorous two-hour walk among fabulously old, gnarled yews, and can still be back in London in time for lunch. I raise my hat to the aesthetic good sense of Sir Leslie Stephen and his companions.

In this branch of the walking movement, as well as all the others, there never seemed to be any question that rambling was a balm to the body and soul that all should be free to enjoy. Yet there was a corresponding darkness too. We see it especially in the eighteenth and nineteenth centuries, for those were years when some walkers were more vulnerable than others, and some had little choice about the location of their rambles. The act of walking sometimes had its savage underside, rooted in poverty, despair and madness.

CHAPTER 4

A Swift Detour: To Briefly Examine Walkers as Deviants, Outcasts and Fugitives – and as Doomed, Wandering Souls

The walker is not always welcome. A stranger arriving on foot in a small community has the power to alarm. In some corners of literature, particularly the Gothic, the solitary tramper is frequently presented as a figure of menace. Preacher Harry Powell in Davis Grubb's novel *Night of the Hunter* is released from prison, intent upon hunting down a fortune hidden by an executed man. This money has been left with the man's children John and Pearl, and the first these children know of Preacher Powell's sinister arrival in their little town is the sound of his footsteps in the foggy night, walking up and down the street outside their house, casting a vast shadow on their bedroom wall as he sings a gospel hymn. The solitary walker sometimes has mythic qualities. Joseph Maturin's popular 1830 Gothic novel *Melmoth the Wanderer* features a figure who has sold his soul to the Devil in return for an extra 150 years of life and is now wandering the earth in search of someone to swap the bargain with. This, in turn, was an echo of the medieval Christian legend of the Wandering Jew. After insulting Jesus as he carried the Cross along the Via Dolorosa, he was doomed to walk all the continents until the time of the Second Coming. Again, we see the idea of walking as something uncanny, connected with rootlessness and a certain moral ambiguity.

As much as the Romantic poets and subsequent Victorian enthusiasts proselytised about the virtues of walking in real life, there was always another side to it; the sense that walking could also be transgressive. The sense, also, that a certain class of walkers somehow symbolically offended a certain social order, and could be viewed by some as threatening. That class of walker, inevitably, was either labouring, or entirely dispossessed. So, running in parallel with the soaring poetic fancies are also accounts – both real and fictional – of the poor and the wretched walking, almost literally, on the fringes of society.

After the Enclosure Acts, there was very much an element of necessity, and of transgression around the entire subject of walking. In centuries past, only the wealthy middle and upper classes could undertake the sorts of tours that everyone now takes for granted. Poor people stayed close to their own communities and were often legally obliged to do so. In the seventeenth century one needed a licence to walk to another village in search of work or lodgings. Even then, there were those who looked upon even the more genteel class of walkers with a combination of distrust and horror. In 1793, German writer Karl Philipp Moritz was staying with a friend in Richmond, Surrey. He announced his intention to walk to Oxford. His friend was 'greatly astonished'. Nonetheless, Moritz set off. Just a couple of miles in, while enquiring if he was going in the right direction for Oxford, he was told 'you'll want a carriage to get you there.' Undaunted, he struck off on a 'fine broad road' into the countryside, bordered with 'lovely green hedges'. But as the miles wore on, he found that every passing coachman was asking if he wanted a lift on the outside of their vehicle, and every farmworker he passed looked at him in puzzlement. On top of this, he added: 'When I passed through a village, the old women in their bewilderment would let out a "God almighty!"'

There is a similar distrust and impatience on show in Dickens' 1841 novel *The Old Curiosity Shop* when saintly Little Nell and her grandfather are compelled to flee London to escape the nightmarish demands of Daniel Quilp upon the pair of them. Initially, it seems to both Nell and the narrator that away from the London stews and the vice lies a bucolic world of innocence and ease, which they will find even though they are travelling on foot. This illusion of yearning immediately dissipates. The little girl and her kleptomaniac grandfather walk across much of England, fleeing from parish to parish, through nightmare industrial landscapes, meeting various colourful characters, and an increasing amount of peril. As the novel – and their walk – progresses, its lethal nature becomes ever more apparent:

> The child walked with more difficulty than she had led her companion to expect, for the pains that racked her joints were of no common severity, and every exertion increased them. But they wrung from her no complaint, or look of suffering; and though the two travellers proceeded very slowly, they did proceed.

Even though they find sanctuary in the end with a kindly schoolmaster in a small village, it is all too late for Little Nell. The walk has broken her. Her journey must soon come to its end. This is an extreme example, but for an author who was himself so enthusiastic about walking, he has the activity often spelling great hardship for his characters. There is Oliver Twist, on the run from the funeral parlour and the Beadle, on his way to London, almost starving in the process. There is Nicholas Nickleby and crippled Smike, struggling their way across the wintry wastes of the Yorkshire moors. *David Copperfield* features a harrowing journey when the young boy David takes it upon himself to walk from London to Dover, a journey of about seventy miles. Along the way, he is swindled, threatened, and gradually has to sell off his clothes to rascally second-hand traders in order to pay for food. His feet are sore with the

unaccustomed exercise, his face is white with chalk, his hair
dusty and tangled; he is forced to sleep beneath the stars. Worse
yet, though, are his fellow pedestrians. We are left in no doubt
that among the lower classes, walking is not merely a token of
great poverty, but also the last redoubt of the low-down drunken
bully.

Things are different for Victorian literature's country folk,
but even then, long epic walks tend to mirror quite vivid physical and emotional states. In Thomas Hardy's *Tess of the
d'Urbervilles*, walking is the natural mode of transport in places
such as the Vale of Blackmoor. Indeed, in the summer months,
it is seen as a source of pleasure: witness Angel Clare and his
priggish brothers, on their 'walking tour' of Wessex. But it is also
a token of privation; and later, when Angel Clare has left his wife
Tess, and she proves too proud to apply to his family for funding, she is obliged to walk the countryside in search of scarce
winter work:

> There was something of the habitude of the wild animal in the
> unreflecting instinct with which she rambled on – disconnecting
> herself by little from her eventful past at every step, obliterating
> her identity … Thus Tess walks on; a figure which is part of the
> landscape; a fieldwoman pure and simple, in winter guise; a grey
> serge cape, a red woollen cravat, a stuff skirt covered by a whitey
> brown rough wrapper, and buff-leather gloves. Every thread of
> that old attire has become faded and thin under the stroke of
> raindrops, the burn of sunbeams, and the stress of winds.

Rather like Little Nell, Tess in the end is forced to escape on foot.
Having murdered Alec, the man who raped her, and having
caught up with her estranged husband Angel, the two of them
(ignoring the modern railway) simply walk away from the town
of Sandbourne (Bournemouth) and into the New Forest. There
is a sense of disengagement about this walk; that both of them

are plunged too deep into shock to properly register where they might be going. They are walkers in a trance. Many miles into this woodland, they find an empty, secluded house. But this fairy-tale sanctuary – where they achieve their long-delayed consummation – cannot last and, once again, they are forced to move on, this time in the middle of the night:

> Though the sky was dense with cloud, a diffused light from some fragment of a moon had hitherto helped them a little. But the moon had now sunk, the clouds seemed to settle almost on their heads, and the night grew as a dark as a cave. However, they found their way along, keeping as much on the turf as possible that their tread might not resound, which it was easy to do, there being no hedge or fence of any kind. All around was open loneliness and black solitude, over which a stiff breeze blew.

They are on Salisbury Plain. And it is here that Angel and Tess find themselves at a moonless Stonehenge, the wind causing the ancient heathen monument to 'hum'. Tess lies upon the sacrificial stone to rest, and falls asleep there. This has been her final walk. This sort of compulsive walking, the automaton trudge as the mind slips its moorings, is found in the writings of the poet John Clare and his *The Journey from Essex* (1841). This searingly sad journal charts his escape from a lunatic asylum (or 'mad house', as he terms it) in Epping Forest, and his subsequent walk all the way up the North Road to Northamptonshire to be reunited with a wife that he refuses to believe is dead.

This journey augurs badly when he takes a wrong turning, seemingly towards London; but then he is on the right road, 'where it was all plain sailing and steering ahead, meeting no enemy and fearing none.' He spends the night in a shed near Stevenage in which he is tormented by an 'uneasy' dream. The next day's walk finds Clare growing weaker through lack of food and drink: 'a Man passed me on horseback in a Slop frock and said "here's another of the broken down haymakers" and threw me a penny to get a half pint of beer which I picked up and thanked him for.' Clare observes 'I seemed to pass the Milestones very quick in the morning – but toward night they seemed to be stretched further asunder.' By the time he is progressing through Bedfordshire, his hunger is growing worse, as indeed is his physical condition. 'So I went on hopping with a crippled foot for the gravel had got into my old shoes one of which had now nearly lost the sole.' Shelter seems elusive, despite various parsons and passers-by attempting to help with directions to barns and sheds. 'It now began to grow dark apace and the odd houses on the road began to light up and show the inside tennants lots very comfortable, and my outside lot very uncomfortable and wretched.'

But it gets progressively more wretched, so much so that 'I was very often half asleep as I went. On the third day I satisfied my hunger by eating the grass by the road side which seemed to taste something like bread. I was hungry and eat heartily till I was satisfied.' There are those who observe him with something like pity: a gypsy woman who warns him that he 'will be noticed'; a young woman and an old relative who argue over whether he is 'shamming' or not and former neighbours from Helpston passing by on a cart who help him out with fivepence, enough to stop off at an inn for bread, cheese and beer. By now, 'my feet was more crippled than ever and I could scarcely make a walk of it over the stones and being half ashamed to sit down in the street, I forced to keep on the move.'

Thus, agonisingly, he finally reaches his destination of Northborough. Journeys end, but lovers do not meet. 'Mary was not there neither could I get any information about her further then the old story of her being dead six years ago.' The walk has ended with the deranged poet both denying yet simultaneously accepting the truth about his wife. Clare died in an asylum in Northampton. His walk encapsulates a certain sort of extremity, the overwhelming need in the face of intolerable grief, to move and keep moving, to walk and walk with some sort of a purpose, no matter how phantasmal it may be.

* * *

Rural walkers could also attract suspicion because of fear. In plague-ridden times, a walking stranger might be a harbinger of the disease coming to the community. This unease and animosity was, in the sixteenth century, firmly embedded in the law. The crime was 'vagrancy' – it was strictly forbidden for anyone to take to the roads and move from village to village for the purposes of begging. In 1572, there was an 'Acte for the punishment of Vacabondes'. This stated:

> All and everye persone and persones beynge whole and mightye in Body and able to labour, having not Land or Maister, nor using any lawfull Marchaundize Crafte or Mysterye whereby hee or shee might get his or her Lyvinge ... whiche ... shall wander abroade and have not lycense of two Justices of the Peace at the leaste ... shalbee taken adjudged and deemed Roges Vacabondes and Sturdy Beggars.[1]

Another term used was 'mendicant', which in the middle ages had been chiefly applied to friars asking for alms.

The eighteenth- and nineteenth-century Enclosure Acts changed not merely the shape and the lie of the land, but also inevitably the lives of so many country dwellers who depended on it. When forced out of work by the new harsh economic systems, some had little choice but to walk looking for alms or work. This form of roaming placed the walker perilously close to the very periphery of society; they would also be sharing those paths with others who had crossed that boundary.

In the era of highwaymen and footpads, strange walkers could turn out to be vicious criminals, looking for new victims.

Karl Philip Moritz, who caused such a stir by walking to Oxford, was very interested in what he considered 'the lowest and vilest class of criminal – the footpads.' He observed that:

> Tragic examples may be read almost daily in English newspapers of poor people met on the road who have been brutally murdered for a few shillings. These thieves probably murder because they are unable to take flight like the highwayman on his horse and so, should anyone live to give information concerning them, they can be pretty easily overtaken by a hue and cry.

As well as haunting the alleys and courts of the big cities, footpads were to be found out on the roads. Hounslow Heath was notorious for its instances of thieving, as was Windsor Forest. The Windsor footpads employed the striking tactic of painting their faces black. They became known as the Wokingham Blacks, and were responsible for a spree not only involving robbery but also murder. Unlike highwaymen, who persist to this day in enjoying a rather romantic reputation, these pedestrian robbers were always on pretty much the same level as modern muggers. Although as Anne Wallace has pointed out:

> The shape of a footpad's life, indeed, is simply another version of that circle of a day's walk confining the more respectable poor. Because the footpads walk, they cannot easily detain or overtake a rider or a coach; their likeliest victims are walkers, probably poor themselves, and so the footpads remain poor, desperate, and pedestrian.

This form of poverty and desperation finds its historical and most emblematic image in the form of the tramp. When you see the phrase 'gentleman of the road', you instantly see the drink-reddened nose, the disintegrating jacket and trousers, the flapping soles of the shoes, the tied up handkerchief at the end of the stick. This figure is imagined recumbent on a grass verge, listening to the bees hum around the wildflowers on a summer's day. The many vagrants who moved through Wordsworth's poetry gave way to Charles Dickens' tramps. In 1860, he wrote about all the different sorts that he had come into contact with. There was 'Soldier Sailor', obviously discharged from military duty; 'the Lads', who are young and travel in gangs and treat authority figures like beadles with contempt. There is the 'Poor Fellow', an old illiterate man on a desperate quest to visit an ill child some miles away, and who asks for help with directions. He receives money by means of help too; and is later discovered insensible outside a public house.

In more recent times, the rural tramp (as opposed to the urban variety) has been the subject of more interest and sympathy. The author Laurie Lee made the acquaintance of a few as he travelled across England in the 1930s on his way to Spain; men with billy-cans blackened with tannin, who were adept at building small fires, and boiling up tea or potatoes. Subsistence for these men would consist of roaming from village to village, asking for money and food along the way. They would find shelter in barns or outbuildings and do odd jobs on farms, such as hay-making, in return for food and money. Even up until the late 1960s, the tramp seemed an organic part of the rural landscape; a figure who wanted little more than his freedom to roam, and also his freedom to be alone, on the fringes. However, the figure of the tramp always disturbs the city dweller in particular, for the tramp stands for what could conceivably happen to any of us; an unforeseen breakdown that could be triggered by job loss, bereavement, intoxicants. It is a combination of catastrophe, and a curious wish-fufilment. So many people, at some point in their lives, feel an overwhelming urge to escape, to walk in a new direction and leave the past firmly behind them. We hear much less about tramps these days. Disturbed former soldiers – such as those encountered by Wordsworth – are these days more likely to be found in prison, having committed small offences purely to be sent there. There is little succour for the gentleman alcoholic among the lanes of southern England now, and one cannot go begging in a gated community.

As to helping out with hay-making, or sleeping in barns: that form of farming is now industrialised. And the barns have been converted. There is no room in the countryside any more for the gentleman of the road. And there is no room on the road itself. Neither tramps nor regular walkers are welcome any longer on the tarmacked thoroughfares that accommodate obscenely large 4x4s.

So we come full circle to the present day. Whereas in remote areas, walkers are not merely welcomed but actively sought out, they seem to have no place on the actual Queen's highway itself. Nothing apparently must be allowed to interfere with the motorist's right to race along every country road at vast speeds. Notice how, when one is leaving a small village on foot, the pavement grows narrower and narrower, until the point at which it disappears altogether. At this point, the walker is on his own. And once again, as with those eighteenth-century vagrants and mendicants, the walker on the roadside verge is also the transgressor; an unwelcome figure.

In the eyes of many of those behind wheels, there is something at best eccentric about the hiker noodling along the side of the verge. Whereas motorists versus cyclists is a war of more direct confrontation, the motorist's ill-will towards the walker seems less to do with his use of the road as the furrow-browed bewilderment he is causing. Try walking along the verge of a moderately busy B-road within the bounds of the M25, for instance, and you will hear a lot of scorn, and quite a few beeped horns. This is especially bad on the roads of Epping; if one has tired of the pathless leafy woodland floor, and of losing one's sense of direction, and of starting to go round in circles, the way out is to get to one of the roads, and walk in a straight line. But the minute you are on that road, the motorists have little time or patience for you. This is to say nothing of the jokers in cars who like to throw eggs at walkers (another Essex speciality). For the moment, the drivers are in the ascendant, and it is the walkers who look like nerdy eccentrics. But things will change though. Perhaps in the manner of militant cyclists, it is time for the outcast oddball walkers to start reclaiming the roads.

In the nineteenth and early-twentieth century – as walking for its own sake acquired more of a beneficial reputation, and walkers gradually became more assertive about where they could walk – one particular area down in the deep west of the country became the focus for the nascent walking movement. In fact, some prophetic Edwardian ramblers could see a future in which this vast tract of land would be open to all. Since then, this area has lost none of its symbolic weight or value, and remains attractive to walkers drawn from all over the world.

CHAPTER 5

A Day Out Among The Tors and Mires of Dartmoor: The Prototype National Park

In 1951, Dartmoor received its National Park designation, after the Peak District and Snowdonia. Now, out of all of them, it's the one that still carries that 1950s tang of jolly yomping and packed lunches wrapped in brown paper.

The atmosphere is simply psychologically different from that, say, of the Cheviot Hills in Northumbria. There, you are aware of a certain hardness, both of prospects and of people. The chill wind biting in from the North Sea adds to an intangible sense of inhospitality. Clearly, the weather on Dartmoor can be brutish, and there are times of the year – when the frost has gouged ruts into the solid soil – that walking is uncomfortable and hard. Yet there is an underlying feeling of friendliness, somehow. Of all the wild regions in England, Dartmoor has historically also been the most welcoming to ramblers. In fact, the history of this land-scape, and that of the ramblers' movement, is knitted closely together. In the late-nineteenth century, Dartmoor was in some senses almost a prototype national park.

I am cheating slightly by coming here in the warm mellowing light of the late summer. This particular rich, mossy stretch of Dartmoor – the dignified pale grey boulders carved by the wind and the rain into fascinatingly contoured shapes, the white spume of fast rushing streams, bright against the green fern – takes me back to a primary school field trip in 1978. We were staying in the absurdly cute Devon seaside town of Dawlish for a week, and every day a coach would come and take us eleven-year-olds off into the wild open countryside. We had wellington boots, but I had rather grown out of mine – still I happily squeezed my feet into them. Then off we set on a breezy, cheery walk near Buckfastleigh.

By the end of it, I was neither breezy not cheery, for my feet, from toes to heels, were pulsing with pain. I didn't make a fuss, because you didn't want to be sent back to the coach, but as a Dartmoor mist swooped in, the teacher couldn't help notice me limping. Back at Dawlish, she advised me to paddle in the salt water of the sea, to ease the blisters. Sound advice. The next day, and in better footwear, I was back out charging around on the moors. There is something about this part of the world that encourages *Blue Peter*-ish enthusiasm. And it has done for a very long time. Dartmoor is the emblem of heartiness in England: it is where you go if you want to get a Duke of Edinburgh award; it is where serious-minded teenagers embark upon character-building all-night hikes. Dartmoor has a sort of fresh-faced, nicely brought-up virtue written all over it.

The story of how it came to be free to all walkers is also the story of the development of another side of the pastime: the newfound ease of travel. The century of steam saw railway routes spreading right across the country in the mid-nineteenth century – the detailed train maps depicting the new lines like veins. Dartmoor became a favoured destination for the equally new mass phenomenon of walking tourists.

In the 1840s, Brunel's Great Western Railway had stretched from Bristol to London, and was now reaching out to envelop the south of Devon, and devour the smaller rail operators. For nature enthusiasts, this was a tremendous boon, especially as it was not too long before the railways were reaching ever further round the edges of the moor, into Okehampton. But the real breakthrough came rather later, in 1911, when even longer distance day excursions by rail from London – specifically aimed at walkers – were introduced. For ordinary Londoners, this would have opened up hitherto unimagined opportunities. After an early start, they could find themselves climbing and exploring this strange and beautiful and faintly alien landscape before lunchtime.

This feat of travel made a whole new world possible to walkers, and it also marked a profound philosophical shift. Once, if you wanted to travel to the other side of the country, you would need not only a great deal of money, but also a great deal of time. For most classes of people, on meagre wages, with no holidays to speak of other than the holy days themselves, such journeys were beyond possibility. With the railways, however, a destination such as Dartmoor became possible to reach from London in the space of a morning; and could be returned from the very same day. The Great Western Railway extended this extraordinary opportunity to London's working classes by means of extremely reasonable fares. The poor could now enjoy the same exhilarating landscapes as the upper classes.

To this day, holiday-making walkers get off the train in their multitudes at Newton Abbot in south Devon; just a few miles up the road stands Hay Tor, an impressive formation of granite that also marks the very start of the moor. This place has a walkers' information centre. But there is rather more to it all than that. To reach Hay Tor, you must walk up a long, steep grassy hill, and when you do so, you realise – along with the scores of other people, all here to do the same thing – that you are approaching this rock as though it was some kind of sacred monument.

The tor is the size of three or four houses, and the grey wrinkled rock brings out a sort of delighted awe. People clamber on it; people walk around it, their hands trailing on its surface; people sit with their backs to it, comforted by the shelter it gives from the wind. It is almost as if the rock itself is imbued with a sort of benevolent identity. It has some quality that makes people want to touch it. Additionally, the view from here is quite wonderful: the hazy blue of the distant sea, plus the valleys of the Teign river.

Beyond the tor lies the moor; on this breezy summer day, it is very much more colourful than you would ever expect. The purple heather is out as are the bright yellow flowers of gorse. These are jumbled in with the rich green fern. The result, I have to say, is startlingly vulgar. The clashing purple and yellow give the area an oddly jarring, 1970s feel. None the less, there is something immensely cheering about the old granite railway tracks (along which the quarried stone was conveyed in the nineteenth century to the river); the deep valleys, which act as the most amazing echo chamber (I can hear several fishermen by the side of the river about quarter of a mile away); and the playful goats, locking horns on a narrow tor ledge and doing their best to push one another off.

The fact is that Dartmoor has been a totemic walking attraction for a very long time, so it seems completely natural that it should also have been such a pivotal part of the post-Second World War settlement that established the ordinary person's right to walk across such wild and remote places. The moor was rather more populous in centuries past, and the land was richer. Even so, by the nineteenth century, the idea of this moor and similar West Country locales was capturing the imagination of popular writers. The turn of the century saw the publication of the moorland ur-text, the work that would bring walkers to Dartmoor not merely from British cities, but from around the world: Arthur Conan Doyle's *The Hound of the Baskervilles*.

Over the great Grimpen Mire there hung a dense white fog. It was drifting slowly in our direction and banked itself up like a wall on that side of us, low, but thick and well defined. The moon shone on it, and it looked like a great shimmering ice-field, with the heads of distant tors and rocks borne upon its surface. Holmes's face was turned towards it and he muttered impatiently as he watched its sluggish drift … rank reeds and lush, slimy water-plants sent an odour of decay and a heavy miasmatic vapour in our faces, while a false step plunged us more than once thigh-high into the dark, quivering mire, which shook for yards in soft undulations around our feet.

Away from lurid romance, yet nonetheless still rather lurid, the moor's greatest chronicler, William Crossing, traversed it ceaselessly in the late nineteenth century. His widely-selling book *A Guide to Dartmoor* (1909) added much to its allure. An evocative passage in a subsequent volume, *The Land of Stream and Tor*, conjured up a juicy scene that could have been scored by Mussorgsky:

First a pattering of big rain drops, and then, apparently at no great distance above our heads, a tremendous peal of thunder. The old moor seemed to tremble beneath the shock, and the hills around echoed and re-echoed the deep roar. Vivid flashes of lightning darted out from the inky clouds, and appeared to strike the dark crags which towered near us, and a drenching rain descended with a loud hissing noise. There was no cessation to the roar of the thunder. Peal after peal crashed out from the heavens, all nature seeming as if in the throes of some tremendous struggle. The storm was most appalling in its severity, and there was no place to which we could turn to shelter from its pitiless fury.[1]

Even today, these sudden storms can create real emergencies. A recent Ten Tors challenge – involving young people hiking over the moor – had to be abandoned, and the youngsters evacuated by helicopter when conditions got too rough: streams and rivers swelled to monstrous cataracts that threatened to burst their banks. Mires are one thing, but a howling supernatural beast is another. The Baskerville hound tapped into something a little older, and something that those keen to yomp across Dartmoor would have been subconsciously keen on: the idea that somehow, wild creatures still roamed these wild places.

There are outbreaks of such wish-fulfilment today; every summer brings newspaper headlines concerning 'the Beast of Bodmin' and 'big cat sightings' in regions as diverse as Cornwall, Gloucestershire and Derbyshire. Sometimes such creatures are seen by farmers; other times, though, it is walkers who are witness to the astonishing sights. An ordinary, cheerful ramble is suddenly transfigured by a glimpse of something alien and utterly unknowable. The entire notion of familiar woodland trails and moorland footpaths is completely overturned by these fleeting, darting incursions of the dangerously exotic.

Such 'big cat' stories may not just be the emanations of fevered summer tabloids. I have been told by an extremely reliable and rather well-known source – whose identity I mean to protect – that there really is something in it. My source owns land in the West Country, not very far from Dartmoor. There have been local sightings of a black puma; indeed, rather more sightings than ever make it to the newspapers. My source's wife was coming along their drive one day when she saw what she thought was their black labrador in the garden. She was annoyed, as the dog at that time was supposed to be kept indoors. As her car drew closer, the 'dog' suddenly leapt gracefully on to a wall, looked back, and then ran off at breathtaking speed. On top of this and countless other sightings, says my source, the body of one of these beautiful creatures was once found. It was decided among the local farmers and landowners to keep it quiet. As my source said: 'Why not just leave the poor buggers alone? They're not doing any harm.' But how did the pumas get into these places at all? Private menageries, says my source. When such things were made illegal in the 1970s, a surprising number of exotic animal owners turfed their beasts out. And clearly some had breeding pairs. Whatever happens, these particular pumas are apparently extremely wary of human company. So why not simply let them enjoy their lives on the open moors? For that reason, everyone in the local community has agreed never to let on to the media.

The idea alone is thrilling. This walker, for instance, daydreams about being confronted with something inexpressibly atavistic, and staring into unfathomable yellow eyes. I am not alone in this. Every few months, we hear voices in Scotland calling for the reintroduction of the wolf – a species that was hunted out back in the seventeenth century.

However, at this moment – rather bathetically – I ought to counter all my swaggering talk of wanting to walk with pumas and confess to a moment of completely shaming cowardice on my Dartmoor trail. It came when, descending from a tor, I had to make my way through a tiny herd of Dartmoor ponies. These are short, fat, brown little Thelwell creatures, munching moor grass; but in one moment, they all looked up at me suddenly, trotted forward, and I leaped sideways off the path out of their way. Yes, they can bite: but not quite as effectively as a puma.

* * *

In historical terms, unlike the moors and the valleys of the north country, where struggles with local landowners and their game-keepers seemed illimitable, Dartmoor was freer simply because the bleak wastes seemed to have been abandoned to the winds. The eerie landscape was marked only with the occasional abandoned tin mine building. Not that there weren't interested parties intent on finding some other use for these vast tracts of heathery wildness. The Duchy of Cornwall seemed ceaselessly interested in afforestation; timber of course was very big business. But a social tide was assuredly on the turn. This found a voice of sorts in 1912 with the forming of the Society for the Preservation of Nature Reserves. To many landowners and businessmen, the very idea of such a body would have been regarded as pure socialism. Whoever owned the land owned its resources, and was free to use it as they pleased. For a body with political backing such as this to begin lobbying for special preservation was a new sort of pressure.

But this was only the beginning. Such middle-class committees, seeking to secure ever larger tracts of lands for the ordinary walker to enjoy, were to proliferate over the next few years. There was an intriguingly prophetic moment from the novelist Arthur Ransome, who wrote an essay for *The Worker* in 1908 concerning areas such as Dartmoor, as well as the great aristocratic estates:

> Instead of the hereditary owner, I imagined the People. Instead of a private park, I imagined I was walking through and enjoying a National park, a kind of English 'Yosemite'. Why not? If we, under our present miserable economic system, can afford to allow one man to own and use such a park, surely the People who owned all the land, nationally and not individually, could afford to indulge in such a luxury.

After the First World War came the creation of the Forestry Commission. In 1926 there followed the even more influential Council for the Preservation of Rural England. The very word 'preservation' carried a charge of anxiety; that the land needed saving. The cloying industrial vapours of the nineteenth century had drifted thickly over into the twentieth. From a belt across the Midlands, and then further north from Manchester to Leeds, the towns were uniformly smirched, the grand Gothic municipal buildings blackened and a blue sky only ever appearing on those days when the manufactories closed. Otherwise the heavy cloud, all those chemicals and all that ash, was unmoving. On top of this there had been the filthy 1914–18 war of trenches and squalor; the men returning from that conflict had been promised better lives, yet the cities were just as noxious as before.

So these committees to do with land use, and with ensuring that green spaces remained green, were far from being filled with delicate aesthetes. This was to do with the well-being of the population; a sense that everyone had a right to have some form of access to the open air, and to be able to roam and ramble across certain wide open areas with minimum hindrance or obstacle.

Although far from any sites of industrial blight, Dartmoor faced its own threats over the years; not merely that of a huge amount of afforestation, but the sequestering of the land by the military, plus pressure from the water companies to set up huge and terrifically unsightly dams that could in turn provide hydro-electric power. By the turn of the century, the ever-expanding military had been a hindrance to local walkers for some time, as attested by the Edwardian Dartmoor historian Sabine Baring-Gould. There was a case in Belstone, near Steeperton Tor, that attracted his attention. He wrote:

> The military authorities coveted this tract for artillery practice … They set up butts, but woman intervened (sic). A very deter-mined lady marched up to them, although the warning red flags fluttered, and planted herself in front of a target, took out of her reticule a packet of ham sandwiches and a flask of cold tea, and declared her intention of spending the day there. In vain did the military protest, entreat, remonstrate; she proceeded to nibble at her sandwiches and defied them to fire. She carried the day.[2]

The moor had long been a special case and had its own group of specialised devotees: the Dartmoor Preservation Association, which had been formed in 1883. By the 1920s, when ramblers were beginning to coalesce into something approaching a national movement, there was the beginning of interest at government level in the idea of certain tracts of land being essentially nationalised – that is, set aside as free spaces for everyone's use. Common lands on an epic scale, upon which there would be no restrictions of access.

In 1929, Labour Prime Minister Ramsay MacDonald set up a parliamentary committee 'to consider and report,' as he directed, 'whether it is desirable and feasible to establish one or more national parks in Great Britain with a view to the preservation of the natural characteristics, including flora and fauna, and to the improvement of recreational facilities for the people; and to advise generally and in particular as to the areas, if any, that are most suitable to purpose.'

* * *

As all these encouraging political developments were taking place in Whitehall and the Palace of Westminster, 1931 was a key moment elsewhere for all walkers: the formation of the National Council of Ramblers' Federations. This consisted of selected members from walking groups up and down the country, and in 1935 was renamed as the altogether slicker-sounding Ramblers' Association. The rancorous aftermath of the Kinder Scout trespass of 1932 had broadly captured the public imagination, and had brought support for walkers, as well as an upswing in enthusiasm for walking generally. A great many people were clearly in need of an organisation – a club, really – to belong to. Whether to receive advice, or to find other people in one's area to walk with, or to campaign alongside when it came to opening up blocked paths, the new and progressive Ramblers' Association presented the inclusive face of the walking movement.

The aims of the Association obviously appealed more to left-leaning voters than others, but it was not about political gestures. Unlike the brilliant Benny Rothman and his colleagues, the members of the Ramblers' Association were not overtly communist. The ultimate aim of the Association was very simple and straightforward: the opening of vast expanses of empty uncultivated land that were out of bounds to over 99 per cent of the population.

It tapped into a new popular appetite for the outdoors. In the mid 1930s, the hugely popular and influential writer J. B. Priestley was moved to nostalgia for his own turn-of-the-century boyhood rambles in Yorkshire; rather freer and easier, we note, than those to be had in Derbyshire. 'The Bradford folk have always gone streaming out to the moors,' he wrote, 'in the old days, when I was a boy there, this enthusiasm for the ... country had bred a race of mighty pedestrians. Everybody went for enormous walks. I have known men who thought nothing of tramping between 30 or 40 miles every Sunday. In those days, the farmhouses would give you a sevenpenny tea, and there was always more on the table than you could eat. Everybody was knowledgeable about the Dales and their walks, and would spend hours discussing the minutest details of these.'[3]

Not everyone was keen. In 1937, philosopher C. E. M. Joad noted sourly of the rambling craze: 'There are fat girls in shorts, youths in gaudy ties and plus fours ... and a café on top of every hill for their accommodation.' Down south, Dartmoor was even more popular with walkers by the mid 1930s, because it had become de-populated, and because the old industries and farm-steads, which had been part of the moor since the thirteenth century, were quietly dying off. By the time Holmes and Watson got there, much of the working moor had disappeared. Conan Doyle had been on hand to turn it into a sort of Gothic play-ground. The 1939 Hollywood version of the *Hound* tale, with Basil Rathbone and Nigel Bruce, perhaps might have sharpened appetites even further.

For walkers all over the country, 1939 also brought a curi-ously regressive parliamentary step, on the very eve of the Second World War. It was a revival of the Access to Mountains Act, the essence of which had first been pushed by James Bryce MP. Ostensibly this should have been a bit of a triumph for the new-born Ramblers' Association – the first legislation that would enable such walkers as the Kinder Scout enthusiasts to stroll across specially designated wild land with impunity. But there were built-in clauses, at the insistence of landowning interests, that actually made it rather hostile to ramblers.

The debate on the subject of access had been hotting up in the national press. The novelist H. G. Wells, in a piece headlined: 'On War Aims – The Rights of Man', in *The Times* in 1939, had this to say:

> Every man, without distinction of race or colour, is entitled to nourishment, housing, covering, medical care and … the right to roam over any kind of country, moorland, mountain, farm, great garden or what not, where his presence will not be destructive of it, its special use, not dangerous to himself, nor seriously inconvenient to his fellow citizens.

The phrase 'right to roam' was to acquire a special resonance in the decades to come. But in parliament, the 1939 Access to Mountains Bill provoked (largely Conservative) opposition, chiefly in the form of Captain Frank Hughes (Hon. Member for Bury St Edmunds in Suffolk) and Col. R. S. Clarke (MP for East Grinstead). Their view was that 'the Bill attacked the whole principle of owning land … it would mean the owner no longer had the right to enjoy his property.' They then went on to defend privately-owned grouse moors, on the grounds that they were beneficial to a wider section of the economy than might appear at first glance: 'Grouse moors provide employment worth £3,500,000 a year … 20–30,000 gamekeepers … cartridge makers and gun-makers.'

Even more importantly to the Conservative landowners was the idea of damage; that townsfolk wandering all over the land could harm crops or nesting sites, leave litter or start fires. 'The individual who owned lands designated in the Bill,' said Col.

Clarke, 'would lose the protection the law gave him against trespass.'[4] More than this, it was felt important to assert that there
was still such a thing as trespass; if a landowner wanted to keep
his land free of all other people, then it was his perfect right to
do so. It is not too difficult to hear the class subtext here, for one
still hears echoes of it in rambling conflicts to this day. In a
pleasingly satirical inversion of this, on the coast of south Wales,
a community of travellers has recently objected to a path
running past their site on the grounds that ramblers are not to
be trusted, and that you can never tell 'what sort of people might
come walking along.'

Class loathing was certainly what veteran rambler John
Bunting and his friends from Sheffield experienced in the 1930s.
It wasn't just for reasons of grouse-spooking that the Duke of
Rutland didn't want these lads on his moors; it was the very fact,
as he would have seen it, of steel worker apprentices, with their
rough language and ways, being on the moors without permission, and liable to indulge in the sort of malicious mischief the
working classes were famous for that made the idea untenable.
Thus the Access to Mountains Act of 1939 at the last minute had
a trespass clause built into it. Any act of intentional trespass, it
stated, could carry a fine of 40 shillings (or £2 – a very heavy
whack back then). It also made trespass a criminal offence, for
the first time, unless it could be proved that the trespass in question was completely inadvertent. There has been speculation
over the years about why trespass *wasn't* a criminal offence
before. Recently, High Court judge and author Stephen Sedley
wrote:

> The answer, I suspect, is hunting. It was – for that matter, it still
> is – one thing for the hunt to hand out compensation to a small-
> holder who has just had his kitchen garden trashed by a horde
> of domesticated quadrupeds in pursuit of a feral one. It is
> another to let the smallholder or the police put the master of

foxhounds in the dock and have him fined, eventually giving him more form than the local flasher.[5]

Obviously the Access to Mountains Act was meant to be some sort of compromise, to make up for the grave inconvenience caused to landowners by having their acres opened up. The penalty applied especially to those who disregarded restrictions laid down in lambing time, the nesting season, and the shooting season. The response to this among walking enthusiasts was bitter. In the magazine *Progressive Rambler*, there was a writer, Phil Barnes, who went under the pseudonym 'Kinder'. In September 1940 – just as the Battle of Britain was giving way to the Blitz – he wrote this:

> The lesson to be learned was that we cannot hope for any real progress towards access to mountains until we have a people's government prepared to place the aspirations of the people before the claims of any vested interests by the rich and powerful. The inescapable conclusion was that the access to mountains was a political issue, and ramblers should not shrink from accepting this unpalatable fact.

Despite the war – or perhaps, more pertinently, because of it – an increasing amount of thought was being given to this question of access to the wilder areas, once the conflict was over. The subject was brooded over by junior ministers and civil servants, as well as the more stalwart members of the walking movement. Walkers could taste the change in the air. 'The meeting produced the following policy statement,' said a Ramblers' Association memo in May 1943. 'The war had profoundly improved the prospects of achieving access to mountains, along with many other socially desirable aims, provided that in the case of access, full advantage was taken of this opportunity by the Ramblers' Association ... the Ramblers' Association should insist that the freedom to roam on moors and mountains was an elementary right of citizenship which a properly planned society should recognise.'

The wording is so redolent of the time: and prophetic too, in a wider sense. For after the war, a new generation of the young middle-classes did indeed try to create this properly planned society – from health to education to town layouts. It was precisely these J. B. Priestley-readers who would go on to sit on government committees.

In 1946, a year after the war ended, the Ramsay MacDonald notion of national parks was picked up again. The extraordinarily colourful wording of a White Paper that would form the basis of the 1949 Access to the Countryside Act illustrates how this passion had seized even the Civil Service. The White Paper concluded,

> If our proposals are accepted, and pass into law, they will confer upon the public a precious gift of greater rights and privileges. They will protect and preserve more simply and yet more adequately than in the past, the footpath engraved upon the face of the land by the footsteps of our ancestors. They will provide long-distance footpaths which may be followed for many miles away from the din and danger of busy motor roads.
>
> In the wilder parts of the country, our recommendations will provide for the greatest freedom of rambling access consistent with other claims in the land. They will enable active people of all ages to wander harmlessly over moor and mountain, over heath and down, and along cliffs and shores, and to discover for themselves the wild and lonely places, and the solace and inspiration they can give to men who have been 'long in city pent'.

This was not merely laying the foundation for a new sort of relationship between landowners and walkers, it was also setting down the principles by which the first national parks could come into existence. There was still stubborn opposition from the landowning side, though. When it came to the 1949 parliamentary debate over access, and its reading in the House of Lords, 'the Duke of Rutland made a curious contribution,' noted Tom Stephenson:

> As the owner of property in the Peak District, he claimed to know that area fairly well and, he said, 'I know of no farmer, or landowner for that matter, who is not prepared to permit ramblers over his land in those areas where it is unlikely that they can do any harm, and provided they behave themselves.' Sheffield ramblers of the day … would have had no difficulty in listing numerous areas where no such liberty existed.

The Duke of Rutland's speech continued thus: 'I would like to ask the noble lord who will be replying what sort of people he envisages will be asked to serve on the National Parks Commission (NPC). It is important that the NPC should be impartial and should be representative of all interests concerned. I sincerely hope that it will not consist only of members of the Trades Union Congress and the Workers Rambling Association.'

A parliamentary agent summed up the fears of the vested interests much more plainly when he declared: 'Have the landowners no rights? This is not Russia you know.'[6] Walkers faced opposition not merely from Dukes, but also from the water boards. Some of the most vexatious disputes over access to land took place near reservoirs high up in moorland. Various water boards wanted to make such land off-limits for fear of the damage that the urban working class could wreak. There was the apprehension that these people might somehow infect the reservoir water with typhoid; or indeed foul it with excreta. It was necessary to call in grown-up scientific opinion to demonstrate that even if some typhoid-ravaged factory worker had swum in a reservoir to his heart's content, it would be pretty much impossible for the typhus organism to survive any length of time in the freezing cold waters.

Prejudices were not easily budged, especially in the north of England, where society seemed so dramatically polarised. As veteran rambler (and in the 1930s, apprentice steel worker) John Bunting observes: 'Why would we have wanted to cause any damage while walking? The lads who *were* trouble went to cause *their* trouble in the towns. Lads from Sheffield who would go up to Hayfield, say, and run around, effing this and that. That type would never be bothered to go walking in the open countryside.'

The issue was a matter of tremendous interest to (primarily) Labour politicians. Mr Bunting remembers going to 1930s ramblers' rallies which were attended by Hugh Dalton and Barbara Castle. After Labour's 1945 landslide, Dalton became Chancellor of the Exchequer, and lost none of his enthusiasm for the walking movement. The same is true of the fiery MP Barbara Castle, who recalled of Dalton that he 'blazed a trail'. These were the politicians who attended so carefully to that 1949 parliamentary debate. They were there to agree when the point was made that in return for freedom, walkers also now had new responsibilities. Lewis Silkin remarked in the House of Commons: 'The public are being put on their honour not to do anything which would create wilful damage to the farming interest. For the first time in the history of this country, there will be a legal right on the part of the public to wander over people's land.' He added, rather inspirationally: 'Now at last we shall be able to see that the mountains of Snowdonia, the lakes and waters of the Broads, the moors and dales of the Peak, the South Downs and the Tors of the West Country belong to the people as a right and not a concession.'

* * *

The 1951 inauguration of the National Parks might be regarded as one of the great triumphs of the walking movement. The country was just emerging from a grinding period of austerity, and while historians always point to London's Festival of Britain as the focus point of a new optimism, the opening up of vast tracts of land for anyone to enjoy unimpeded must have been the far greater tonic to those who had endured grim city winters. The National Parks illustrate an aspect of the new Atomic Age. On Britain's coast, alien-looking establishments of white concrete with names like Windscale were springing up to usher in a new, and to many scientifically incomprehensible, era of nuclear energy. Meanwhile, the National Parks were there to boost health and fitness and happiness through the appreciation of nature. Moreover, in a sense, they too were futuristic, for they hinted at a time to come when the land would be there as much for our leisure as to be worked. Leisure was to become one of the keywords of the age; a belief that in a computerised future, we would all have much more time on our hands, much more time to appreciate the great outdoors.

What you hear less of is the element of a quiet class triumph, although it was unquestionably there. As with so much else in that post-war period – from the restructuring of the Welfare State onwards – the middle classes thought radical thoughts to improve the lives of the working classes. And if that meant inconveniencing a much-weakened upper class, then so much the better. Just as the war destroyed the nation's finances, so too many aristocratic landowners found those immediate post-war years difficult. Not merely was the money tighter, but staff were becoming far harder to recruit. Apart from anything else, why would anyone go into service – with its miserable hours and threadbare pay – when there were far better wages and working conditions to be found in the suddenly plentiful factories making consumer goods? As a result, the old landed estates were becoming very much more difficult to maintain.

Much as many aristocrats were forced to go to the National Trust for help in preserving their homes, so this new policy of access to land might well have been something of a relief to men like the Duke of Rutland and the Duke of Devonshire, who saw parts of the Peak District in essence being nationalised. Access to the public seemed a perfectly reasonable price to pay for the opportunity to hang on, rather than sell up.

For the walking movement, however, this was by no means the end of it. While the National Parks were (and still are) a superb sanctuary for millions of urban dwellers, they were still only a very small proportion of the country. The dedicated walker wanted to explore, to satisfy curiosity – to see what lay over the hills and far away. There was so much of the land still to see, to know, to experience. Walkers wanted greater freedoms yet.

While the terrible depredations of the war had encouraged the belief that British urban populations deserved better – the bombing acting as the catalyst for a wholesale demolition of slum districts up and down the land – so the sleeker modernity of this post-war settlement gradually brought greater material wealth. This in turn brought with it greater ease of travel, by means of the motorcar. The effect this had on one part of the country, the Lake District, can still be felt now. In the 1950s, a bespectacled and rather irascible former town clerk loved these hills so much that he decided to catalogue and record them in a series of beautifully produced little books, which were to become the focus of a vast and curious cult that persists today.

CHAPTER 6

Seatoller to Haystacks, Underskiddaw to Dodd Point: The Lake District and the Cults of Wordsworth, Wainwright and Withnail

It is a wildly inconvenient moment to develop vertigo. I crouch, paralysed, clinging onto some cold brown heather growing out of the turf beside me, on a narrow ledge-like path that seems to be right on the edge of a sheer abyss hundreds of feet up – my head is definitely swimming.

How could this place have inspired so much sublime poetry, so many lovingly written guides? How did such a landscape change from being regarded as stern and harsh up to the eighteenth century to being an area now renowned the world over for its subtle charm and beauty? And how can this be the place that suddenly became the totemic destination for so many millions of post-war walkers? If I look down, I can see not merely the steep gully stretching beneath me but also, if I turn my head a little, a distant lake and some fields that seem extraordinarily far down. It is like looking out of an aeroplane window; the prospect is one of mountain tops and deep, deep valleys with tiny wriggling roads and speck-like cars. I had never quite expected this from the Lake District. You hear of such things in Scotland, but here? The mountain whose side I seem to be clinging to is near Haystacks, which lies behind the high ground of Honister Pass, near Lake Derwent.

More vexingly, this was one of the favourite spots of Alfred Wainwright. I try to get a grip of myself, and continue to clamber up a narrow, slate path that is moist with last night's sleet, while imagining the disdain that Wainwright would have felt for me. A little further up this slippy, unsteady path, with that vertiginous drop just one step to my right side, I now realise that I am one of these walkers that you read about; the ones who think every landscape, every path, is feasible, and available. Wainwright knew better; he knew that there were days when these hills could kill the unwary.

In 1930, Alfred Wainwright was a young clerk, gangling and ginger-haired, working in the Municipal Treasury office of Blackburn Town Council. The air of this town was dense with factory chimney smoke. Every day, in the soporific routine of the office, Wainwright and his young colleagues would intersperse poring over accounting figures with discussions about the girls that they 'most wanted to give it to.' Aged twenty-three, Wainwright and his cousin, Eric Beardsall, decided it was time for a hiking holiday. He had never before been to the Lake District. The first goal was Orrest Head. 'It was a moment of magic,' wrote Wainwright in his autobiography,

a revelation so unexpected that I stood transfixed, unable to believe my eyes. I saw mountain ranges, one after another, the nearer starkly etched, those beyond fading into the blue distance. Rich woodlands, emerald pastures and the shimmering waters of the lake below added to a pageant of loveliness, a glorious panorama that held me enthralled ... There were no big factories and tall chimneys and crowded tenements to disfigure a scene of supreme beauty, and there was a profound stillness and tranquillity. There was no sound other than the singing of larks overhead.[1]

Ten years later, in 1941, now married to Ruth and with one child, the Wainwright family moved to Kendal, where he worked at the Borough Council, in a senior accounting position. By 1952 – at the age of forty-five – he embarked upon writing and illustrating the *Pictorial Guides to the Lakeland Fells*, books that would confer upon him a form of immortality. They were, and are still, adored by countless readers.

To pick up one of these volumes now is to marvel not only at exquisite artistry and vivid, honest prose, but also at the sheer, supernatural levels of care and patience that must have gone into their production. Each of the seven books in this sequence – hardbacked, pocket-sized – contain carefully handwritten text, laid out around detailed contour maps and extraordinaily evoca- tive and accurate drawings of each of the mountains and lakes. Book Seven contains a perfectly illustrated 'Ascent from Honister Pass', the very path that I am currently paralysed upon. 'This is a remarkably easy walk,' remarks Wainwright blithely in that perfect handwritten print. 'All the family will enjoy it, irrespect- ive of age.' It was also the case almost as soon as these books were first published that they were enjoyed by families, irrespective of age.

Wainwright's name and the Lake District are now absolutely interchangeable. And now, as I am half standing, half crouching, on the edge of a mountain not far from Wainwright's favourite spot, and where his ashes were scattered, I can't help wondering both about the enthusiastic cult around his writing, and the cult of the Lake District itself. Why, among so many other dramatic landscapes in Britain, is this one so favoured by walkers? And why does Wainwright's work continue to resonate? The answer to both questions is to do with an unconscious narrative of landscape: even for those who have never been, these dark fells have a similar hold on the rambler's imagination as the fantastic- al landscape of Middle Earth. We are aware of these mountains and ice-cold lakes as a region, compact, delineated. There is a

sense of apartness, unsulliedness and also, curiously, of a kind
of innocence. Preposterous, really, when one considers the reality of the teeming lakes and gridlocked roads of summertime;
but the Lake District and Wainwright now give the most reso-
lutely un-poetic among us the licence to experience a tightly-
regulated, highly linear form of romanticism. Walkers are
encouraged to clamber around these bunched, towering, snag-
gletoothed crags; to sit like Wainwright upon their summits and
survey patchwork views; but not to get soppy about them.

Enthralling and evocative though Wainwright's deceptively
simple prose and rich illustrations are, there was underneath it
a rather more complex and strange character. It was not that he
was solitary; he was always happy when his son Peter accompanied him on his treks through the Fells. And indeed he had good
friends and an especial partiality for attractive women walkers
with pretty bottoms. These excursions were to an extent the
journeys of a man turning his back on a world that he did not
much care for.

You might say: who can blame him? Surely anyone who had
left the lung-coating air of Blackburn would be grateful for the
music of running streams and the wide expanses of constantly
changing sky? And who wouldn't become rather indignant if
they clambered all that way up a mountain only to be greeted
with the sight of other walkers guzzling 'crisps and fizzy pop'
(particular Wainwright dislikes) and paying scant attention to
the glories of the views all around them? It went a little further
than this though. Wainwright had a sort of acutely intelligent
autodidact gruffness that in an unfavourable light might equally
have been termed arrogance. This was coupled with an aversion
to direct contact with strangers. He hated telephone calls, and
would certainly never conduct any kind of business, even
making appointments, over the phone. Even if the BBC wanted
to make contact, they were advised that it was best to do so by
letter. Domestically, he was more hopeless than any caricatured

northern male. He did not know how to cook an egg; he did not know how to make tea. 'Not knowing', of course, means never having had to find out. But when you read his carefully calibrated prose, his evocations of the charms of Ennerdale, the soaring beauty of the view from Hay Stacks, even when you admire that calligraphy (a skill of his since schooldays), you wonder if a reluctance to engage with a wider world is a trait common to other walkers?

The fact that his wife Ruth was driven to leave him in the mid-1960s compounds the sense that here was a man who had allowed his love for the hills to crowd out everything else. Heartbreakingly, as they discussed what sort of modest financial settlement Alfred should make with her, Ruth suggested that she might pop back to the house one day a week to do his housework. The antipathy ran deep. In his later years, he donated quite a large amount of his income to animal welfare charities – always the clearest indicator of someone who has little time for humanity.

As Wainwright's friend, Molly Lefebure, told his biographer Hunter Davies, 'I gathered from stray remarks he had an empty married life. He was very lonely, communication with others could never have been easy for him. He felt secure with his pen, his typewriter and the knowledge that the postbox was between him and the recipient of his letters. At a safe distance, he could relax and let himself go.' She went on, 'what I didn't like about him was his conceit, which got worse as he got older. I don't mean as a person, but as a writer. He did begin to think he was God, or Moses, laying down the law on Lakeland, telling his readers, "You will be treading in my footsteps."'[2]

Those footsteps! There has been continuing controversy in recent years concerning the popularity of those footsteps, and how they are now leading to erosion on Wainwright's favourite footpaths. His supporters dismiss this, first with the assertion that a certain amount of erosion would be natural anyway, thanks to the sheep. Secondly, they argue, the sheer level of attention means a concomitant level of care. Even the path that I am clinging to uncertainly right now, my fingers numb from holding on to the cold, cold rock, is one of the most lovingly preserved and tended in the world.

*   *   *

Writing all seven volumes of the Pictorial Guides would, Wainwright calculated in 1952, take thirteen years to complete; miniaturist masterpieces. And he was exactly right. What he did not imagine was that these cleverly produced books would so very quickly become huge national hits, going through countless reprints, new editions and millions of copies. He was an amazing stickler for layout, and variety, and ensuring that each right-hand page ended with a full stop, so the reader would not have to turn over and lose focus on the illustration.

Fundamentally, what he did somehow was to snatch the Lake District away from the romanticism of William Wordsworth. If anything other than a helpless love of this part of the world linked the two men, it was a certain prickliness of temperament. As difficult and shirty as Wainwright could be, Wordsworth could be worse, and on a much more magisterial scale. Wordsworth had almost single-handedly drawn the public's attention to the wild wonders of this previously neglected part of the country – through the soaring poetry of the Lyrical Ballads, written with Samuel Taylor Coleridge in 1798, the epic *Prelude* of 1805, and not least, his own specially written guide book to the Lakes of 1810. Wordsworth some years after that bitterly complained about the coming of the railways that would bring hordes of visitors to the area. As the Kendal to Windermere line was prepared for construction in the 1840s, Wordsworth argued that urban holidaymakers would not benefit. 'The good is not to be obtained by transferring … uneducated persons in large bodies to particular spots,' he wrote. Instead, he argued, such folk would perhaps derive more from 'little excursions with their wives and children among neighbouring fields, whither the whole of each family might stroll.'[3]

Wordsworth went rather further in a letter to the editor of *The Morning Post* in 1844, when work on the railway line had been suspended. He had been listening to the argument that standing in the way of the railway was a grave injustice to the labouring poor, denying them all that natural beauty. Wordsworth didn't see it that way. 'The directors of railway companies are always ready to devise or encourage entertainments for tempting the humbler classes to leave their homes,' he wrote, 'we should have wrestling matches, horse and boat races without number, and pot-houses and beer-houses … The injury which would thus be done to morals, both among this influx of strangers and the lower class of inhabitants, is obvious.'

I wonder what Wordsworth would think now? Obviously Coniston and Grasmere are not, as yet, renowned for their wrestling matches or beer houses; none the less, in the high summer, when the roads are clogged, and the waters of the lakes are filled with chugging boats, it is quite difficult to see what Wordsworth described as the area's 'character of seclusion and retirement.' Glossy brochures in local Lake District hotels point not to walking routes, but to a whole mini-economy of specialised museums, art galleries, shopping centres, restaurants, and child-friendly indoor attractions, some centred around Beatrix Potter, another famous Lake District inhabitant. You can see why Wordsworth would yearn for purity; but is it reverse snobbery to point out that one poet's purity is another family's rain-trudging boredom? Is it so very awful that the local economy now seems so heavily geared towards the less active sort of visitor?

More than anyone else, William Wordsworth created the Lake District; by which I mean through the force of his language, he turned a landscape previously regarded as forbidding, gloomy and barren, into an airy and *innocent* realm where the spirit might find freedom. 'Fair seed-time had my soul,' as he was 'wandering half the night among the Cliffs/And the smooth Hollows'. And even the charge of menace that these vast dark hills might be seen to carry is transformed by Wordsworth instead into a form of magical awe, such as the passage in *The Prelude* when his younger self iceskates beneath a darkening winter sky, and the noise finds an answering echo in those blackened hills that 'tinkle like iron.'

Wordsworth was not the first walker to have noticed the singular beauty of this harsh land. In the mid to late-eighteenth century, the area became fashionable among the smarter cognoscenti. In 1768, the roaming Reverend William Gilpin, who had walked Snowdonia and other challenging regions, declared that the Lake District had 'that kind of beauty which is agreeable in a picture.' Some time before Wordsworth wrote his lines on Tintern Abbey, Gilpin had got there first; on another of his tours, he pointed out the pleasing aspects of that melancholy decay. While in Arthur Young's *Six Month's Tour Through the North of England*, published in 1770, Young enthused over the 'sublime' and the 'picturesque' aspects of the scenery. Thomas Gray was very detailed in his walks through Helvellyn, Grasmere and Ambleside, comparing dramatic rockfaces and waterfalls favourably with the Alps.

It was not merely the romantic poets who proclaimed this hitherto unacknowledged wild beauty; it was artists too. Among them were Gainsborough and Joseph Wright of Derby, vying to produce the most suitably dramatic canvases of such sublime landscapes, often in lurid lights of bronze or darkest blue, with wind-torn trees and violent gushing waters. So among the monied class, tourists started heading for the region, and even by the 1780s, there were pleasure boats ploughing up and down the lakes.

When Samuel Taylor Coleridge, Wordsworth's collaborator in the *Lyrical Ballads* of 1798, was living in Keswick, he viewed this procession of the well-off and the artistic with a faintly jaundiced eye, though he expressed the hope that they did at least keep 'their hearts awake.' According to writer Jenny Uglow, this fashionable parade of visitors slowed with the outbreak of the Napoleonic wars. However, it might equally be asserted that the same wars brought a halt to the continental Grand Tours, and thus left a lot of rich young British men travelling instead to the remote corners of the British Isles in search of the sublime. Whatever the case, it was really left to the nascent genius of Wordsworth to bring this particular branch of romanticism out to the full. Unlike the metaphysical poets, or the Georgians, the Romantics looked at nature in her extremity and found that such sublimity could awaken a soaring spirituality in the beholder; as long, that is, as that person was completely alive to what he was seeing. Wordsworth and Coleridge drew their deepest inspiration from the darkness of the hills.

Keats was another of the Romantics to find that rigorous walking helped one to appreciate the profounder beauties of nature. On one occasion, in 1818, he walked from Lancaster to Inverness, roughly a distance of 600 miles. Such a journey at that time was fraught with risks to health, and indeed Keats came down with throat ulcers. He managed to negotiate a wild landscape, with Highland roads that had only recently been set in order by the English military, with the help of their mapmaking department the Ordnance Survey.

Meanwhile, Wordsworth, having done so much to influence the spirit of the age, was later at pains to point out that a romantic sensibility was not necessarily a natural one, somehow implanted at birth. He was also extremely aware that the completeness of his own approach had been pioneering. He quoted the eighteenth-century poet John Gray's dismayed reaction to the crags of Borrowdale: 'Let us not speak of them, but look and pass on.' He also quoted a woman with whom he had sometimes lodged at Keswick. 'Bless me!' she said, 'folk are always talking about prospects: when I was young, there was never a thing neamed.'

Wordsworth was quite clear in his *Guide to the Lakes* on the point of how the humbler classes might look at things:

A vivid perception of romantic scenery is neither inherent in mankind, nor a necessary consequence of even a comprehensive education. It is benignly ordained that green fields, clear blue skies, running streams of pure water, rich groves and woods, orchards, and all the ordinary varieties of rural nature, should find an easy way to the affections of all men, and more or less so from early childhood till the senses are impaired by old age and the sources of mere earthly enjoyment have in a great measure failed. But a taste beyond this, however desirable it may be that everyone should possess it, is not to be implanted at once; it must be gradually developed both in nations and individuals. Rocks and mountains, torrents and widespread waters, and all those features of nature which go to the composition of such scenes as this part of England is distinguished for, cannot, in their finer relations to the human mind, be comprehended, or even very imperfectly conceived, without processes of culture or opportunities of observation in some degree habitual ... it is noticeable what trifling conventional prepossessions will, in common minds, not only preclude pleasure from the sight of natural beauty, but will even turn it into an object of disgust.

Wordsworth seemed to be saying that only a very few could genuinely appreciate the soul of this place. So, 150 years after that, what was Alfred Wainwright saying? His approach right from the start was in many ways the very opposite of poetry. His aim was not to excavate soul or spirit from the hills, to imbue the mountains with a sense of brooding majesty. His aim was simply to capture, as exactly as he could, the myriad of details from rocks to flowers to glittering tarns that could trigger delight in others. Beauty there was, certainly, but it was beauty that he sought to catalogue, yard by yard, in intense, microscopic exactitude.

Many of Wainwright's perceptive and sharply observed pen and ink illustrations in the guide are, in part, self-portraits; depicting him, back to the frame, seated against a boulder, and looking out over distant ranges of hills. These illustrations helped to persuade countless thousands of people to come to this part of the world, to drink in such views themselves. And now here I am. The start of my attempt to follow in Wainwright's steps – to try to see this landscape as he saw it – is very different to the Wainwright image of the peace and stillness to be found at the tops of those hills.

*   *   *

You can get a bus to the village of Seatoller, just south of Derwent Water, and begin the walk from there. The village itself is not much more than a road and three or four whitewashed houses. Immediately the road points upwards, first through some trees, and a small gushing valley of icy fresh water and overhanging branches. Quite quickly, you are above the tree line, and the gradient isn't letting up. Now you see a prospect before you of white and black hills; the white being last night's snow. This is the road zigzagging up to the Honister Pass; now you are in a tree-less land of yellow-grey grass and mossy tussocks. You are reminded of all those eighteenth-century figures who gazed at views like this and shuddered with horror. But when you are swaddled in a waterproof and jeans and great thick boots, with great thick socks, the urge to climb as far as you can is extremely strong. There is a magnetic power in these hills; you cannot help but be drawn upwards.

This bleak road is often impassable in the winter. I am on it in early March and even now, at the cusp of spring, there has been sleet and hail that will not budge. I approach the entrance to the Honister slate mine, and the car park is adorned with fancy slate carvings and signs. Here too is a brilliantly sparse looking Youth Hostel – single storey, grey, the bunk beds visible through the windows. Unlike many others of its type, this construction seems a proper 1930s throwback; the basic comfort of shelter, and very little else.

It is here, as I leave the road and start climbing the stony path, that I am reminded forcibly that this is no uncharted wilderness I am heading into: both the tastefully carved wooden sign, pointing to Haystacks and Grey Garth, and the carefully constructed stone path itself, tell you that this route has been put here for your benefit. Still, I currently have this spot to myself, and this in itself sweeps away one of my Lake District preconceptions: that every path and every hill would be jammed with walkers, saying 'good morning' to one another.

The incline on the path at first is a little sharper than I expected, but there is the corresponding pleasure of hearing the slate stones beneath my feet grinding together. Soon I find that I have been climbing one side of a vast valley; the other side of it looms enormous and dark, scattered with flint. None of this seemed apparent from the road. But then I am over the first brow of this hill, and suddenly, everything is changed again. The valley behind has now disappeared from view. What lies ahead looks rather more rugged than anything I had expected from the Lake District.

There is the first sense of the *unheimlich*; really, what this amounts to is a gelid pool of water on the grey slate path; the water is milky, half frozen by the sleet. It also gathers in the hollows of brown moss and the darker slate around. Ahead lies more slate; further on is a rugged bothy of stone, with an unexpectedly ornamental front gate. The roof of this property is half off. No one can shelter here now, and it looks as though no one has done so for years.

A new, shallow valley presents itself, framed by looming peaks of bright white and jet black and brown. It is the angles that are a little unexpected; whereas most hills have their softer, rounder edges, here are perpendicular points of Gothic sharpness touching the sky, upright and somehow clustered, pressed together like the striations in the limestone beneath my feet. Around me, the lichen on the grey stones and vast boulders seems luminously green; a trick of the constantly changing light, perhaps, as the clouds swarm and bustle overhead. Then there is the apparent absence of any animal life. I have not seen a thing; not a hare, nor a bird. It is apparently just me up here, all alone. There has not even been the scaly flash of a newt in a tarn. At this point, I am standing on a sort of undulating stony plain, framed by these cathedral-like hills. The path ahead dips down into a hollow, through which rushes what is no doubt some of the freshest water in the world. Then the distant path climbs again, up a hill of dark brown, dotted with grey boulders.

Now the ascent is much easier, but the wind is maddening, chiefly because of its irregularity. For a few minutes, it will blast icily, steadily; but then disconcertingly it will stop and the cold air will be still and suddenly the ringing ears are able to pick up other noises, such as the faraway rush of falling water or even the occasional overhead military plane. The wind gusts gruffly again and there is a curious smell – could it possibly be the sea? There is a disconcerting hint in the scent of salt and (this really cannot be so) seaweed. Then the wind stops abruptly, and once again the silence is filled with a constant gurgling. I have now climbed to a further level, stonier yet, and the clouds above are moving with supernatural speed.

It is now that I approach a tarn. The surface riffles as the wind, without warning, starts blasting again. Apparently newts make their homes in the water up here, though as I get close to the water, I find the moss and heather that I am standing upon are already half submerged, and so it's rather tricky to get closer

105

for a proper look. In this shrewd wind, and with my footsteps in the sleet behind, I have no wish to get my feet wet. It would take them a very long time to warm up again. Onwards, across another tumbling stream, and here is where I seem to have entered a realm of optical illusion. The path that I see before me leads upwards once more – a trail of big, loose stones and coarse dark brown heather and turf, poking out of the wall of the hill. So I am upon it, and walk steadily upwards for a few hundred yards. Then I turn my head slightly from the path before me. And that is when the vertigo hits. Where exactly did that astounding, severe drop materialise from?

It is all fabulously unsettling. I climb a little further, my feet feeling for reassurance among large, moist stones, looking up at the dark crag rising above me. I try to reason it out. The path is perfectly wide enough to walk up without clinging pathetically to cold stones and unruly sprigs of heather. Just avoid looking to the right, that's all. Of course, it is impossible not to see that vast valley, and the grey lake, so far below. Then the wind starts buffeting again. It feels aggressive. I think to myself, absurdly: 'I bet Melvyn Bragg wouldn't stop here.' Then, after another shockingly strong gust, I give up. I have recalled the recent news-paper story about the man who fell off a hill and bounced pretty much all the way down. He survived, miraculously, with minor injuries. The indignity, though, must have been spectacular. That frustrated itch – when one curtails a walk – is extraordin-ary. You can almost feel it physically, at the back of your brain; that sense that turning back is wrong, and that one must simply press further and further forward. Even as I begin my crab-like descent of this steep path, I hesitate again, look back, and think: how can I leave this? How can I turn away without having seen what lies over the hill? It is the thread that pulls all walkers; that irrational need to see the valley beyond.

However, sweet reason wins. The minute I am back at that tarn, just a few hundred yards away, any sense of vertigo dissipates. I do notice, however, that I am lighter on my feet. The relief of getting off that ledge has added a literal spring to my step. And now there is intermittent sunshine, I can now see the most extraordinary thing happening to some of the slate on a hill in the distance. Before it was grey-black; now it is a deep sea green. The colour is mesmerising, all the more so for seeming illusory. Is it a trick of the Lakes light? As I draw closer, I see that this must be slate that has been hewn from the mine below and taken for whatever reason up the hill. That very dark green seems to give the stone an almost metaphysical depth. I could stand here and look at it all day. In fact, later on, back down in Keswick, I see a few of the local buildings have been constructed from this very slate. The colour has worn a little but it is no less arresting.

As I walk back, though, down through these damp, stony hollows, hemmed in by all those sharp spire peaks, I can see how this sort of landscape mirrored something in Alfred Wainwright's soul. Fresh and open and beautiful though it is, there is something unyielding and intransigent in the landscape here, a lack of forgiveness.

*   *   *

At the turn of the last century, these parts were much favoured by the Oxbridge educated liberal intelligentsia – men such as Raymond Asquith and Herbert Samuel. They used the hills to play a human version of 'hare and hounds'; in other words, they would hunt each other down. The game would involve serious climbs, and even more dramatic and fast-paced descents. I am not sure Wainwright would have looked kindly on tomfoolery of this sort. The land was there to be taken seriously, not to be used as a playground. 'All I ask for, at the end,' wrote Wainwright in 1966, is a long, last resting place by the side of Innominate Tarn, on Haystacks, where the water gently laps the gravelly shore and the heather blooms and Pillar and Gable keep unfailing watch. A quiet place, a lonely place. I shall go to it, for the last time, and be carried: someone who knew me in life will take me there and empty me out of a little box and leave me there alone. And if you, dear reader, should get a bit of grit in your boot as you are crossing Haystacks in the years to come, please treat it with respect. It might be me.

Wainwright died in 1991. His remains have been crossed and recrossed countless times by countless walkers since. The area is, to many, a form of shrine.

Both Wainwright, and Wordsworth a century before him, could see the paradoxical results of their work. The secluded paths that had provided their inspiration were now sought out by countless others. In Wordsworth's 1810 *Guide to the Lakes*, he ruefully reflected 'It was well for the undisturbed pleasure of the Poet that he had no forebodings of the change which was soon to take place.' This was the influx of walkers that he had unwittingly encouraged. He continued: 'It might have been hoped that these words, indicating how much the charm of what *was* depended on what was *not*, would of themselves have preserved the ancient franchises of this and other kindred mountain retirements from trespass; or (shall I dare say?) would have secured scenes so consecrated from profanation'. But no, the vulgar travellers insisted upon coming. 'The lakes had now become celebrated,' he added, 'visitors flocked hither from all parts of England; the fancies of some were smitten so deeply that they became settlers; and the Islands of Derwent-Water and Windermere, as they offered the strongest temptation, were the first places seized upon, and were instantly defaced by the intrusion'.

Today's walkers in the Lake District might hear very precise echoes of this cry. Defacement and intrusion are the accusations that have been ceaselessly thrown at ramblers. Many ramblers might stop to consider that even if Wordsworth's anguish was primarily aesthetic, it was still obviously coloured by a form of snobbery. There are also passages in his *Guide* which again amusingly mirror modern day stances. Whereas many hillwalkers today loathe the spectacle of vast white windfarms, the huge blades scything circles through highland air, so the poet was infuriated by another white addition to the landscape, new to his generation: that of the whitewashed cottage.

These are now so much part of the Lakeland and northern landscape that it is possible you have never even especially noticed their whiteness before. From a distance, a whitewashed cottage nestling at the base of a vast green hill seems as organic and perfectly placed as the white specks of sheep wandering all over the grass. This, however, is not how Wordsworth saw it:

> The objections to white, as a colour, in large spots or masses in landscape, especially in a mountainous country, are insurmountable ... In Nature, pure white is scarcely ever found but in small objects, such as flowers: or in those which are transitory, as the clouds, foam of rivers, and snow ... white destroys the *gradations* of distance ... Five or six white houses, scattered over a valley, by their obtrusiveness, dot the surface and divide it into triangles, or other mathematical figures, haunting the eye, and disturbing that repose which might otherwise be perfect ... it is after sunset, at the coming on of twilight, that white objects are most to be complained of. The solemnity and quietness of Nature at that time are always marred, and often destroyed by them.[4]

Yet for all his complaints, these sorts of passages also serve as a useful illustration of just how *little* the Lakes have changed, in essence, since his time. The white that Wordsworth would find most jarring now, I suspect, is the white of the fat contrails left crisscrossed over the pure blue sky by jumbo jets flying silently 24,000 feet above. Go just a few miles to the west, though, and we have another outbreak of whiteness in the landscape, and I am not at all sure how Wordsworth might have reacted to it: this is in the form of the nuclear power station Sellafield, first known as Windscale when it opened in the 1940s. Parts of this colossal coastal structure were pure white, and silver, and would have contrasted strongly with the dark green of the Irish Sea. Then, just a few miles to the east, there is that other great standby of post-war Britain: the motorway.

The curious thing about the writings of Alfred Wainwright is that the land he loved was – at the very time he was popularising it for millions – bordered by these two vast symbols of jet-age modernity. The motorway has enabled millions of people, inspired by Wainwright's writing, to drive to the Lake District with the greatest ease, thus ensuring in the summer months that very few may wander lonely. And the looming bulk of Sellafield is that other great totem from the post-war years: the belief when it was built that science and technology – the ability to wrestle with the atom – pointed to a new future. Our lives would be cleaner, brighter, with less manual labour, more leisure hours – and indeed, more time to explore newly appreciated areas such as the Lakes.

It might be suggested – as Wainwright's books started appearing during a time of Conservative government – that the political complexion of a lot of walkers had transformed by the mid 1950s. Instead of being broadly socialist in outlook, eager both for fresh air and a sense of reclaiming the land, many new walkers had a measure of affluence; among them would have been the middle classes who had voted for Attlee in 1945 in their moment of radicalism, but then began reaping the huge upswing in material wealth that came during this time.

The Lake District was set aside as a National Park in 1951; then came the essentially conservative writings of Wainwright, which involved free movement across a landscape, no conflict with landed interests, and the slightly ironic commodification of the entire area. The Lake District became a place, in a sense, for walkers to consume, as they would consume anything else. In contrast to the struggles of Tom Stephenson and the Kinder Scout pioneers, Wainwright's eager readers did not want to push for more access, so much as to simply enjoy a land that seemed completely open already. In doing so, and in writing these books, Wainwright has now conferred upon the Lakes an entire industry.

We can't talk about Wordsworth and Wainwright without giving at least a fleeting acknowledgement to *Withnail*. In the cult comedy film *Withnail and I* (1986), set in 1969, the eponymous out-of-work actor and his friend Marwood escape London and go to a cottage in the Lake District owned by Withnail's Uncle Monty. Almost instantly their notion of a tranquil retreat from druggy urban squalor is destroyed by a fresh, rural nightmare. The locals are grim, the countryside is wet, the men are faced with the prospect of killing a chicken to eat. Even when they have done so, things aren't straightforward. 'Shouldn't it be balder?' enquires Withnail, looking at the badly plucked bird. The local pub is frequented by a sinister poacher with an eel down his trousers, Marwood is cornered by a 'randy' bull and Withnail wails 'we've gone on holiday by mistake!'

The film had tremendous resonance among many committed townies: the farmer, his leg tied up in polythene; the glowering distrust on both sides; the unwritten rules of the country. Unlike Wainwright and Wordsworth, *Withnail* makes this landscape alien and hostile, and inimical to ideas of civilisation. It is very much a town-dweller's view of the countryside and, what is more, a countryside that is emphatically not there for the convenience of tourists. The unexpected arrival of Uncle Monty brings a whole new nightmare for Marwood: 'I mean to have you, boy – even if it be burglary'. Though it seems that, otherwise, the predatory Monty is actually rather at home among the lakes. There is only one moment of relative rural tranquillity: when Marwood takes off alone to explore, and finds himself gazing down on Ullswater. He smiles gently. He has found a moment of genuine peace. Later on, after the village pub chucking out time, and in the darkness, Withnail desecrates this view with a repeated holler of 'Bastards!' across the valley. The fundamental comic point is that it is a dreadful error for town-dwellers to think that they can 'rejuvenate', as Marwood puts it, in the country. Earlier in the film, by London Zoo, Withnail exclaims 'What's the point of the country? I'm in a park and I'm still half-dead.'

Perhaps a little ironically, one of the film's greatest lines – when a drunken Withnail, in a village tearoom, demands 'We want the finest wines available to humanity. And we want them here, and we want them now!' – has become a self-fulfilling prophecy: the Lake District is these days something of a foodie paradise, with no shortage either of expensive vintages or venison in jus. Again, it is possible to see the ghosts of both Wordsworth and Wainwright pursing their lips.

The clouds are still gliding fast across the sky and I am grateful for my big black cagoule. There are some other walkers now, over the far side of the slope, picking their way up the path through the heather. They are wearing bright red, high-visibility jackets, as indeed were so many of the walkers around the lake. By contrast, I am wearing what might be described as a low-visibility jacket. Why would walkers want to be quite so conspicuous against the landscape? And how did this fashion sub-genre – walking gear – develop?

CHAPTER 7

Rhossili to Llanrhidian: In the Gower Peninsula to Consider the Surprisingly Long History of Walking Gear – While Wearing Quite Unsuitable Clothes

It wasn't all that long ago when an anorak was simply an anorak. It was either thin, or quilted; collared or hooded. It had a zip and pockets and possibly, if you were feeling flush, a fleecy lining. So when you headed out into the wind and the rain for a walk, there was nothing in the way of dithering over clothing choices. You simply zipped up that unremarkable anorak and got on with it.

In a more consumer-led age, it's naive to imagine that we could ever return to such blissful simplicity. Every form of hobby or recreational activity now comes with a dizzying array of kit. Runners will know only too well the tyranny of choice: the absurd array of trainers, shorts and T-shirts, each making their own mountebank claims for improving speed and reducing chafing and for 'wicking' sweat. And these days, the walker is now presented with warehouses full of specialised gear, from special 'thermic' trousers to the very latest in water bottle ergonomics. If you are a serious walker, you are very much made to feel that you have to wear the precision-designed uniform. Or that somehow, if you don't, you won't be doing it right.

This is why I have decided on this occasion to visit a part of the world which is very slightly set back from the trendiest weekend rambling routes; a place where one might expect to find a more old-fashioned kind of walker, not dressed head to toe in black Neoprene. In fact, there is a pleasing feeling of déjà vu in the prospect before me. I am high up, on firm, sprung turf, looking out over the silver sheen of the sea. It is not so much a feeling I have been here before as a sense that I am in an earlier time – perhaps the 1950s. It is the seaside, but the very wholesome face of the seaside. This is the far tip of the Gower peninsula in south Wales. The light, for this deep autumnal time of year, is bright and warm; even in November, the sun takes that little bit longer to set on the people of the west. As it happens, I am quite wrong about fashion. There are a few other walkers stumping around – older than me, yes, but in clothes that are defiantly up to date. These people are in light waterproof trousers, and in fleeces that are not too thick and not too thin. Some fleeces are even sleeveless, allowing for even greater flexibility in matters of temperature and comfort. Such clothes are tribal badges. They can even have an element of fetishism about them. One old friend of mine used to swear by his Rohan blouson and trousers, and by the way that they could be scrunched up into a ball the size of a tin can. He was ceaselessly impressed with this tin can aspect.

However, out here on this dramatic promontory, with darker clouds inking themselves on to the sky in the distance, I have rejected such utilitarian comfiness. Indeed, for reasons to do with a certain sense of angry resistance – I never cared for the way these new-fangled fleeces gradually invaded all the woolly jumper shops – I am dressed absurdly in overcoat, cardigan and jeans. This is the opposite of Baden-Powell. Be Unprepared. All the more so considering that I am standing upon one of the most reliably soaking places in the British Isles.

Nearly sixty years ago, the Gower peninsula – this narrow jut of verdant, bountiful land, poking into the wild Atlantic sea just beyond the city of Swansea – was granted a great honour. In 1956, it was the first place in the country to be designated an

Area of Outstanding Natural Beauty. AONBs were intended as cousins to the new National Parks, in that these areas too would be accorded certain levels of planning protection, and given help with conservation and improvements. So Glamorgan County Council, in cahoots with The Gower Society, started pressing the National Parks Commission, clearly rather harder than other areas managed. Incidentally, the phrase 'Area of Outstanding Natural Beauty' can now pull one up a little; is such a subjective judgement best reached by anonymous committee? Isn't it even a little impertinent? Whatever the case, in 1956, other such Areas-To-Be must have looked on with envy.

The Gower peninsula conforms to a very particular and traditional sense of beauty, I think, in that this is a landscape of remoteness, combined with a sort of Celtic primitivism (this comes in the form of numerous Neolithic burial mounds, as opposed to the local people, I hasten to add). The peninsula coast is also burrowed through with caves, some of which held deep religious and sacred significance. Gaze out from one at a vast, reddening sun dipping over a sea of inkiest blue, and you will understand why. These gentle valleys, high patches of gorsey, ferny moorland, apparently ancient woodland, combined with tiny smatterings of little villages, ruins of small medieval castles and rich salt marshes teeming with life, all conform to that post-nineteenth century sense of an urban escape. This was a place where the soul, as well as the body, might be recreated. It has certainly been good enough for local-girl-turned-Hollywood-actress, Catherine Zeta Jones, to keep a home there; and to visit faithfully and regularly with husband Michael Douglas and family. Another famous fan, though rather longer ago, was John Wesley. Not to mention, centuries back, a significant chunk of the population of north Devon, who took to their boats, sailed over the Bristol Channel, and decided to stay.

This accounts for the area's historically English feel, despite it being clasped deep within the bosom of proud Cymru. Up until the nineteenth century, the peninsula was divided neatly between English-speakers in the south, and Welsh-speakers in the north. In 1933, the nascent National Trust was even swifter than the Gower Society to spot the picturesque possibilities of the peninsula, and since then it has been stealthily colonising the place, piece by piece, path by path. The result is that it is something of a walker's paradise. Access is pretty free and easy in most parts.

Indeed, you can tell by the different ages and styles of the walking signposts all over this landscape – ranging from old green painted metal, to modern eco-friendly stencilled timber – just how long ramblers have been welcome. It is claimed that the area gets some three million visitors a year, mainly in the form of holidaymakers searching out those beaches of pale gold, and more recently, the surfing fraternity on its quest for those waves of silver. Despite all this, the Gower peninsula is still a curiously overlooked sliver of land. And I am here on an extremely windy day to test out my wider theory – one that goes to the very roots of walking – that one doesn't actually need special clothes in which to go rambling.

What to wear when one goes walking has exercised many. In the eighteenth century, the Reverend Gilpin relayed how he favoured a long coat with many pockets for his perambulations on the Welsh mountains. The pockets were there to carry emergency supplies of food and drink. The coat was not built for comfort. Nor indeed were the fashions that came later. Even in the nineteenth century, thick tweed was clearly the thing, and for working class walking groups, it was sometimes found that 'Sunday best' was most suitable, as it put the emphasis on warmth, as well as practicality. Exposure to the elements is not quite the ordeal that it used to be for walkers.

Those Kinder Scout daredevils back in the 1930s, for instance; photographs show the men cheerfully attired in thick jackets and fairisle jumpers, all uncomfortably water absorbent. Any rain shower must have added several stone to their weight. Also, in the 1930s, when the fashion for rambling moved deeper into the middle classes, pamphlets and books and posters were illustrated with pictures of men and women wearing semi military honey-coloured walking gear: shirt or blouse, shorts, long socks, shoes looking rather like brogues, and for the lady, a jaunty scarlet neck scarf. In one famous illustration, an advertisement for the Ramblers' Association itself, a man and a woman are striding up a green slope, looking upwards, with smiles at the prospect of the hill to come. Behind them lie perfect fields and a charming village. There is something redolent of totalitarian 1930s propaganda in this image; interestingly, it was during this pre-war period, as newsreel footage of physically fit young Germans was shown in British cinemas, that the British government used such imagery to cajole its own young people into improving their fitness. With an increasingly resurgent and bellicose Germany in the process of rearming, ministers in Whitehall were concerned that young people did not have enough basic fitness for even the most undemanding of military routines. So it was that good long hikes, along with other types of recreation such as PT and climbing, were quietly encouraged through films and posters.

It was also around the 1930s that walkers began to hear the first unkind jeers from non-walkers; the tittering both about the pastime itself and particularly the clothes worn to enjoy it. For women at that time, there was one immediately pressing sartorial issue: shorts were considered by some to be revolutionary, and by others to be absolutely disgraceful. One woman rambler recalled 'In those days, girls did not wear shorts, and we had several people stop their cars and take snaps of us. We also had abuse hurled at us for being hussies and showing our knees.' Knees and the like, for either sex, were soon the subject of scorn and satire. In October 1934, there was a letter written to *The Times* that was to spark off some furious debate. It was about walkers and their aesthetic sense. 'Why do our lean-limbed young men and shapely damsels make themselves so ugly in potato colour and khaki while merely taking a walk?' The question was posed by one W. Russell Flint, a member of the Royal Academy, who clearly had delicate sensibilities.

In general terms, in those pre-Second World War years, hearty walking gear of the shorts and neckerchief variety was obviously only suitable for the warmer months. What about the rest of the year? It was almost as soon as walking had gained a fashionable currency, in the early-nineteenth century, that the business of specially tailoring clothing for miserable weather was addressed. One Charles Mackintosh had patented his first waterproof coat as long ago as the 1820s. This first version, unfortunately, had a tendency to melt when worn in exceptionally warm weather. It was improved with vulcanised rubber in the 1840s. Even then, it was always just a little too hot and cumbersome for the purposes of stout long-distance walks. Even so, the prototypes and the principle were there. The old hazards of getting caught in terrific cold downpours – as illustrated in Jane Austen's *Sense and Sensibility* and Charlotte Brontë's *Jane Eyre*, when characters are exposed to terrible weather and either a) get ill or b) die – were mitigated a little. Nonetheless, right the way up to the end of the Second World War, the average walker would be kitted out simply with heavy woollens, and some good stout boots. The technology that came in the 1940s and 50s was to change all that in a revolutionary way.

The revolution was plastic. Even up until the 1950s, a real Mackintosh – of the bright yellow or shiny black variety still favoured by some fishermen – was a reassuringly heavy beast, as were oilskins. The new science brought forth much more flexible garments – ones that could be scrunched up into a bag when not needed. They were called pac-a-macs; how fun and sophisticated that must have sounded at first and how very swiftly those three syllables became a byword for a certain sort of naff hardiness.

Next came the cagoule. We might at a pinch argue that – apart from the car – this is the one single thing that made long-distance walking a much more realistic prospect for millions. For without the dragging weight of heavy rain gear – which could be intolerably hot on even vaguely warm days, and a savage nuisance if it didn't actually rain at all – there was a new sense of liberation. Unfortunately, with liberation came what many saw as ugliness. For any fan of brightly coloured cagoules, there were just as many people who thought them both revolting, and beneath contempt. Faced with the cagoule, the upper-middle classes subtly fought back with their appropriation of the dark green Barbour waxed jacket. Here at last was an upper-crust anorak – a garment that combined rain-worthiness with quiet dignity. They have rather slyly returned recently, along with their quilted cousin the Husky, but this time to the high streets not the hills. But back in the 1960s and 70s, the rustling cagoule became a sort of metonym for an especially unloved form of walker, blotting landscapes effortlessly, simply by moving across them dressed in fluorescent blue and purple.

One glaring example of this prejudice is found in the 1969 film comedy *Carry On Camping*. While the majority of the protaganists, from Sid James to Barbara Windsor, make their way to the Paradise Campsite via car or coach, it is left to regular eccentric Charles Hawtrey to represent the walking interest. His character, Charlie Muggins, is dressed in distressingly brief beige shorts (revealing pipe-cleaner legs) and a freakishly large yellow pac-a-mac. He clanks along with various tin mugs and little pots attached to his knapsack. Through the fields this misfit wanders; and when he is walking along the road, he is jeered by Betty Marsden.

'Get off the road, get off the road!' she shouts. Given that her own character is on a tandem bicycle with Terry Scott, we can see precisely how low on the scale screenwriter Talbot Rothwell considers Hawtrey's rambler. Even by the standards of Carry On grotesques, Charlie Muggins is almost anarchic in his refusal to conform to social norms; an object of distrust even to Terry Scott.

These days, walking gear is hi-tec, hi-spec and almost fetishistic in terms of the accessories and specialised terms and equipment. Something like the 'Lite-Speed' jacket is a kaleidoscope of special features: 'Scotchlight' reflective dots create 'a 360-degree reflective effect' and 'Pertex microlight fabrics' give all round 'wind-proofness' and 'high breathability'. Similarly, a walker's trousers these days have come a long way from hearty tweed and wool. 'Terra Thermic Pants', for instance, offer a 'zoned, warm and wicking lining.' They also boast a 'Tactel shell with double layers', 'DryActiv Suede micro-fleece/mesh lining in strategic points', 'webbing belt', and 'zipped mesh lined' pockets. Many modern trousers also make a brave claim for having eliminated rustling noises. That, in all seriousness, would be a selling point for me; there are few things more aggravating on a perfectly quiet hill than the noise of one's own legs, encased in synthetic fibres, fissling like crisp packets.

Parenthetically, another relatively recent rambling development – and one that I confess I find a little puzzling – has been the arrival of the Walking Pole. On long hill-walks, their use is clear enough; these slender, multicoloured shoulder-height wands are obviously descendants of the shepherd's crook. It is when I see them being used on undemanding Home Counties footpaths that I begin to wonder about the true, full benefit. But many walkers, including my stepmother, love them; friends of mine say that they help improve pace, as well as posture. There's no slouching with the poles.

There is one other consistent historical point about walkers' clothing though, right up to the present day, with its fashion for tight lycra leggings: and that is the curious sexlessness of the uniform. Whether it was the man or the woman in khaki; or, today, the man and the woman in layers of close-fitting, dark coloured synthetic fibres – it's not what you might call an elegant or alluring look. None the less, it is one of those things that presses at the back of the minds of non-walkers – that walkers simply look strangely, determinedly androgynous.

Is the clothing really that important though? Obviously it is for anyone setting out to clamber around Glencoe or the Cairngorms, when one is always at risk of fog or of serious temperature drops. But a normal walk? In rather steadier climes? Serious ramblers will tell you that they are not simply wearing these clothes as a uniform, or as some form of identifying symbol. They will tell you that the pleasure of walking can actually be sluiced away if the clothes are wrong.

There is a soggy personal flashback that I cannot shake off: I recall, about twelve years ago, a trip to the Isle of Skye (some way north of Arran, but still very much in that west coast rainbelt) with a friend. It was summer, and the weather had been, rather unusually, consistently fine. On the morning we set out from a village on the north tip of the island to walk along a vast empty beach of dark stone, there was no reason to suppose that the sun high in the sky would be disappearing. So I wore (oh, the idiocy!) a corduroy jacket and tweedy trousers. A mile further on, and my friend and I were on that beach. To our backs, a pale grey cliff; before us, the expanse of dark pebbles, and then the khaki ocean, flecked with white. The sky was darkening very suddenly, and the wind was picking up. We could see the rainstorm out at sea, a thick curtain of black, being drawn across the water. There was not enough time for us to make it the mile back to the village.

The rainstorm swept in. It did so with a violence that almost took our breath away. It was impossible to see more than three yards ahead. The downpour teemed like deafening applause and fast rivulets of water, akin to mountain streams, ran down the back of my shirt. It is impossible to convey just how stupid I felt without that waterproof. So will I be feeling stupid and soaked again today, out here in the extremities of Wales? Should the clouds gather, I am rather counting on the overcoat to mitigate some of the moisture. The cord jacket under that will be a secondary barrier, so with any luck the shirt will get damp but not bedraggled. The fact is that no matter what good sense tells you, there are days when you simply don't want to wear uniform. And those fleeces and Gore-tex jackets and waterproof trousers – no matter how snug and practical – are both too samey and too stridently purposeful. These clothes say, I think: I am here to walk, and nothing else. My coat and scarf, conversely, say in this howling wind that I am a bit daft.

* * *

Rhossili is a tiny village right at the foremost tip of the Gower peninsula. It is a sort of Land's End, but without any of the commercialised horror. There is a pleasant little hotel, some crisply whitewashed houses, a discreet lifeguards' lookout, and a twee little National Trust shop, there for the supply of emergency mug coasters and novelty tea towels. In the summer, this particular place is a surfers' paradise. In November, not so much so, although stand atop this cliff and far below, a lone surfer – a speck on the vast grey beach that sweeps away – is trooping some quarter of a mile out to sea at low tide. That's the spirit!

The main attraction for walkers here is the Worm's Head – a jutting rectangle of dark rock fringed with a haircut of green grass. The promontory is the size of several office blocks, poking out of the sea, and attached to the mainland by means of a limestone natural causeway. From the top of the cliff, it looks like a road made of coal and around it, silver in the autumn light, are the in-rushing waves. The Head itself, when seen from a proper distance, looks like a giant dark submarine surfacing from the sea. The poet Dylan Thomas, who lived just a few miles and across some estuarial water from here, was especially enthusiastic about this place when he was a boy:

> There was monstrous thick grass that made us spring-heeled, and we laughed and bounced on it, scaring the sheep who ran up and down the battered sides like goats … even on the calmest day, a wind blew along the Worm. At the end of the humped and serpentine body, more gulls than I had ever seen before cried over their new dead and the droppings of ages.[1]

These days, there is a small stone-built hut up here on the top of the cliff that overlooks the limestone Worm and the causeway, and there are men in there who are constantly looking down during daylight hours in case of trouble. You may, when the tide is far out, venture down and along the black causeway onto the block of Worm's Head itself; but you are required to come back when the tide is coming in. One local, of a certain vintage, tells me that it was quite different when he was a boy. Many years ago, he and a group of friends once ventured out on to the rock. Then the tide came in, and they were stuck there for 12 hours, right the way through a warm summer's night. Nor were they any the worse for the adventure, until they got home, and their panic-crazed parents confronted them. Haven't mobile phones taken the fun out of everything? Moreover, the lifting of stranded walkers off the Worm's Head via coastguard helicopter is a costly business.

My elderly correspondent was not alone in having this adventure, and I slightly wonder if his own exciting account might not have been coloured a little by a very similar adventure experienced by Dylan Thomas when he was a boy:

> I stayed on that Worm from dusk to midnight, sitting on that top grass, frightened to go further in because of the rats and because of things that I am ashamed to be frightened of. Then the tips of

the reef began to poke out of the water and, perilously, I climbed along them to the shore.

There is that touch of Enid Blyton about this rock; from the dancing, prancing porpoises sometimes to be seen capering in the waters around, to the flumped figures of grey seals, spread out across the black rocks, to the curious blowhole. Throw sand at this hole, and it will be blown away in the opposite direction, as if the rock had just exhaled sharply; it is to do with tides and air currents beneath the rock. Until the 1960s, there was a vast herring gull colony here; it was gradually depleted by visitors, many of whom helped themselves to eggs. In 1948, a local wrote complaining to Glamorgan County Council:

> As tenant of Worm's Head, I am writing to you to ask if anything can be down to protect the wild birds on the Head. I understand there is a bye-law passed for that purpose but not put in force. At present people from town come down and rob the nests by the hundreds and I want to see it stopped.[2]

And lo, it was, and with remarkable success. Indeed, thanks to the tightening of laws concerning such things, the Worm's Head is now a colony to many other species, including kittiwakes, fulmars and guillemots. With the occasional human interlopers now being rather more sensitive about such matters, these beautiful birds are able to go about their business without fear of molestation. To balance this abundance of flying fauna, there is also an extraordinary range of flora, including pink sea-campion, knotweed, spear thistle, fern-grass, ribwort plantain and golden samphire, all clinging on, flowers shaken violently from side to side by the aggressive winds blowing off the Bristol Channel.

Everywhere there is wind. This is a land of wind. It cannot be escaped. Even as the November sun shines heroically, the wind whines in one's ear. There is nothing close to silence here. The wind doesn't drop; and the distant sea roars and murmurs. Go in the other direction from the coastal path that sweeps around for about ten miles to the Mumbles – all springy turf and sheep with dirty bottoms – and you have a wider variety of Gower peninsula walking options. The first is a vertiginous concrete staircase leading down from the hotel, and down the cliff to the silver sand below, and to what must be one of the most spectacular beaches in Britain. Rising up from this vast, empty, lonely beach is a hill of russet and dirty green, a blend of fern and gorse; dark rock and red soil. Thousands upon thousands of years ago, the sandy hummocks at the base of this hill would have been at the water's edge. The tide has drawn out inexorably – due to geology, and post-glacial rebound. In broad terms, the west of the country has been rising out of the water, while the east has slowly been dunked in. On this very blowy November day, with the clouds haring off to the west out over the ocean, I have this enormous beach to myself save for one other distant walker. The silver sand is mesmeric in itself, there are Lawrence of Arabia style ripples of it in the swift wind, snaking and writhing across the darker wet sand beneath. Here, the wind is so absurdly insistent, that even the sound of the sea is muted.

About a mile along and it is now time to glance back, like Lot's Wife, and gasp at the prospect of the Worm's Head promontory. It is lit from behind by the thin aluminium light of an autumn sun, the dark bulk of the little island surrounded by a glowing corona of sea mist. Little wonder that this area is filled with sacred Neolithic burial sites. On an afternoon like this, you might gaze at such a view and feel, in the words of G. K. Chesterton, that you are looking out towards islands yet dreamier than our own. As I am currently also dressed rather like Chesterton, I am feeling smug about my cosy clothing arrangements, except the scarf which – no matter how firmly knotted and tucked into the overcoat – seems determined to fly away with that gale.

This view of the Worm's Head was voted by *Country Life* magazine as one of Britain's top favourites. Sometimes the boxing and labelling of beauty is maddening. And also – by stamping the words 'chocolate box' so firmly on a place – these sorts of meaningless surveys subtly empty the landscape of its truer meaning. To look upon a prospect like this is not simply a question of widening the eyes and saying 'oooh'. There are other, emotional responses. Especially on a day such as this, when the lemony sun is low, the wind is whistling, and you find yourself quite alone.

We often forget just how eerie wide, lonely beaches can be. Because of the vast prospects – of churning sea, and of sand, and dunes – the sense of isolation is intensified when you are completely alone. It is a primordial world where neither man nor animal counts for anything. M. R. James saw this unsettling potential in the grey Suffolk coastline. In 'Oh Whistle and I'll Come To You, My Lad', the trouble starts for the hero on a pebbled beach in the twilight as he is followed by a distant dim silhouette. There is further supernatural upset on the lonely beach at Seaburgh in 'A Warning To The Curious', where the unfortunate anti-hero has his head stoved in by a vengeful force conjured by an Anglo-Saxon king.

In happier terms, what we have at Rhossili is a rather socially superior stretch of shoreline, one that has resisted being vulgar-ised. This is hardcore coast. Not the namby-pamby sort to lie around on, but one to be walked along with every breath draw-ing in lungfuls of insanely rich, fresh air. Coming off the beach, one finds the start of the marshland that gradually creeps around the estuarial side of the peninsula, and a road to the village of Llangennith. For the walker, paths branch off in all directions. Up another gorsey hill is a trail that leads to a view of the estuary, and out on to Dylan Thomas territory, and all the boggy marshy ground beneath. Other paths scoot off in the direction of rich pasture, and of tail-swaying horses. Ramblers are not short of options; yet this landscape seems a little short of ramblers today. There is not a brightly coloured anorak anywhere to be seen.

You notice, when you enter a village like Llangennith, the way that the people there quietly and quickly size you up. The fact that I am not wearing a brightly coloured anorak or a fleece clearly presents a fleeting anomaly, a flicker of puzzlement. I don't conform to the understood image of walkers. As I say, the look in the eye is there for the merest fraction of a second; but of course this is how we all read the shorthand of one another's clothes. The road out of Llangennith winds up another invigorating hill, at the summit of which we say hello once more to the wind. Now you are out on the sort of moorland that one associates with Exmoor; complete with stunted, arachnoid trees, their spines bent over under the wind, their limbs almost horizontal and stiff. Yet my very old overcoat – the lining is going and little threads of it trail out from beneath the hem – and my Marks and Spencer cardigan, are bearing up extremely well. Indeed, slightly too well, for there are points when I find myself a little clammy and moist. Once more, as I walk along the side of the road towards the village of Llanrhidian, both fellow walkers and drivers seem unable to place me, and seem uncertain when they pass. Who is this fellow in a dark overcoat with a knapsack on his back?

A colourful rambler is instantly placeable, and takes his position very firmly in the modern post-agricultural landscape. Like a farm labourer, we know the rambler's business exactly, and are therefore at ease around him. Given current levels of crime in the countryside generally – from burglary to animal rustling – the appearance of any stranger in less easily identifiable clothing is an understandable trigger for suspicion. In social terms, the mores of appropriate walking clothing – and the sorts of garments that were considered acceptable – were drolly considered 100 years ago by A. H. Sidgwick in an essay entitled 'Walking Equipment'.

> The subject bristles with controversial points … the structure and fortification of boots; the requisite number of pairs of socks; the rival claims of long trousers and short trousers, with the subvariants of short trousers buckling at the knees, short trousers with box-cloth continuations, and short trousers with homogeneous continuations; the configuration of coats; the shape of hats (if any); the functions of waistcoats; the necessity of ties.[3]

When it is put like that, I feel almost naked. Even Sidgwick was keenly aware of the importance of a certain sort of 'uniformity' – even if it carried a suspicious flavour of 'political allegory' – and the fact is that by not dressing the part, I am somehow proclaiming that I am not really a proper walker. It would be like playing golf in tasteful clothes.

I am still striding along on the unseasonably lovely November Gower day. And as I reach Llanrhidian, the sun, now low, is still psychologically warming. To my faint vexation, I have rather missed out on the extraordinary range of Neolithic tombs that this sliver of land has to offer. There is the famous example of Goat's Hole cave at Paviland where, in 1823, the Reverend William Buckland came across a most valuable find. First erroneously described as 'The Red Lady', this was the skeleton of a man that had been buried with all manner of ornamental seashells and items of jewellery. The skeleton was red because it had been covered in ochre. The astounding thing about this find was its age: it is estimated that the man to whom the red skeleton belonged was placed in the cave some 28,000 years ago – just before, in fact, the area was overrun with ice sheets.

Because of tides, the cave can only be visited at restricted times now; but there is no shortage of other barrows, including two on Rhossili Down, and, in the south-east of the area, at Penmaen Burrows and Parc le Breos. The stones that mark these places are mini Stonehenges, yet somehow more sombre and, curiously, more credible. They stand, undisturbed, on a land that has subtly transformed around them through the ages. Other stones have been disturbed, though, centuries ago, by farming activities, and the memory of them lives on in place names like Stone Park.

In the last thirty years or so, South Wales has performed the most dazzling turn around – negotiating the end of its industrial usefulness with grace, while presenting itself fresh not as a land of slag-heaps and open-cast mines, but of rare butterflies, of clean unspoilt beaches, of green hilly walks leading to unexpected treasures such as ruined castles.

Despite the low temperature – and despite the fact that in walking terms, I was really quite the dandy boulevardier – I have to say that there was one specific drawback which would make me think more practically in the future: sweat. Even in November, a scramble up a sand dune, a yomp across a beach, a turn on the high moorland or just going up and down hills produced quite a gloss, which like the rainwater on Skye, I could feel trickling down my back. Sweat on a November day? There's little to grumble about there. And the landscape of the Gower peninsula is as uniformly beguiling as people have always said. But what about those parts of the country that people don't enthuse about? What kind of walking is there to be had in places that have acquired reputations for being ugly, lowering or even, in extreme cases, oddly menacing?

CHAPTER 8

Higham to Cooling: The Hoo Peninsula, North Kent, in Search of Beauty in Ugliness

Despite the trend for labelling certain areas as 'outstanding', notions of what constitutes a beautiful landscape are prone to quiet shifts of fashion. Take a recent example, that of the Fens. Before the 1980s, there were not a great many people who would have regarded the flatlands of Cambridgeshire and Lincolnshire as attractive places to visit, still less as a walking destination. The level lines of the horizon, the perspective of the straight rivers and ditches, added to the black soil and the wide, often grey skies, were considered to induce a mild form of depression. Many strange stories, about the region and its people, were in circulation.

Daniel Defoe took against the area in his eighteenth century tour: 'but for the Healthyness or Pleasantness of it, I have no more to say than this, that I was very glad to get out of it, and out of the rest of the Fen country; for 'tis a horrid air for a stranger to breathe in.' This was a landscape of strange folk tales, of Jack o' lanterns and Will o' the wisps. It had a sense of the *unheimlich* about it, something just beyond the edge of comfort. Could it really have taken just one novel to have swept away those views? Oddly enough, I think I can make the case that Graham Swift's bestselling, critically acclaimed novel *Waterland*, published in 1983, did more to rescue the region and turn it into a honeypot for visitors and walkers than any amount of local tourist board advertising could have done. Richly layered with history, *Waterland* was the story of the Fens past and present. Even now it makes me think of fishing for eels at midnight.

Something similar is now happening to the hitherto deeply unloved sumplands of the Thames Estuary. What once was a place synonymous with both ugliness and illness is now being looked at in a subtly different way by many curious walkers. Flatlands punctuated with pylons, oil holders, even the occasional crisp, dirty orange, burnt out shell of a car in the mud of the river foreshore. A few years ago, most would have turned away from all these with a shudder. Now, such things intrigue and hold the eye. Before we explore why this should be, it is worth returning briefly to the eighteenth century, when the aesthetics of natural landscape were being formed.

In the late-eighteenth century, as the men of the Ordnance Survey were transporting great optical measuring instruments of bronze around the country, there were other inventions used by gentlemen of leisure through which to peruse nature's works. Some, such as the *camera obscura* – the projection on to a flat white screen or canvas of an outdoor scene, by means of mirrors – are still with us in spirit. The obscura was a means of observing the immediate surroundings not only in comfort but also an unusual amount of detail from an interior vantage point and allowing a bird's eye view – the philosophical forerunner of the BBC's *Springwatch*. There was also a device invented by the painter James de Loutherbourg, called the *Eidophusikon*. This created a sort of panorama which featured, according to Brownlow, 'moving pictures ... shown within a proscenium, by means of a combination of Argand lamps, coloured gauzes, lacquered glass and receding planes which reproduced scenes with realistic atmospheric effects.' The notion was to summon, with a sort of primitive three-dimensional effect, images of ideal landscapes.

The most intriguing of all these instruments was one that gentlemen and ladies would take with them on their excursions: the Claude Glass, named after the seventeenth-century French landscape painter Claude Lorraine. This was a small tinted convex mirror, with a black backing, which imbued the landscape with ideal qualities – golden-hued – of a Claude painting. The peripatetic Reverend Gilpin noted its uses while travelling in a coach:

> They are like the visions of the imagination; or the brilliant landscapes of a dream. Forms, and colours in brightest array, fleet before us; and if the transient glance of a good composition happen to unite with them, we should give any price to fix and appropriate the scene.[1]

The poet Thomas Gray used a similar instrument and, after his tour of the Lakes in 1769 with the contraption, is quoted about one rather dicey incident, by Brownlow: 'I fell down on my back across a dirty lane with my glass open in one hand, but broke only my knuckles; stay'd never the less, and saw the sun set in all its glory.' It now seems rather extraordinary that men of fine taste should feel the need to view landscapes through a certain trick mirror, with coloured glass, rather than simply enjoying the unadorned view. Yet in that age of Capability Brown, Humphry Repton, and the Landscape Movement, certain notions concerning perspective and symmetry were obviously lingering. Even a prospect like that of the Lake District was considered to look better if viewed through a man-made device.

There were always going to be some areas, though, that would be beyond even these phantasmagorias, where picturesque notions of ruins and decay would be dispelled sharply by a utilitarian bleakness. So we turn to the case of the Thames Estuary – a deeply uncherished, depressed landscape praised by very few. Two hundred years ago, London's docks gradually gave way in the east to a vista of grey spongy marshes and slopping inlets. On the south side of the river, the Isles of Grain and Sheppey acquired reputations in the sixteenth and seventeenth centuries for miasma and disease.

Joseph Conrad's Marlow, in *Heart of Darkness*, famously declares that 'this also has been one of the dark places of the earth'; and indeed Conrad himself lived in that dark place, in the Essex village of Stanford-le-Hope, for a while. Today, on the north side of the estuary, the formerly drab Rainham Marsh – landfill site, shooting ranges, fat seagulls, bored teenagers, sullen pylons – has been appropriated by the RSPB (complete with a trendy timber-built twitching block). The birdwatchers have noticed that the area actually contains a breathtaking amount of biodiversity not only in terms of birds, but also insects and much-loved rarities like the water-vole. Neighbouring Purfleet is getting some sort of Royal Opera House spin-off effort; even the town of Grays, dominated by the nearby oil depot, and by the inescapable Queen Elizabeth II Dartford Bridge, now has a certain culty cachet thanks to its most famous son, the comedian Russell Brand.

On the Kent side, by comparison, the Isles of Grain and Sheppey maintain their reputations for a slightly eerie remoteness and quietness. Grain, and the area around Cliffe, generally known as the Hoo peninsula, is especially fascinating, for it inspired one of the most famous landscapes in English fiction: that of young Pip Pirrip in *Great Expectations*.

Ours was the marsh country, down by the river, within, as the river wound, twenty miles of the sea … this bleak place overgrown with nettles was the churchyard … the dark flat wilderness beyond the churchyard, intersected with dykes and mounds and gates, with scattered cattle feeding upon it, was the marshes; and that the low leaden line beyond, was the river; and that the distant savage lair from which the wind was rushing, was the sea.

As I get off the train at Higham, and turn right to find myself, after just 200 yards or so, in very gentle, flat grey countryside, in the murk of a late December day, it seems to me that there can be little dispute that the real location of Pip's shivering nightmare was the village of Cooling, some four miles off. Other candidates have been put forward, but most agree that this still weirdly cut off spot, complete not only with old church and churchyard but also the ruined remnants of a castle, is the most likely.

My aim is to see it on exactly the same sort of day that Pip was describing in that opening chapter – a low winter's afternoon in the old churchyard, by the five little children's graves that inspired Dickens directly. Later, Pip relates that despite a sign pointing towards his village, no one ever seemed to follow that pointing wooden finger. This would also seem to be the case today.

Incidentally, before heading to that church, a very swift local diversion will take you faster to a river's edge with a unique and perhaps not altogether comfortable atmosphere. If you bear left towards a village called Church Street, the road will pass unexpected orchards, and you will find yourself crossing a single railway line, which still carries freight and coal, back and forth from a vast, pale industrial operation somewhere in the distance. Beyond this line is the marsh country; there are ditches and embankments and black rivulets, and cocoa brown muddy paths running through narrow aisles of prickly hawthorns. There is a nice parallel, on a winter's afternoon, between Pip's later, almost hallucinatory, glimpses of big sailing ships apparently moving across the land, and the sight that greets me now of a huge oil tanker, seemingly gliding across the grass nearby. A few yards on, and you can see that there is a stubby green embankment and dyke to be climbed; and that when you do so, you are very suddenly looking at the wide and silent Thames, northwards across to the Essex shoreline. The vessels that move through these waters do so incredibly quietly; the main noise you hear is that of skinny marsh birds, wheeling and crying. In the middle-distance is a prospect that seems to mirror the ominous black prison hulks of Pip's day: the dark rectangular bulk of Tilbury Power Station on the north shore. At night, this power station glows from within, a benign vanilla light is reflected on the rushing tidal water. In the day, it is here as a reminder that this is still a working river.

Back on the road from Higham, eastwards to Pip's church-yard at Cooling (Dickens quite frequently alighted at Higham station) you are drawn into another genre of landscape, of gentle hills and rows of shivering poplars and rich ploughed soil and flat fields glowing emerald with winter greens. There are green signposts everywhere signalling very properly laid out footpaths, complete with their own serial numbers. Equally though, as you reach the top of this gentle incline, near the villages of Cliffe and Cooling, you once more enter a world that seems a little less relaxed. There are remarkable numbers of signs on the edges of fields warning that there is 'no right of access' to them. On this shivery day, with the echoing pops of distant gunshots carried on the gelid breeze, this is a tiny area that seems very keen on keeping itself to itself. On the road from Cliffe to Cooling – looking out over a vast expanse of frosted cabbages and kale – you also catch glimpses of oil refinery chimneys, of the squat white cylinders of oil holders, so reminiscent of 1950s *Quatermass* sci-fi thrillers. These lie across the river; once more we see Pip's optical illusion, not merely of big buildings, but of vast oil tankers moving in a stately fashion apparently through marshy rivulets.

As I reach the all important church – St James', Cooling – the sky is bright though the wind is as raw as that conjured by Dickens. Here are the five little lozenge shaped horizontal gravestones alluded to in that first chapter; here are the trees that bowed and creaked under the wind and so frightened our young hero; and there in the distance, are the marshes. All-Hallows! Is there anywhere else in England with such a delightfully Gothic name? Here is the great tombstone that one can very easily imagine Magwitch hiding behind, and dangling Pip upside down from. Yet there is one thing Dickens has failed to mention – and that is just how pretty the church is. Perhaps such structures back then seemed more commonplace, and therefore utilitarian as opposed to aesthetically pleasing. Unusually for a country church these days, it is kept open most of the time, even though it is a very long while since any proper services were held in here. Inside there is a rich silence, though one might also imagine it in the darkness of a stormy day, as one perhaps takes shelter, and watches the reds in the stained glass window at the back glowing a dull blood ruby.

Just 100 years ago, this area had an evil reputation that would have kept a great many away, and that was for disease. The five little graves in that churchyard were for the Comport children, each killed by 'marsh fever' or 'the ague' or, as is now thought, by malaria carried by mosquitoes. The estuary was one of the busiest waterways in the world, carrying vessels from all parts of the globe; the mosquitoes, it seems, came with them.

The last recorded case of malaria on Grain was as late as 1918, thought to have been brought to the area by soldiers returning from Greece. An eighteenth-century historian wrote of marsh-dwelling people, that 'it is not unusual to see a poor man, his wife, and whole family of five or six children hovering over their fire in their hovel, shaking with an ague all at the same time.'[2] In *Great Expectations*, one of the escapee convicts is found by Pip hiding in the marshes, and is similarly shivering with fever. The irony is that the man might well be better off aboard the prison hulk than out here in this wilderness of disease.

Such stuff is catnip to the modern walker. Much in the way that we see the eighteenth-century Romantic imagination being sparked by views of 'ruins' and 'wastes' – decaying roofless monasteries, derelict woodland chapels – so the modern post-industrial imagination is drawn to a place which seems to be in some ways an eddy of time – a weirdly silent place that, despite being surrounded with the tokens of old messy industry, seems somehow to have sidestepped that age, and remains haunted with memories of miasma and mists. The attractions of melancholy can never be overstated. Often the walker is not simply looking for the uplift of bright wild flowers, or the simple pleasures of hilltop views: they are looking for something a little more complex to ponder. A dreary landscape cannot depress the spirits of the curious; nor can its baleful qualities follow the walker back home.

A little further east, towards the mighty power station at Kingsnorth and the big dock of Thamesport, there is an unloved stretch of former industrial land where an oil refinery once stood; the soil is still infused with all sorts of toxic chemicals. It is very strictly fenced off and no one has had access to it since about 1985. Ironically, this one discrete area – devoid of humankind – now teems with wildlife that can be found almost nowhere else. Conservationists are calling it a 'miniature lost world'. Inhabitants include the white eye-stripe hover-fly, the brown-banded carder bee, and Mellet's downy-back beetle. Here the rambler is not up against angry farmers, but against implacable security guards watching monitor screens, police surveillance and blank-faced corporations. This, for some ramblers, makes the lure of the area stronger. Have they not the straightforward liberty to explore this little known shoreline? There is also the enthusiasm of pressure groups like BugLife, which seek to catalogue and protect rare species of insect and the interest that their work generates attracts yet more walkers.

The poetry of bleakness is obviously not new. When I first read *Great Expectations*, as a teenager, and on every subsequent reading, the impressions I gained of this landscape were as follows: icy, windy, flat, colourless, remote, not pretty, watery,

138

marshy, rather hostile, inimical to any sort of comfort. Of course Dickens was only using this area as the launching point for his imagination, and we also have to bear in mind that the novel was set many decades before 1860, when it was written. Still, the landscape we have now is one of a very singular beauty and it is no wonder the locals of Cliffe, Cooling, and Hadstow so vociferously oppose another London airport being sited here. The local community has understandably reached for the great untouchable defence of the modern age: biodiversity. Before coming here, I had assumed that there were simply too few people living in the area to care one way or another. Now I see, as a walker, that the people who do live around here guard it with a kind of intense jealousy.

There is something about estuaries, wrote Joseph Conrad in 1906, 'that appeal[s] strongly to an adventurous imagination.' And even in his day, there was not much that was pleasing to the eye on this incredibly busy stretch of river, though 'the dispiriting ugliness' was only 'a repulsive mask':

> The estuary of the Thames is not beautiful; it has no noble features, no romantic grandeur of aspect, no smiling geniality; but it is wide open, spacious, inviting, hospitable at the first glance, with a strange air of mysteriousness that hangs about it to this very day ... here and there a lonely wooden jetty where petroleum ships discharge their dangerous cargoes, and the oil storage tanks, low and round with slightly-domed roofs, peep over the edge of the foreshore, as it were a village of Central African huts imitated in iron. Bordered by the black and shining mud-flats, the level marsh extends for miles.[3]

Fear is not a commonplace emotion among recreational walkers, yet there are some places that hold a distinctly odd atmosphere. Among them is the riverside stonework of Cliffe Fort, looking out over the estuary. Originally built in 1860 as a defensive position on the river, and added to in the 1940s for the Second World War, this vast, abandoned, ruined structure is somehow supremely unwelcoming – especially to the solitary walker on a dim winter's afternoon. Inside, the old fort still has vaulted corridors, heavy stone cellars and courtyards that crackle with glass; outside, its glass-less, darkened windows face out on to the grey water like old blind eyes.

Incidentally, you feel a similar sense of abandonment on the north bank of the Thames too, on the Essex river path that winds from Purfleet to Grays, underneath the Queen Elizabeth II Bridge and past an oil depot. This path – on the immediate face of it – is extremely displeasing; a blend of concrete embankments, rusted barbed wire, rotting jetties and, a few yards inland, huge mysterious metal structures, industrial cathedrals with dizzyingly tall chimneys and mazes of pipelines. But that is exactly the element that gives this landscape a new, intriguing aesthetic dimension. As with all those eighteenth-century writers and poets, the walker is faced with the sublime, and all the 'terror' that it conjures up. Instead of dark unconquerable mountains, the sublime in this landscape is formed of nameless industry, some of it now closed down, decaying: clanging metal, rust and silos. This territory is alien to most walkers, and many respond to it with a form of pleasurable unease. We imagine blight, and noise, and the strange tang of pervasive chemical smells. Even as these vast structures continue their obscure functions in silence, their overbearing presence still utterly dominates the riverscape. Here, on this dingy concrete path, there is a very faint echo of that old Noel Coward line: 'Ghosts beside our starlit Thames, who lived and loved and died'. There is another key element of the sublime on this Thames path: sheer, unadulterated awe. It comes from the most unlikely source. Seen from a great distance, there is something delicate and almost fragile about the Queen Elizabeth Bridge as it arcs high above the water. Walk along this riverside path and at one point you find yourself standing directly beneath it. Look up and you will find yourself almost falling over; the vertigo is so powerful as to make you recoil. Far above your head – some 150 feet or so? – is the dark concrete underside of this mighty construction. You have nothing to fall from, and your feet are firm. Yet look upwards again, your head right back, and you might well find your insides gripped with something akin to panic. It is fantastically irrational, and fascinating. More than this, it is curiously satisfying.

This is also a path which accommodates teenagers accompanied by a thick fug of cannabis smoke: one of the more disagreeable and unnerving sights for the average walker. Yet even the awkwardness of this moment – middle-aged rambler passes sardonic hoodies, all parties watchful – can be part of the satisfaction of the day. It brings into focus the blank pale oil containers, squat and fat and silent; the colourful (and at times extraordinarily poetic) graffiti on that pockmarked concrete. It sharpens the beige smoky light reflected on the Thames, and heightens the delicate slurping noise of the river against the artificial banks. That odd tinge of sepia in the air is reminiscent both of old photographs, and of the idea of the Claude Glass.

* * *

Back on the estuary's south side, on the Hoo peninsula, the river is said to have shifted a little since young Pip's day; Cooling is now some two miles away from the water's edge, whereas the water apparently used to lap rather closer. A curious element for walkers of a certain age is nostalgia; anyone visiting here forty years ago would have been less impressed with estuarine industry, and would have regarded it as noisy and polluting. But now, in our era of global banking, out-of-town retail centres, and identical offices, such industry now looks rather heroic and bold. In terms of current industry, look at the giant white globe that dominates a certain stretch of the Suffolk coast near

Aldeburgh. In the 1970s and 1980s this was, to many, a symbol of genuine horror, for it is the site of the Sizewell B nuclear power station. But time and familiarity do their own work and now there are equally as many people in the area, as well as visitors, who regard that same unearthly white globe as a thing of aesthetic pleasure.

One other – arguably outmoded – industrial feature of the British landscape that causes regular controversy among walkers and local residents alike is electricity pylons. There are parts of the Hoo peninsula where these dominate to an unusual degree; tall and angular, marching from several directions towards the power station. This is another leitmotif of the modern estuary; pylons everywhere, including some giants on the Essex side. Pylons were introduced to Britain in 1928; as you would expect, they received a chilly reception, despite being designed with the utmost care by the Central Electricity Board, and one Sir Reginald Blomfield. He had seen images of the pioneering square pylons of America, and he knew that such a shape would be altogether too alien and jarring here. So he set about designing that distinctive 'pyramid' or even 'Christmas tree' shape. It wasn't enough. Among the protesting letter writers to *The Times* were Rudyard Kipling, Hilaire Belloc and John Maynard Keynes. According to the Central Electricity Board, these signatories were 'impractical aesthetes'. Their opposition was roundly ignored. And the CEB prevailed.

From around that period we also have a poem from Stephen Spender, simply entitled 'The Pylons': 'Now over these small hills they have built/The concrete/That trails black wire;/Pylons, those pillars/Bare, like nude, giant girls that have no secret.' Even as late as the 1950s, when lines of pylons were introduced to the wilder corners of Scotland, there were aesthetic objections and cries of horror from local conservationists and walking groups, claiming that the pylons would turn prospective visitors away. There is an incredibly evocative Giles cartoon from a 1950s edition of the *Daily Express*: it depicts a country view, in full, dark, rainy black ink. Under the grey skies and these torrents of rain, the landscape before us, all sodden fields and meadows, is jostling with the bare outlines of dozens of pylons; a line of them stretches grimly off over the horizon, like invading H. G. Wells aliens. To a conservative like Giles, such things represented a barbaric despoliation of the countryside – a Stalinist invasion of brutal industry. But in the case of the remoter Scottish Highlands, pylons were introducing electricity for the very first time.

In some quarters the passionate opposition to pylons continues, mainly in the face of a proposed new generation of super-pylons; twice the size of their antecedents, poised to sling their lines across the country and to loom over the flint-grey waves of the English Channel. Bill Bryson has been campaigning energetically against a new generation of such structures being erected in Wales. But there are some walkers who regard them almost as modern sculpture, and who carefully catalogue all the different types to be found around the countryside. As with most of these things, such enthusiasts can be found with tremendous ease on the Internet. In a small way, pylons stand as a metonym for the wider truth: that yesterday's industrial outrage becomes today's cherished landmark.

CHAPTER 9

A Brief Detour into the Lures and Attractions of Walking at Night

'Night is my time for walking,' declares the narrator of the first few chapters of Dickens' *The Old Curiosity Shop*. It is through the city that he processes, obsessively pacing the sloppy, reeking pavements, alive to every sign of poverty and distress in those thick industrial fogs. Dickens himself was also something of a night walker. On one occasion, late in his career, he set off from his home in central London at 2 a.m., in the dark. By lunchtime, or thereabouts, he was in Rochester, near his childhood home of Chatham.

There is something disconcerting about the idea of night walking; we subconsciously link it with sleepwalking. With the somnambulist, who rises from his bed and walks around as though awake, there is the troubling idea of a lack of control. The deepest recesses of the mind are directing the body, without the conscious brain knowing anything about it. Anyone who has ever had episodes of this condition will testify to how unnerving it is to wake up to find oneself standing in one's kitchen, or by the front door, in the dark, perhaps holding something inexplicable like a mop. Though a conscious activity, night walking has a similar feel to it; as though it is more a subconscious impulse. Many years ago I made two such walks in the middle of the night in Wales. Both showed me an unsuspected world that changed my view of the familiar daytime landscape. The first was in the countryside around the village of Lampeter – a wooded, gently hilly landscape. It was the autumn, and about 4 a.m. when, unable to sleep, I got up, dressed, and headed outside, wrapped up in a big overcoat and a thick scarf. I was not especially aware of the topography, and so simply followed my nose, first along the main road that led out of the village, and thence along a succession of ever smaller lanes. The sky was blue-black and clear and starry, so the darkness had a faint silvery sheen; what was most astonishing to me, however, was the richness of the silence. As the little road rose and dipped, I listened out for anything other than the sound of my own footsteps. Surely I would hear the movement of small animals? Of birds stirring in their nests? But there was nothing. I could even hear the sound of my own breathing.

Because of high hedgerows, and trees, there was not often much open landscape to be viewed, but it didn't matter. What was extraordinary was this sense of walking outside of nature; patrolling it, when I, like all the birds and the animals, should be resting. I must have walked some distance and for some time because there came that moment – it always seems curiously abrupt – when the trees and the branches and the road beneath me became more distinct, as around me there were suddenly chirrups and songs; the first suggestion of dawn. My walk had been roughly circular, and I returned to Lampeter where the village was awakening. I felt, as night-time walkers do, that I had already been up all day – not tired, but full of the experience of a day.

Another occasion was with a university friend at Aberystwyth, just up the road from Lampeter. Aberystwyth is a coastal town and boasts a rather brilliant coastal path, running both north and south. My friend and I had both been studying late in the run-up to exams; it was about 1.30 a.m. and she suggested a walk. Both of us thought it would simply involve an amble down to the seafront to have a look at the waves. But as we got further immersed in conversation, to do with Russian Formalism and deconstruction (those were the days!), we turned south, and started heading out of town, over the harbour bridge, and then up the hill that looked out over the sea. Pretty soon, on those darkened clifftops with the moon reflected on the tranquil, far-away whispers of waves, the literary criticism gave way to a sort of mesmerism. High up on this night-time cliff, underneath wink-ing stars, listening to the sea far below, our voices were lowered in appreciation. What had previously been a bracing view was now something entirely different, with an almost numinous quality.

Rather than go back the same way, we cut inland, downwards along a path that led into a small patch of woodland. The path was clear and the branches were discernible against the night sky. In the middle of this wood was a very large Victorian house; it had the look not of a private home, but of some specially constructed institution. There was a green light visible in one of the upstairs rooms but the rest of the place was darkened. My friend and I wondered – with some curious anxiety – if we were trespassing. Again, in the darkness, it felt as though an element of reason had been suspended, that somehow different rules applied; that this dark wood and this strange house were some-how a place that was closer to dream than to consciousness. The path led on, and then out on to a road that led back to the lights of the town. And, subtly, that walk changed our relationship with the town. It gave the place a sense of depth that we had never credited it with before. Beyond the seafront and the struggling little shops and the noisy nightlife of the pubs, there was a land-scape that could be strange and sombre; romantic and rather hypnotic.

Political journalist and author Matthew d'Ancona recalled that when his first child was a very small baby – disinclined to sleep at night – he used to put the child in its pram and venture out on to the orange lit streets of east London, where he was living. This is a rather frazzling experience common to many fathers. No matter how unrelaxing those darkened streets may seem to the parent, they are perversely soothing to the infant in the pram. Having said that, any father lucky enough to live in the region of London's Primrose Hill will know that the Hill itself, though a bit of a climb with a baby, is rewarding for both parties: the infant, cosy and wrapped up in the night air, and the father, gazing down over the abstract lights of the city.

Generally speaking, night walking in the city is often anthropologically fascinating; from the all-night kebab shops to the nervy remnants of clubbing activity to the blurred cheeriness and careful gait of the very drunk, to the occasional wandering insomniac, eyes barely registering the night. There were those, in the 1970s, who made a habit of walking up Swain's Lane in Highgate late at night; the reason for this was that the Victorian cemetery was rumoured to be haunted by a vampire. These thrill-seeking night walkers would march up to the wrought-iron gates, and dare themselves to peer through to the streets of tombs beyond for as long as they could withstand the dread. The story was that some had seen a white-faced, dark garbed figure moving around near the Cedar of Lebanon crescent, and that this figure's presence was accompanied by a weird note in the night air, like a finger being run around the rim of a wine glass. After becoming suitably freaked, these late-night trampers would then climb further, to the comforting lights of Highgate village.

Just a couple of miles west of this, a night time walk becomes one of the most celebrated opening chapters in English literature: that of Wilkie Collins' *The Woman In White*. The hero, up in the then northern edge of London, in Hampstead, is about to make his way back to the city in the darkness of Hampstead Heath:

The moon was full and broad in the dark blue, starless sky; and the broken ground of the Heath looked wild enough in the mysterious light, to be hundreds of miles away from the great city that lay beneath it ... I determined to stroll home in the purer air, by the most roundabout way I could take; to follow the white, winding paths across the lonely Heath ... I was strolling along the lonely high road ... when in one moment every drop of blood in my body was brought to a stop by the touch of a hand laid lightly and suddenly on my shoulder from behind me.

Walking at night will always have that unsettling quality because it implies a certain mental dislocation. It is allied with the torment of insomnia. Those who walk through the dark are one degree apart from the material world that they move through; they walk through a landscape through which imagination may be heightened, and perspective lost.

There were similar moments of dark romanticism to be found during the London Blitz. Virginia Woolf had been especially affected by the German bombing; her house in north Bloomsbury had been sliced open while she and husband Leonard were in Sussex. Those bombing nights held some form of ghastly fascination for her, and this manifested in night time walks of disturbing fervour. 'After a dinner party in Westminster,' recalled William Somerset Maugham, '[Virginia] insisted on walking home alone during an air raid. Anxious for her safety, I followed her, and saw her, lit up by the flashes of gunfire, standing in the road and raising her arms to the sky.' Yet night-walking can bring clarity that the daylight crowds out. Two old friends of mine, brought up in rural Oxfordshire, often took to the Ridgeway on moonlit summer nights; in the silence, under that transformed landscape, they could talk in a way that the jumble of daylight life would not often allow. Either they would make their plans for pop stardom, or discuss philosophical points; but the point was that the chalky road beneath their feet, and the distant black silhouettes of hills, and the bright red pinpoints of television transmitters, seem to suspend the world in time. These were not conversations that they could have had sitting in a pub; they only worked out there, as they marched, the walk into the dark perhaps reflecting the shapeless but boundless possibilities of discovery.

CHAPTER 10

*Exploring the Preternatural Forest of Dean
and Woodland Legends – While Examining
the Beguiling History of Youth Hostels
and B & Bs*

Old woodland evokes sharply atavistic emotions. Forests are at the very core of countless children's stories; archetypes with the deepest and most sinuous of roots. To walkers, wild woods are irresistible, and this is partly why we protect such places so fiercely now. While the farmed countryside, treasured and loved by ramblers as it is, will always have an element of the quotidian, wild wood seems to take walkers somewhere else. You can lose your way physically while losing yourself in reverie. There is also that edge of anarchy: unlike the open countryside, forests – whether they are privately owned or not – feel as though they belong to everyone and no one. The trees have their own presence and dignity, older and more enduring than any ephemeral property deeds or leases.

Woodland offers the walker something more rewarding and complex than a simple linear trek. Even the very least committed amblers and dawdlers – the weekend trippers in the family MPVs – are drawn irresistibly to those chunkily signposted 'woodland trails' to be found all over the country. This is tangentially to do with modern environmental sensibility. The deliberate cutting down of an old tree can be felt as keenly as an amputation. That is only a part of it, though, and overlooks the important fact that we felt this way about the wild woods a very long time before the term 'environment' was ever used. Obviously we are drawn to the mellow subterranean colours, the diffused light, the silence and the chance of seeing rare plants. But there is a great deal more there too.

The nature of some forests can prevent walkers ever feeling wholly tranquil within them. That is also part of the pleasure. The Royal Forest of Dean, for instance, has one of the most curious reputations of anywhere in the British Isles. You wouldn't perhaps immediately know it on a bright day as you clamber around those lush green hillsides of the Wye Valley, or wander around the upbeat museums devoted to the area's mining history. Plough further into those rich thickets, which seemingly stretch for illimitable miles, and you begin to feel that sense of apartness. Someone recently described the Forest of Dean as a sort of independent republic, locked away in a patch of land that lies between the rivers Severn and Wye. The reputation might perhaps be best described as a sort of inwardness; that those who live in the Forest have little care for anything that happens outside of it. Possibly this identity is the result of a combination of remoteness (there are few main roads) and the eccentric nature of the very woodland itself. Walkers will see this most strikingly in Puzzle Wood, near Cinderford: fantastically gnarled trees form natural corridors with vast grey boulders and soft moss. Elsewhere, near the village of St Briavels, there is an expanse of protected woodland called Hudnalls Wood, containing a rich array of beech, oak and elm.

The walkers who come to stay at St Briavels are chiefly here for the many miles of woodlands. The village is almost ringed with them. For those who have never been to the Forest of Dean, the area sounds slightly too abstract to really get a purchase on. The minute you plunge into it, the storybook feel of the locale swiftly steals over you. If walking is partly about escapism, then the sort of imaginative escape offered in these parts is nearly overwhelming. Little wonder that vast woodlands such as these have echoed throughout British literature and art.

Hudnalls Wood lies on the great gorge of the Wye that twists and turns through this quiet world. From St Briavels, you can gaze out across the vast thickly wooded valley, and imagine quite easily that it is the sort of fantasy land that you see portrayed naffly on the covers of novels involving men in robes with swords, and wizards (oh, and quickly shake your head to dispel the image; it's a form of desecration). When Hudnalls Wood is approached from the tiny road that leads to St Briavels Common – there is barely enough room for one car, let alone two – the feeling of otherness is heightened.

A green sign proclaiming a 'restricted byway' points right-wards. You turn – and then look down into a beguiling prospect. You find yourself descending through a natural pergola, a passage of dim green, tightly-wound tree life leading sharply downwards. This is a footpath that resembles the old hollow ways that can still be found in Dorset and other parts of the West Country. The sharp gradient gives rise to quite another impression: that you are descending into some kind of jade underworld. This sense is intensified dramatically after a few yards when suddenly, the path brings you to the edge of an extraordinarily lush, tree-filled crevasse. You can go left or right at this point, along a tiny muddy stony ledge, looking down at quite a drop – but you cannot see its full extent, simply because the view is jammed with trees sprouting out of the steep hillside. It is a forest flipped sideways. There is an old and oddly sacred atmosphere here – one that any walker can savour when the strange and unique history of the area is known.

One of the Forest's most famous sons is the late television playwright Dennis Potter. In 1962 – a few years before he composed the Forest-set *Blue Remembered Hills* – he wrote a short, polemical book about the area's past, and its deeply uncertain future. In the early 1960s, even among all the soughing woodland, mining was still a very strong ongoing concern and the major employer for some miles. Coal was the economic engine of all these little towns, which lay physically and spiritually somewhere between the brash modernism of England and the close chapel-bound psyche of Wales. In one passage, Potter describes a time when his miner father, and his father's old mentor, were walking back home after work. It was dark, and the two men were making their way in silence through the murk of the woods:

> All the old Forest stories, the tales told to children, the mining superstitions related to danger at work, the country superstitions based on isolation and history and religion, welled out of them to create an old and unknowable fear ... it is (or was) a small part of the strong feeling of being 'a Forester', something complex and unique, something that outsiders were rarely expected to understand.[1]

The mines are all gone now, save for a few individual private concerns. In 1962, Potter saw this end coming, but could not quite bear it: 'It is not enough to say that the Forest's future must be that of a tourist playground surrounded by a few ugly villages inhabited by employed young women and out-of-work old men.' To be fair, even if it is a draw to many, the Forest is not quite so vulgarised as to be considered a 'playground'. And in the early weeks of 2011, it found itself in a rather different position as the focus of an intense political campaign.

The Coalition government was proposing to sell off chunks of Forestry Commission land, meaning that hectares could end up in the possession of private owners who could conceivably then restrict access; the very notion sparked a very middle class form of outrage – letters to the grander newspapers, local authors writing articles. The Forest of Dean came to symbolise all that we appear to hold most sacrosanct about woodland: not merely the right to roam, but also that of land that is owned by no one, with old trees that grow free – rather than regimented lines of soulless commercial conifers stifling other varieties of woodland plants. The campaign to 'save the woodland' tapped into a long held myth that England until the Middle Ages was one vast land of wild forests; that kings, commoners and deer all roamed in bosky bliss; that Shakespeare's Forest of Arden, with all its associations of spiritual freedom, was in some way an English Eden from which we had yet to be expelled.

Certainly the Foresters (as the locals are termed) have been vocal in asserting their ancient rights. And they have attracted much support from elsewhere. There is, among ramblers and conservationists alike, an anxiety that Britain is steadily losing swathes of its native forests, and has been for centuries. In wider terms, though, could there be some historical misunderstanding about the range and extent of ancient woodlands? In his ground-breaking 1955 history, *The Making of the English Landscape*, W. G. Hoskins asserted that when 'we read that one Durham man alone was said in 1629 to have felled more than thirty thousand oaks in his lifetime, and reflect that similar destruction was going on in all the ironworking districts of England – in the Weald, the Forest of Dean, round Birmingham and Sheffield, and in the Clee Hills – we can envisage something of the extent of woodland lost between 1500 and 1688.' In addition to this, 'the revolutionary improvements in farming in the sixteenth and seventeenth centuries led to large tracts of woodland being grubbed up for corn and cattle.'[2]

Even back in the nineteenth century, there were those who felt a nostalgia for woodland that they felt sure had disappeared many aeons beforehand. Thus William Wordsworth in 1810, writing of how the landscape of England had changed:

Formerly the whole country must have been covered with wood to a great height up the mountains; where native Scotch firs must have grown in great profusion, as they do in the northern part of Scotland to this day. But not one of these old inhabitants has existed, perhaps, for some hundreds of years; the beautiful traces, however, of the universal sylvan appearance the country formerly had, yet survive in the native coppice-woods that have been protected by enclosures, and also in the forest-trees and hollies which, though disappearing fast, are yet scattered over the enclosed and unenclosed part of the mountains.

The question still remains though: what was the extent of those original woodlands? More recently, the naturalist and landscape historian Professor Oliver Rackham has taken a slightly different view, ingeniously extrapolating from the Domesday Book that, in the eleventh century, England was composed of 35 per cent arable land, 15 per cent woodland and wood pasture, and 1 per cent meadow. Pasture came in at an estimated 30%. The rest was 'mountains, heaths, moorland and fen.'[3] So while it is perfectly obvious that old forests have been whittled down over the course of the centuries the landscape, some argue, still might not have changed all that dramatically over the last millennium. On top of this, we may be getting tangled up in thickets of linguistic confusion. 'To the medievals,' wrote Professor Rackham, 'a Forest was a place of deer, not a place of trees.' As such, the term 'forest' could also include moorlands and heath – look at today's 'forest of Dartmoor' as confirmation.

As we have seen from recent protests, woodland holds such a strong grip on the national imagination because it chimes so deeply with anarchy, and openness, and freedom. From the legend of Robin Hood and his outlaws to *Just William* and *his* outlaws – it is easy to see the romantic pull of the forest. Children love woods because this is territory that they can make their own. They can climb the trees, make shelters out of sight of the grown-ups. Natural wildwood defies order; it is the exact opposite to the regimentation of agriculture and the strictures of land ownership.

Places such as Hudnalls Wood, and other parts of the Wye Valley, can have an interesting psychological effect upon the walker too. Just as ridgeways and escarpments and blowy heaths have a tendency to temporarily empty the mind, deep old woodland can conversely set the mind working. The sound of soft footfall on twig or moss, the feel of snaking tree roots pressing into the arches of the foot, even the semi-light seeping through the canopy above, encourage inward reflection. The mind does not skitter when one is walking through woodland; rather, it slows down, works at a more considered pace. There are individual moments of pure, utterly unconscious delight: the tiny glimpse of bright blue from above through the thick green leaves; the even more fleeting glimpse, from far above, of the coiling, dark blue River Wye. There are also moments of silent surprise. For instance, having picked my way gingerly along the narrow ledge near the top of Hudnalls Wood, absorbing the fantastical shapes of the old trees (one pokes a thick branch out across the path like a giant squid), I suddenly find myself in a clearing, filled with profoundly pink rhododendrons, and intense red roses. There is neat grass, and clipped bushes, and more blood-red flowers, and an open sky. The contrast makes you blink. Then the path descends into thicker woods, deep green depths. The word Tolkienesque would be perfectly applicable here, since parts of *Lord of the Rings* were indeed said to have been inspired by visits to the Forest of Dean.

Even though the path is clear, the way through the woods is rarely straightforward. There is always an obstacle, be it the thick red trunks of fallen trees, or collapsed branches, or the mulchy mud around streams that gurgle humorously; walkers are forced to make a hundred tiny decisions as they move forwards. Unlike the wide open hill tops, where the conscious mind can disappear into a trance of abstraction, woodland requires you to stay alert, and near the surface of consciousness.

Most walkers have been steeped in images and stories of woodland since early childhood, via such diverse means as *Hansel and Gretel*, *Little Red Riding Hood*, and Rupert Bear's 'Nutwood'. Forests are partly how, as youngsters, we come to understand the world. We have also been immersed, as a culture, in literary forests that carry a similar charge to the old fairy tales. It is extremely natural that walkers should, even on a subconscious level, seek out a similarly transfiguring experience. In Shakespeare's plays, characters come to the woods to enter a different sort of world. People get lost; they are lured onto false paths; they encounter ambiguous figures. From *A Midsummer Night's Dream* to *As You Like It*, we see in the landscape of Shakespeare's imagination that the woodland – the Forest of Arden – is a place where people can finally, truly, be themselves.

In other stories, the forests are also often a labyrinth, in which moral choices have to be made, or grave jeopardy faced. In Book III of Edmund Spenser's *The Faerie Queene*, the forest into which the squire rides is vast and wild; he is unaware that deadly enemies are hiding among the trees, waiting to strike him down. The wounded squire is discovered by a beautiful wood nymph. She sees that she must use her arts to treat the injured man, and to take him to her woodland fastness. Here, the forest is associated not merely with hermetic and feminine knowledge, of herbs, simples and enchantments; but here under these canopies also run deep erotic undercurrents. This is not to suggest that ramblers are in search of similar erotic undercurrents – we leave that for the more specialised outdoor enthusiasts. In a slightly broader sense, though, many walkers exploring woodland are certainly looking for a homeopathic elixir of that feeling of mystery, that sense of entering another realm conjured by Rudyard Kipling in 'The Way Through The Woods': 'Yet if you enter the woods/Of a summer evening late/When the night-air cools on the trout-ringed pools/Where the otter whistles his mate ...'

The labyrinthine nature of woodland is important; there have been times, when I have been strolling through Epping Forest, to the north east of London, when I have found myself lost. Even on a sunny early autumn afternoon, amid the richness of the last summer colours, such disorientation in the geographical sense can be a little unsettling. When you stop moving, and stand still, there are moments when the rest of the forest is perfectly still as well. Not even the stir of a small animal or a bird can be heard. It is as though time has been paused. Then there is the faintly unsettling sensation of hearing other people – perhaps a family with small children, giggling and laughing – but never quite seeing them through the trees. Are they really there? Or are they some manifestation of the forest itself?

* * *

The seclusion and privacy of the Forest of Dean lure in other sorts of tree lovers too. It is not so unusual to come across white witches in a clearing, performing rites on certain sacred calendar days. Whatever our reasons for being there, there is the very specific aesthetic pleasure of following a woodland path; that sense both of being away from one's everyday world, yet also being rather hemmed in within a new one. You lose your sense of direction here very quickly, and also your sense of distance. The walker gives himself up to woodland. The mind is still working, still making those tiny decisions, but the feet and the legs are somehow yielding to the shapes of those paths, following their curves as though preconditioned.

Here in the Wye Valley, in a landscape so fretted with ancient mystery and geological curiosity – our eyes are constantly flickering over the path beyond, either to rest on the fantastical ridged carvings of an old oak or yew, or to gaze upon the green glowing moss on a sensuously rounded boulder on the forest floor. There is such a thing as the 'Sculpture Trail' in this Forest – an arts project in which various creations wrought from wood and steel have been purposefully placed at certain points. And given that these pieces are intended to represent the Forest's industrial past, it is all very commendable. There are perfectly natural sculptures here too; from the occasional free-standing boulder, that will put you in mind of Arthurian legend, and the *Sword in The Stone*; to the rich lichen climbing the branch of an old tree. 'Trees in more rural areas should have grey, brown, green and yellow lichens,' wrote Professor Oliver Rackham. In these parts, it seems luminous in the rich semi-darkness.

Another great attraction for walkers – one that works lightly on the imagination as they explore – is that this Royal Forest can boast an almost Ruritanian past; we think of the conquering Normans, who, in their love of hunting, introduced Forest Law here in the twelfth century. This meant that they appointed the wonderfully named Verderers – men whose job it was to look after the deer and wild boar populations. The Royal Forest of Dean remained a rich hunting ground throughout the Tudor period, though there was also industry, in the form of iron ore, timber and, to a limited degree, coal. As the demand for coal went up at the dawn of the new industrial age, there was already a tradition in place that any man aged over the age of twenty-one, who had worked for a year and a day down a mine, had the right to become a 'freeminer' – that is, one who had his own small portion of coal or ore that he could dig from the ground.

Here too are ancient burial grounds. The main thing we hear through all historical accounts is that there exists a sense of apartness, uniqueness. It is this quality that is so irresistible to walkers. For in such a place, the rambler feels the prospect of self-transformation, of being lifted out of themselves.

While we enjoy forests there is also buried deep within our culture an innate wariness of woodland dwellers. You hear it in modern urban rumours and in nineteenth century tales about gipsy brigands. Yet this ambiguity has also found expression in one of the greatest of our national myths. Once the star of minstrels' ballads, and still the central hero figure in big screen films and television series alike, Robin Hood is the ultimate expression of the schizophrenic approach to woodland – the freedom it offers, yet also the sense that to live there makes one an outcast from society.

Thanks to this medieval ballad turned sylvan legend, the most famous of all England's woodland remains Sherwood Forest, even if it is only a scrap of what it apparently used to be. Nor could the forest live up to the expectations of Daniel Defoe in the eighteenth century: 'This Forest does not add to the fruitfulness of the County,' he wrote, 'for 'tis now, as it were, given up to Waste.' By this, he meant bare heathland: 'Even the Woods which formerly made it so famous for Thieves, are Wasted; and if there was such a man as Robin Hood, a famous Out Law and Deer Stealer, that so many years harboured here, he would hardly find Shelter for one week, if he was now to have been there; nor is there any store of Deer.'

* * *

Back in the 1980s, a party of sixth formers from my west London school came down to St Briavels for a long weekend, on the pretext of some geographical themed weekend, though really more for a laugh. We stayed in the St Briavels youth hostel, a fancy affair consisting of a twelfth-century keep – a small castle – filled with all the paraphernalia of bunk beds and very sparsely equipped kitchens. King John once used the place as a hunting lodge. Gamely, the hostel now keeps such associations going with weekly medieval Banquets. There is still a grand courtyard, and although water no longer ripples in the moat, the shape of it remains, giving the place a very regal sense of separateness. It is a cross between an imposing National Trust antiquity and a Mike Leigh film set. It seems in some ways to symbolise what is so very fine about the Youth Hostel Movement, and why it seems to have been part of the walker's landscape for rather longer than it actually has. When I was first there, in 1984, things were rather sober. Youth hostels were uniformly unlicensed, and alcohol was strictly forbidden on the premises. That did not stop us smuggling grog in our suitcases; one girl even brought along a bottle of Cointreau. There are no limits to the horrors of teenage drinking tastes. But the teetotal element is part of what made these establishments such a draw to more serious-minded young people in the 1930s, when the Youth Hostel Movement, inspired by pioneering establishments in Europe, really got underway. The idea of these hostels originated at a meeting of the Liverpool and District Ramblers' Federation in 1929. It attracted interest from various bodies such as the National Council of Social Service and, shortly afterwards, the Youth Hostel Association (YHA) was formed.

The first hostel was in Wales: Pennant Hall in the Conwy Valley, which opened in December 1930. Soon after there were 73 hostels, all over the country; by 1933, there were 180. The first President of the YHA was historian G. M. Trevelyan – himself a fervent walker who was wont to trick guests staying with him in Northumberland into undertaking 30-mile hikes. In 1931, he gave a radio broadcast on the BBC, to explain the philosophy behind this new movement. The intention, he said, was to help young city dwellers of limited means. He wanted them to get 'a greater knowledge, care and love of the countryside', to rediscover their rural roots. The only way to do this effectively, he argued, was to stay in the countryside for three or four days. With hostels roughly 15 miles apart, 'the walker can easily get from one to another in a day.'[4]

Trevelyan, an energetic and passionate Oxford academic, was the brother of Charles Trevelyan, an MP who in 1908 had tried to follow in the footsteps of James Bryce in an attempt to get together a Bill to allow access to English moorlands and uplands. Trevelyan was a spiritual heir to the Sunday Tramps, but he brought a more elegiac approach to his love for the land. In his view, it was a beauty that was fast disappearing. By the 1930s, towns and cities across the country were experiencing a huge building boom; it seemed to people like Trevelyan that these urban masses were enveloping and suffocating the surrounding countryside.

He had, a few years previously, written an essay that he was later to dismiss as 'exceedingly mad' – yet the points he made were finding echoes in commentators all over the country. He asserted that since the mid nineteenth century, 'a population living in country cottages and small towns' had been replaced by 'a population living a wholly artificial life in great cities.' These great cities rather resembled, in his imagination, the subterranean hell inhabited by H. G. Well's Morlocks – a world not merely of squalor and smog, but also of pubs and public drunkenness, loutish newspapers and low music halls. The city, he wrote, represented 'ugliness, vulgarity, materialism, the insipid negation of everything that has been accounted good in the past history of man.'[5]

There are some in the country who would find that difficult to disagree with even today. But there was also a note of melancholia abroad about the essence of English natural beauty being on the brink of being lost forever. This sense of imminent loss is, we realise, quite a constant theme in the story of walking.

In Trevelyan's *History of England*, written after the First World War, there is a swooping passage where he reaches right back into the roots of the English countryside in order to tell us exactly what we have destroyed:

What a place it must have been, that virgin woodland wilderness of Anglo-Saxon England ... still harbouring God's plenty of all manner of beautiful birds and beasts, and still rioting in the vast wealth of trees and flowers – treasures which modern man, careless of his best inheritance, has abolished, and is still abolishing, as fast as new tools and methods of destruction can be invented.

Here, we can clearly make out the resonant aftershock of the Somme, of Passchendaele, of those haunted, shattered landscapes reduced to mud and blood and bone. Trevelyan conflated the inexorable march of industry with the industry of death that was the mark of the horror of the Great War.

Yet that conflict also brought with it an unexpected social repercussion that would facilitate Trevelyan's desire for the masses to enjoy the land. The war had ripped away a significant proportion of the young male upper classes, and in the post-war years, many of the great aristocratic estates would be broken up. For the first time since the Enclosure Acts, the future of many areas of countryside was looking uncertain.

In 1925, Trevelyan became involved with another enduring institution – the National Trust. He was especially interested in Lord Brownlow's Ashridge estate in the Chilterns: an example of an old estate that was selling up in the aftermath of the war. Trevelyan, using all his influence, persuaded various philanthropists both to contribute and to campaign for the Ashridge estate to go to the National Trust. It did so and is now a favourite among walkers. It is the Youth Hostellers who owe Trevelyan a special debt of gratitude. In 1936, he wrote an introduction to *Walking Tours and Hostels in England* – a few paragraphs which encapsulated everything that he wanted the explorers of the land to enjoy:

I especially want to recommend [this book] to those who have discovered the Youth Hostel Association and its Hostels and are already fortunate enough to be enrolled as members … for there is no movement I believe to be better or more necessary than ours during these latter days. Mankind, particularly in our island, has been locked up in the great cities away from nature and from its health and beauty. Our race, almost more than any other, is denied the natural use of its limbs which machinery displaces, is denied the enjoyment of the old human instincts, the delight in sunset and sunrise, noontide and dew, woodland, field and running stream, valleys, woods and hills.

For hundreds of thousands of years, mankind was bred on the lap of Nature. It is only in this last century that he has suddenly been seized upon and locked away from his mother earth, locked away from God's country in man's ugly artificial towns, where he sees nothing of Nature but a thin strip of sky between the chimney pots. It is not, and it cannot come to good.[6]

His words – and the fast growing network of hostels – caught something of a national mood. As veteran rambler John Bunting recalls, in places like Sheffield the young people divided into those who wanted to spend their time dancing, and those who were desperate to jump on their bikes and cycle into the country-side. These new youth hostels presented the lower-paid with a fantastic new holiday possibility. Instead of heading to the pleas-ure beaches, there was now a chance to investigate the deep coun-tryside properly, at no great cost. This is what Mr Bunting and his friends did when young; they took a few days off and cycled a huge distance over the north, staying at youth hostels along the way and embarking on epic hikes from each fresh location.

In the 1930s, a night's stay would cost one shilling. A small charge was also made if you sat down for an evening meal or breakfast. You could also pay a minimal amount for a specially prepared packed lunch if you were heading off for a long hike. Certainly, the accommodation was rather austere – starting as it meant to go on, the bedrooms consisted of single sex dormitories, filled with bunk beds. In some hostels, the roofs were rather rackety and had holes. But if you were a young man or woman, from a heavily industrialised town, then in most cases you were actually coming from accommodation that was even sparser: crowded houses, shared bathrooms, outside lavatories, damp, mildew, insufficient heating. Conversely, the prospect of a youth hostel – clean, bright, out in the open – would have looked to some rather luxurious.

One early enthusiast summed it up:

The Youth Hostel spirit I cannot accurately convey, it has to be
experienced. It is social in that it brings together walkers and
cyclists in fellowship with a minimum of restriction. But, most
of all, it contributes to the service of beauty – not the outward
beauty of our national heritage, for which we in this generation
have to be vigilant trustees, but the inward beauty, which in
words depends on simplicity – I mean the true simplicity of a
rightly and nobly ordered mind and character.

One edition of *The Ramblers' Handbook* went a little further
with this almost poetic sentiment: '[The YHA] opens the way to
the sea and the hills for those who know only the smell of the
streets and the noise of the traffic … it enables a young man or
woman to plan and carry out their own escape from the towns.'

In this, we again also catch a scent of non-conformism, of the
enthusiastic teetotal movement. Moreover, many hostels had a
very strict 'lights out' policy; some as early as 10 p.m.
Paradoxically, these rigid rules brought a fresh level of freedom
to a growing constituency of female walkers. For with any hint
of licentiousness firmly eradicated, hostels all over the country
were regarded as proper and respectable places. The YHA helped
to open up the countryside for young female friends from all
backgrounds, who could now take off and find a place to go far
from the demands of the men in their lives, or the expectations
of men in the seaside resorts such as Blackpool. The strictly
segregated sleeping arrangements firmly dispelled even any
thoughts of wild promiscuity. Old-fashioned ideas of chaperon-
ing were melting away; the modern world was starting to
acknowledge that girls were every bit as entitled as boys to enjoy
holidays with friends.

On top of this, for all the austerity of the facilities, there were
some startlingly grand youth hostels to be found. Because of

help from bodies such as The Forestry Commission, as well as charitable concerns like the Cadbury Trust and the Carnegie Trust, properties were either donated or lent out on leases. Which is why hostels could end up in locations as spectacular as St Briavels castle; this fresh use rather came to the rescue of an otherwise decaying, expensive to run structure.

Come the 1940s and 50s – and accelerating in the 1960s and 70s – a new genre of youth hostel visitor began to emerge: the middle-aged, middle class, *Guardian*-reading walking enthusiast. Rather than succumb to the vulgar siren calls of foreign beach holidays, these hardy folk, often with their children, would pitch up, clanking their own knives and forks (for the kitchens in youth hostels were sparsely equipped).

Naturally, the inception of the National Parks in the early 1950s brought a concomitant upswing in interest, for here were millions of acres of wild walking territory dotted with youth hostels. Again, Trevelyan had been a noisy enthusiast for the Parks and had made all sorts of representations to the then Chancellor Hugh Dalton, another keen walker. Meanwhile, hostels became such familiar establishments that it was soon as though they had been around for a century, rather than just a couple of decades.

The new wave of middle class youth hostellers in the 1960s and 70s were highly conscious of the environment, and matters of pollution. Youth hostels offered a sort of socialist purity, where all classes could mingle in a perfectly level environment – the same kitchen and dining room, the same bunk beds and dormitories. They were also favoured by the sort of walker who is now pretty much extinct: the hitch-hiker. In the 1960s and 70s, when private car ownership had leaped up, the first few yards of every motorway in the land would feature figures standing with cardboard placards, bearing in hope the name of a destination. And there were always drivers who were willing to pick up hitch-hikers. The general understanding was that the hiker would have to listen to the driver who would deliver an uninterrupted, never-ending monologue, on a subject of his pleasing. But this is perhaps unfair. Most hikers were young, most car owners were just a little older; and both understood the ecology of the road – that a car with a single driver was somehow wasteful.

Now, of course, fear of crime on both sides – the wary hiker anxious about where they are being driven, the wary driver anxious that they will be hijacked and that the vehicle will be stolen, or worse – means that hitch-hiking has virtually died out. But it is not just a fear of crime; the other thing that has happened in the intervening years is an intensified sense of private property and private space, of which the car is an extension. You would now no more invite a stranger into your car than you would your home. The space belongs to you and your family; it is not there to be shared with others.

That is exactly what makes the continued success of the YHA such a fascinating phenomenon. It seems to be the one area of British life where the notion of shared space is still absolutely intrinsic to the entire thing. To a man of John Bunting's generation, the notion of sleeping in a room with several other completely unknown men was simply a fact of life. Now it seems quite extraordinary. In subtler ways, the times have changed. While there are still many bleaker YHA outposts, such as the Honister youth hostel which resembles nothing so much as an Antarctic expedition, places like St Briavels have quietly evolved. Yes, there are still dorms and bunks and basic washing facilities. But there is now wifi – and you are also allowed to drink.

*   *   *

In St Briavels, just across the road from the spectacular castle, is a bed and breakfast establishment. It advertises the fact that the rooms have en-suite facilities, as well as kettles. Even now the idea of space, of privacy, of the primacy of property, is what makes the very notion of the bed and breakfast establishment – like hostels, so long a part of the rambling tapestry – so intriguing. Especially when it seems that the cost of a room in such a house is pretty much the same as that of a room in an anonymous, economy hotel. If anything, the bed and breakfast has just as strong a claim on the collective imaginations of walkers as the youth hostel. How can it not? The idea of paying to stay in a private home, to flit through for one or two nights, to sample the hosts' breakfast menu, to abide by the personal rules of complete strangers, is rather beguiling.

Bed and breakfasts – or guesthouses – sprang up with the nineteenth century growth of the seaside resort, and with the coming of the paid holiday. In the 1880s, thanks to the introduction of Wakes Weeks – a week in which mills closed so that all the machinery could be checked and repaired – working class holidaymakers streamed to Blackpool in their hundreds of thousands. There were a very large number of guesthouses near the centre to accommodate them. Far from being fancy, these houses, in which rooms would be rented out, were often as overcrowded and insanitary as the dwellings that the workers left behind. The streets, with their warrens of backyards, were similarly unfancy. What these houses did have was a certain rackety atmosphere of fun and escape. Families would be thrown together and just a few yards away lay all the gaudy pleasures of fairgrounds and street entertainers.

It was only a little later on that the mythos of the boardinghouse landlady began to develop; the sharp-tongued harridan who would tyrannise her paying guests into conforming to the house rules. This gorgon would be the gatekeeper, forbidding both drunkenness and any kind of sexual freedom. She started to rise to prominence as a comic caricature in the 1930s, a music hall figure of fun. The appeal lay in the idea of honest working people defying unjust authoritarianism; at work it was the foreman, and on holiday, it was the boarding house Medusa.

Now, the seaside boarding house – as opposed to the inland bed and breakfast – has a reputation for straightforward licentiousness. The bed and breakfast, on the other hand, is a curious institution that in some ways appears to have stayed lodged in a certain post-war cast of mind. In place of the raucous, plain-speaking nature of the seaside guesthouse, there is something a little quieter, more reserved, and certainly more middle class about a bed and breakfast.

There are some bed and breakfasts that live in ramblers' lore; those that cater for the die-hard, regular Pennine Way or Yorkshire Dales walkers, for instance. A walker of my acquaintance who regularly rambles with his wife in Yorkshire is constantly e-mailing me about his recommended establishments along the routes – houses that he and his wife have been visiting for years. Owing to factors such as early retirement, and better health – or the desire for it – in old age, walkers have more time for their expeditions than they used to. Perhaps walkers are keeping the dual traditions of bed and breakfasts and youth hostels going long after both might have been expected to fade away.

Today, we have a real 'big society' of walkers, who are so at ease in each other's company that all of today's social norms concerning personal space – individual bedrooms and fully equipped en suite bathrooms – don't really come into it. For the seasoned walker, half the fun of a youth hostel is the impossibility of a full night's sleep. The frozen limit of anti-social behaviour is loud snoring. If anyone wants to see how Britons used to live in the 1950s, they need only join the YHA and stay at St Briavels. Ignore the wifi and the drink, and the spirit of the place is exactly the same; from the plain wooden tables to the large notice boards advertising hearty outdoor activities, making full and creative use of those vast woodlands, the place reeks of a certain kind of apple-cheeked virtue. These days, one need not venture into deep country to find such qualities; for thanks to years of environmental awareness, there is now an increasing amount of virtue also to be found hidden within big cities, as numbers of walkers are finding.

CHAPTER 11

A Quick Detour Through Regenerated Cities and the Art of Urban Rambling

I could tell, at weekends in the summer months, that something had changed in the East End area where I live. Gathering around the locks of the Grand Union Canal, which open out here into the Thames at Limehouse, were groups of walkers of a certain age. They were precisely the walkers you would see on National Park trails, or in Woodland Trust areas: dressed practically, with carefully calibrated shoes, back-packs, and armed with colourful walking poles. What I found striking was the idea that these ramblers would want to spend their Saturdays gazing upon reclaimed urban wilderness – redundant docks and wharfs and warehouses bulldozed to make way for 'riverside lifestyle choices' – as opposed to meadows and murmuring brooks. Then I thought about it and realised that these apparently new walking trends are not new at all; many ramblers have always been fascinated with cities and their walking possibilities.

In my case, the pacing of the streets has been a question of a gnawing need to know; London-born, I felt it almost a duty to walk as much of the city as I could. To explore not merely the tight, dark streets of Lambeth, Southwark, and Elephant and Castle – and all those other places with almost folkloric reputations of resonance. But also those long terraces of 1930s houses that stretch illimitably, over Harlesden in the west, Ilford in the east. It is only by walking the city that you can detect how different areas change abruptly and dramatically street by street; how different cultures can be found on both sides of one railway line.

Only through long hikes can you appreciate the awesome multiplicity of London identities. How the Turk-Cypriot flavour of Stoke Newington so swiftly gives way to the orthodox Judaism of Stamford Hill, and thence to West African Seven Sisters. Different roads and streets and terraces and markets move past the walker like a diorama; a procession of vivid images – store fronts with displays of fruit in plastic bowls; evangelical churches in abandoned 1960s office buildings, signs proclaiming 'The Celestial Chapel of the Blazing Chariot'; suddenly smart little parades of shops with knowing cupcake boutiques, and then the rather tattier parades, with their fried chicken shops, to be found on the city's frazzled fringes: Chadwell Heath, Welling, Feltham.

An urban walk – be it in London, or along the canal paths of Birmingham, or around Manchester and Liverpool and Gateshead – all those coiling white pedestrian bridges and old flour mills transformed into museums – oddly fulfils as much of that rambling pleasure as any game struggle across sucking moorland. The hills and views of the city, by and large, are not dramatic, it is true. But what you lack in wildlife and greenery, you gain in the ceaseless fascinations of architecture, and history, not to mention the human face. On top of this, in these post-industrial times, we might have to rethink the notion of nature and the city; for even though the wildlife is not immediately obvious, it is most certainly there, more thriving and diverse than at pretty much any other time in history. Back from the brink of extinction are sparrows and blue tits; more exotically, hawks are to be found nesting in the sheltered parts of high-rise office buildings. A ramble through any of the old London ceme-teries – from Highgate in the north to Nunhead in the south – will reveal an astonishing range of birds and wildflowers. In the 1950s, there were days when people could not see the hands in front of their faces thanks to industrial smog; now, with industry all but gone, London's woods and rivers and parks are teeming with life. The Camley Street nature reserve at the back of King's Cross, and backing on to a formerly derelict area of canal and warehouses, now boasts reed warblers, mallards and bats. The walker in this area can very easily envisage the idea of unstoppable nature pushing her way up from beneath the cracks in the paving.

The same is true of the old Midlands sumplands, that stretch of the country between Birmingham and Wolverhampton that not so long ago seemed to be one long rusty scrapyard. Parts of Birmingham's canal system can change any walker's preconceptions. For those of us who don't live there, Birmingham is synonymous with a nightmarishly grim railway station, a ringroad dominated city centre and broken down redbrick relics of the city's once formidable industrial past. You would imagine that these – plus the hard-to-love tower blocks in the distance – are now what constitutes Birmingham's soul. The canals, as they so often tend to, neatly upend this preconception. For once you get away from the dual carriageways and the horrible station, and on to those defiantly antique paths which force you to crouch under low bridges, you see a city proud of its history and keen to polish up those dignified old redbrick warehouses and manufactories.

The restoration of the canals both in the Midlands and throughout the country is one of the more breathtaking success stories of the last fifty years. Local enthusiasts and volunteers, equipped with little more than drills, shovels and wild bloody-mindedness, took these abandoned decaying waterways and made them not merely viable, but actually a huge part of England's tourism industry. Men and women – local and visitors – piled into old sluices and locks, removing shopping trolleys, burnt out cars, and worse. They repaired leaking crumbling stonework, rebuilt lock gates and ensured that the waters were pumped through fresh once more. It was not so long ago that many urban canals were complete no go areas, haunted by drunks and prostitutes. Now there are more longboats piling up and down canal waters than there were 100 years ago. For walkers, entire new ways of exploring not merely the countryside, but the relics of industrial urban areas, have been opened up.

There have also been social changes; all broadly in the walker's favour. In the 1970s and 1980s, London ramblers knew better than to venture along the Regent's Canal from Dalston to Hackney; some of the path ran alongside some of the capital's most troubled areas. Stolen cars burning by the side of the towpath were not uncommon. Local children would amuse themselves by tipping breezeblocks off the small canal bridges. In addition to a familiar repertory company of harmless old boozers claiming ownership of the waterside benches was a new generation of less predictable drug addicts. Now, at the weekends, there is virtually walkers' gridlock on this towpath; a cacophony of angry ting-tings from frustrated middle class cyclists attempting to get round the pedestrians. The walkers stop to admire the early-nineteenth-century bridges, stare at the now-compulsory waterside warehouse-flat conversions, and break for cappuccinos in waterside cafés that were once old textile factories. There are drawbacks. Up until the late 1990s there were still the ghosts of old industry here, the echoing sense of the canal itself being used. But the path today looks a little like one of those estate agent computer simulations, with smiling, middle class people enjoying urban regeneration. If one wants to feel secure, one must sacrifice a little authenticity.

For urban walkers, the notion of trespass is subtly (and amusingly) reversed. Obviously we walkers know that we cannot traipse through back gardens or front gardens or indeed anywhere that involves any kind of fence. Nor would anyone want to. Naturally. The areas where urban walkers sometimes feel most chary about intruding on are labyrinthine old council estates from the 1960s and 70s. And not because of fear of crime, but simply because of the sense that they are somehow not allowed.

There is a good example of this to be found in Poplar, east London. It is called the Lansbury Estate in honour of the pioneering Labour politician George Lansbury. As these 1960s estates go, it is neither repellent nor attractive – just a very large quantity of utilitarian square houses, and tower blocks that are not especially towering. For the walker – and there are both individuals and groups now seeking out such locations – the place is quite literally a maze. A cut across a small patch of greenery would appear to lead to a path between a tower block and a terrace; but it does not. You turn a corner, and you are in a high-walled dead end, filled with bins. Similarly, down a few more of these twisting paths, you cross a car park, heading for a road you can see beyond. But there is a fence in the way and you are forced to retrace all those steps. During all of this, you feel as though you are trespassing. There is no reason why you should. There are no signs forbidding casual pedestrianism. But this is none the less the abiding impression, and it is very much to do with the way that urban territory is marked out. It is the subliminal message of graffiti, but also buried deep within this use of space. Paths can only have been blocked off to discourage casual use. May that dead end be a lesson to you. If you do not live here, you have no business being here.

A little further east along the river, you will find curious hardcore urban walkers exploring the vast, dense maze that is the Thamesmead estate. Thamesmead – a cruelly lovely name for a place that has become the byword for all things unloved about council estates – is built on marshland. At its northern edge laps the silent River Thames. Through its closes and cul-de-sacs flow little channels of water, made to look like canals. All around are vast fortresses of pale grey concrete, stained in places with overflow pipe water, and punctuated with little windows. To the south lie other obstacles to the walker's path, including the southern outfall sewage pipe and the baleful bulk of Belmarsh prison.

None of this is pretty; more importantly, none of this is remotely welcoming to the casual explorer, on foot. Thamesmead has been designed for cars and buses; very often pavements simply disappear, and the reluctant pedestrian is forced down into dark underpasses. Statistically, the chances of being mugged are not especially higher here than a lot of other places. But the lack of a sense of a community on an old marsh cut off from the rest of the city gives the place a rather lawless feel. So there are dedicated walkers who come to experience this, plus also to gaze upon an architectural experiment that is now widely reviled.

Also popular in London – and slightly more easygoing in terms of atmosphere – are the old 'railway walks', paths on old trackbeds that used to run through the suburbs. Especially pleasing is the Finsbury Park to Highgate 'Parkland Walk', which follows a steady upward incline, and gives the walker occasional glimpses of the backs of houses that they would have been seen from a train window as recently as 1970. Not far from the Highgate path is the Highgate Woods to Alexandra Palace reclaimed railway line – even more rewarding, as this grants one views right the way down to the distant Square Mile, and across east towards Stratford and the Olympic site. An even more remarkable story of renewal can be found down at that very site – though the sleek, soulless Olympics cannot, and must not, claim any credit. For much of the late nineteenth and twentieth centuries, the River Lea – which runs steadfastly down from Hertfordshire, through north-east London and the East End down to the Thames – was one of the most poisoned rivers in Britain. Along its banks, dirty industry – from the ordnance factories of Enfield, to the noxious glue factories of the Bow Backs – would spew reeking waste into those narrow, brackish waters. The area that is now partly occupied by the Olympic Park – Fish Island – was, by the 1950s, a hellhole of pollution, and the waters were dead.

Successive recessions, added to a dawning environmental consciousness, began to change things. The ordnance factories closed down, heavier industry rusted, decayed and was blown away. The path along the River Lea – a patchwork of potholes, broken glass and extravagant weeds – became the haunt of derelicts and keen urban runners. It was also noticed that in the absence of industry, the water now flowed cleanly enough to encourage species to return. Now, in place of the country walk, we have dedicated groups of ramblers tracing that River Lea path, from the eighteenth century Three Mills, at Bow, up to Waltham Forest, and along the way noting such extraordinary curiosities as cormorants, kingfishers and exquisite dragonflies, as well as the clear waters playing host to pike and an array of other fish. *Rus in Urbe*: the virtues of the country, and the rejuvenating effect of seeing the varieties of nature, are brought instead to the old Walthamstow Marshes. There are special walking tours led by natural history experts trailing up and down the River Lea now. They explore the meads near Waltham Abbey; they cheerfully march along in the shadow of the looming waste disposal incineration centre on the North Circular Road; and they eagerly hike about in search of exotic plants on the Tottenham marshes beside the old power station.

Not all attempts at urban regeneration have been so benign or pedestrian-friendly, though: it is only about seventy years ago that Sir Patrick Abercrombie – in thrall to the idea of building a new city in the aftermath of the Blitz – advocated constructing vast motorways right through the centre of London. Mercifully he was stopped; apart from the sinuous grey concrete snake of the Westway gliding over west London rooftops, and the uncompromisingly bruising A12 bulldozering its way through the terraces of the east, the capital always broadly favoured the walker. Other cities throughout England and Scotland were not so fortunate.

Newcastle is shot through with dirty grey dual carriageways. In the late 1950s and early 1960s, it was clearly decided that the pedestrian was a second-class citizen, and that nothing must impede the motorist. Similar nightmare roads were pushed through Glasgow. Other towns, such as Derby and Chesterfield, had concrete necklaces of ringroads fitted. The net result of all these tinkerings – the one-way systems, the vast roundabouts, the flyovers – was an urban landscape filled with dark under-passes, long subterranean passages that the walker would have no choice but to traverse. Now the walker is at last prevailing. In towns and cities up and down the country, subways are being blocked off and filled in, and decent systems of traffic lights are being installed on the surface. Town planners appear to be acknowledging that it is not fair to terrorise pedestrians. This is just as well, for the only way that one can really keep checking the pulse of a city is by walking its streets, noting new develop-ments and the quiet demolition of others. Only the walker – never the driver – will see how dramatically the urban landscape of England has changed over the last fifty years.

Some cities have been reinvented and rebuilt to a degree that would make anyone from the 1940s gape with incomprehen-sion. Sheffield, once a smoggy city of steel burning industry, now glistens with white high-rise towers, silvery water features and carefully landscaped steps. The forbidding concrete estate on the hill above the station is itself receiving a Day-Glo refit. Down in the west, Cardiff has been thoroughly overhauled; once again, we find white high-rises and silvery water features and landscaped steps. Only the walker can fully appreciate just how alienating complete modernity can be. How weird it is to return to a town that you thought you knew, and find that all the famil-iar landmarks are now either jostling against vast new architec-tural projects or have been overwhelmed by them. From the giant dimpled luxury superstore in Birmingham to the gaunt, metallic, glittering corporate towers that now jab at the clouds in Leeds, pulling the eye away from the old municipal glories beneath, the pace of change in the British urban landscape over the last fifteen years or so has been extraordinary. In time, once all these fresh landmarks have lost their novelty, the cities will subsume them once more. For now, walkers must acquaint themselves anew with roads and high streets that they thought they knew. This is a simple matter of reorientation. On a happier note, it also gives the rambler fresh views and prospects to assimilate. So in many ways, this is a golden age for the urban walker; whole new territories are opened up on the edges of city centres, with the development of 'quays' and the renovation of disused docks and industrial canals. Where once the banks of the River Clyde were used for the epic labour of boatbuilding, there are now nicely paved riverside walks, punctuated with the occasional old crane, left there for ornamental purposes. The 'Clyde Walk' has been a long time in preparation. First mooted in the early 1970s, it was a good thirty years before any sorts of results in terms of path creation materialised. Meanwhile, some 60 miles to the east on the River Tay at Dundee, the once forbidding river edges are now – finally – thrown open to eager walkers, who can enjoy both the furious Tay estuary, and the view of the epic, curving railway bridge across it, as well as pure blasts of invigorating North Sea air.

Whereas a walk out in the wild can connect one with an ancient past, a walk in the core of a city will impress more recent eras upon you. There are those who make for the City of London on quiet Sunday mornings; the Square Mile has a road and passageway layout that has survived since medieval times, if not before. In the silence of that morning air, anyone moving through this jumbled warren, darting down from Moorgate to Aldgate, through tiny passageways and hidden courtyards, by way of Guildhall – a mash-up of medieval pomp and late 1950s gaucheness – or any one of the innumerable churches that survived the Blitz, will be confronted with history. Ironically, thanks to the Blitz, the City is now reconnected with its Roman forebears; for the Luftwaffe bombs exposed many sections of the old, long buried Roman wall. Today, walkers can look down on these sections from pavements above.

For the last few years, there has been a cult enthusiasm among younger urban walkers for 'psychogeography' – which very loosely seems to mean divining the old spirit of each street, or each district, and seeing the invisible lines of historical – or even occult – energy that connect them. Rather than being an exclusively modern phenomenon, these psychogeographers – like those who enjoy the bleakness of the Thames Estuary – are actually romantics, in the old-fashioned poetic sense. To these walkers, boarded-up disused hospitals, or derelict small factories, old railway arches, or power stations, are pretty much the urban equivalent of the ruins of Tintern Abbey. They use the term 'entropy' but what this really means is the picturesque quality of abandonment or obsolescence. Groups such as Urban 75 – a jolly sounding bunch who, like Leslie Stephens's Sunday Tramps, occasionally escape London's bonds into the Home Counties, and then post cheerful accounts of these rambles on the Internet – are the embodiment of what seems to be a growing walking enthusiasm. They embrace the dustier, more neglected corners of the city. For the last two centuries, our footsteps have been directed out of town; now, increasingly, they are being directed into it. Some urban landscapes are now deemed every bit as beautiful as Hambledon Hill.

It is only comparatively recently that Londoners en masse have been tempted out into the country at all. There is a distinguished tradition of cockneys especially preferring to remain securely within the sound of Bow Bells. In the late nineteenth century, there were music hall songs about this antipathy to the countryside. In one ditty, a drunk man climbs aboard a late-night tram and wakes to find himself, horror struck, at the end of the line among the fields beyond Upminster. Men and women who would think nothing of walking miles across the city either to work or to visit families and friends would not countenance similar jaunts across fields. There are some rambling groups today – in the East End especially – that seem to specialise in staying within London's borders, and exploring instead the ever changing, shifting city. Some urban walkers, for instance, are sometimes drawn to 'regenerated' sites simply because local history has been thoroughly eradicated, and something entirely new has materialised, bringing with it new paths and roads. One such ramblers' magnet that has dispensed with heritage – other than a few cranes and the occasional eighteenth-century warehouse transformed into millionaire bankers' apartments – is the financial district of Canary Wharf, which is perched on top of London's extinct economic engine, the great docks.

Water remains; but now it dazzles in the reflected light of vast skyscrapers, each dedicated to those esoteric financial arts. The other point of fascination for walkers is their own status upon this vast estate, which stretches fully a good mile wide. At the edge of the Isle of Dogs, on the access roads leading in to Canary Wharf, there are vast yellow signs. They proclaim that this is strictly private property. That there is no automatic right of way. That there are certainly no bridleways or designated footpaths. In other words, you are there only as long as the management of Canary Wharf deem you suitable. When this 'Manhattan on Thames' started to rise in the late 1980s, there were a few eagle-eyed observers who wondered about the legality of taking such a vast tract of land, upon which ran public roads, and in effect privatising it to the extent that even the pavements were under the jurisdiction of faceless financiers, as opposed to Parliament. Walkers might want to ponder that now as they march by the sides of these reclaimed docks. One word of caution to anyone who likes to go walking with a dog: you might be permitted, just, in the open air. But try entering any one of the dinky Canary Wharf 'parks' or indeed any enclosed area, such as the Docklands Light Railway, and you will find yourself instantly surrounded by faux policemen, wearing faux police outfits – security guards dragged up to look like real constabulary. Dogs are not permitted. In that sense, there are parts of the city that are every bit as hostile to the walker as the old Farmer Giles bidding people to get off his land. Where rural walkers have slowly made incursions into restricted territory, urban walkers still meet with surprising obstacles. One now wonders how Tom Stephenson – one of the most influential figures in the walking movement – might have tackled such flagrant intransigence.

CHAPTER 12

In the Steps of Tom Stephenson Along Britain's Many Ways – and Paying Tribute to Generations of Self-Taught Botanists

Kitty – a ferociously opinionated middle-aged comic character created by Victoria Wood – declared in one sketch that she had walked 'the entire length of The Pennine Way in slingbacks in an attempt to publicise mental health'. Many others who now set out on this 272-mile adventure seem to be publicising their own mental health. It is estimated that those who do succeed in conquering its full length are rather an elite group: around two thousand a year.

A colleague of mine walked it some years ago with friends. The excursion started badly on the first night when their tent was pretty much torn asunder by a shrivelling wind, slicing across the moor. By the morning, there was snow on their sleeping bags. A little over two weeks later, after they had hauled themselves through innumerable bogs, they reached the end. At the northernmost point of the path, at Kirk Yelthom, in the Borders, there is a pub where, legend has it, Alfred Wainwright left an unusual bequest: for the landlord to supply a free half pint of beer to any walker who had completed the Way. My colleague claimed his drink. The landlord, he said, seemed rather glum about it.

The fact that such a path exists is a fitting memorial for a man who arguably did as much for the walking movement as Alfred

Wainwright. This man was Tom Stephenson: a journalist who had covered the Kinder Scout trespass, and who threw himself into the organised walking movement, sitting on government committees and becoming president of the Ramblers' Association in 1948. Stephenson was remarkable not merely for his commitment to the cause of walking, and of free access for all; he was also the perfect representative of an entire class of people who had, in effect, educated themselves through the countryside. How Stephenson rose to positions of such prominence and how he brought his great dream for a mighty Pennine path to fruition, can best be understood through the landscape that he loved the most. For Stephenson only had time for the uplands; they were elevating, in all possible senses.

Although he had to wait some thirty years for his long-distance Pennine trail scheme to come off – having first had the idea in 1935 – it is clear that by the mid 1960s, the time was more than ripe. In 1965 and the years immediately afterwards – from the opening of The Pennine Way, to the establishment in 1969 of the West Highland Way and in 1971 of the Offa's Dyke trail – there was a further explosion of enthusiasm for walking and hiking. This was helped enormously by the fact that car ownership had multiplied so dramatically. Walkers no longer had to rely on train timetables, or on obscure branch lines. Indeed, many of those obscure branch lines had now been shut. Now it was within the means of the average walker to bundle everyone into the car, drive out of the town, locate some country with some kind of parking space, and head out into it, without worrying about time.

To rural communities at that time, the prospect of all these urban visitors was viewed as being akin to a hostile invasion and rising anxiety about careless, ignorant townies among farmers led to a barrage of publicity concerning The Country Code. When I was growing up in the 1970s, the gaps between children's television programmes were filled with Public Information films, many of which concerned the innumerable trangressions of town folk. One such film was a cartoon featuring what can only be described as a comically plebian couple. There was a ferrety man and his rather plump, tarty blonde partner. Around them were the remains of their picnic, which they clearly had no intention of picking up. Meanwhile, the man was absent-mindedly removing the stones from the drystone wall behind him; and the tarty wife was amused by the sight of the cattle passing through the gate that she had left wide open. They were confronted by an apoplectic cartoon farmer. The townies could not understand why he was so angry. The chief prejudice among country dwellers seemed to be this: that people from towns were not only common and stupid, they were also malicious. And that their only purpose for being in the country was to cause havoc.

The mistrust was growing on both sides. By the mid-1960s inception of The Pennine Way, there was coincidentally, in some metropolitan quarters, the first inkling of suspicion about farmers and their modernised methods, and about the impact that these new methods would have on the landscape. In the immediate aftermath of the Second World War, farmers had been high in general public esteem as a result of their extraordinary efforts with the land. Just twenty years later, however, and members of small but influential groups like The Soil Association were reading a pioneering American book by scientist Rachel Carson called *Silent Spring*. Carson's thesis was that a new generation of pesticides were causing immense damage; her theme was picked up in Britain where by that time over 200 kinds of pesticide were in use. The farmers concerned were simply responding to a greater consumer demand for more and better quality produce; as today, most shoppers wanted perfect, unblemished vegetables, not misshapen ones. The effect of this blunt chemical intervention on the land, as the pioneer environmentalists saw it (and as later evidence shows), was catastrophic.

Modernisation brought an end to many of the once familiar features of rural life. Figures such as wheelwrights – who had still been very much there in the war years, and even beyond – now lost their livelihoods, for the farms no longer had need of horses. Blacksmiths too were forced into retirement. For ramblers with a love of the countryside, there was more than the simple dislocation of modernism. Thanks to the developing industry of agrochemicals – producing fertilisers, weedkillers, and anti-insect poisons – smaller farms started to give way to much larger concerns. With a combination of the new farming machinery and pesticides, farmers could now amalgamate fields; there was no longer any reason for any diversity in crop production. The Midland counties in particular began to be transformed into vast cereal production centres. As well as being unutterably depressing to the eye, they were also blotting out many old paths; and the byways that were left were too dreary and monotonous – and soundless – to be enjoyed.

The reason that walkers were now more likely to hear the hum of distant motorways rather than the drone of insects was the knock-on effect of agro-industry: the coming of these US-style prairies had also resulted in the destruction of the hedgerows. Up until about 1990, around 230,000 miles of hedgerow was uprooted and destroyed. The impact on countless other species, from birds of prey to insects, was almost unfathomable.

So even as walkers made for the country in greater numbers throughout the 1960s, a small number of them were also starting to see that fast changing system of fields and meadows through an adjusted perspective; a perspective that was adjusted for them. By contrast, the pioneering Pennine Way path offered, serendipitously, a much more unspoilt prospect. Up on the high ground, they walked far from any offensive view of other tokens of modern agricultural methods: the vast industrial looking barns, the enormous combine harvesters, the long, low hen-batteries, the stark concrete and metal of the milking sheds. It is striking that in a decade otherwise so fixated on the 'white heat' of the technological future, and on the virtues of scientific progress, the Pennine Way was offering ramblers not merely the freedom of so many hundreds of miles, but also something in the way of a reassuringly old-fashioned rural heritage trail. It showed, through the smaller hill farms, that some agricultural traditions were hardier than others, and that there were parts of Britain that were still free from transistors and computers.

The rough brown hills of the Cheviots, at the far end of the Pennine Way, seem to discourage sentimentality, and to shrug off any woolly notions of romanticism. Though an eighteenth-century walking poem by Mark Akenside called 'The Pleasures of the Imagination' sought to draw out the deeper, more reson-ant attractions of the region:

> O ye dales
> Of Tyne, and ye most ancient woodlands; where,
> Oft as the giant flood obliquely strides,
> And his banks open, and his lawns extend,
> Stops short the pleased traveller to view,
> Presiding o'er the scene, some rustic tower
> Founded by Norman or by Saxon hands.

Akenside – and many other subsequent writers, including G. M. Trevelyan – sought to soften the hardness of this part of the world by invoking history: from the presence of the Romans and their ancient Wall to those 'rustic towers' of the Normans and Saxons. The subliminal comfort is there in the sense that people have always been drawn to these gale scoured hills. Any walker with no idea of that history might assume – while trembling in those freezing winds – that the opposite was true.

* * *

You sense that there was little in the way of sentimentality about Tom Stephenson. I now find myself wondering how he had been inspired to create this particular trail in the first place. In some ways, the forces that impelled him were fiercer than those that guided figures such as Benny Rothman. For Stephenson was the very image – an almost nineteenth century image – of the auto-didact walker-botanist. His formative experiences – including conscientious objection, and prison – made his rise to national prominence all the more remarkable and admirable. Indeed, we can see now that he was one of the more emblematic left-wing English figures of the last century.

Tom Stephenson was born in 1893 in Chorley, Lancashire; his father was an engraver in a calico printing works. The father was a heavy drinker – his son recalled that he spent more time in the pub than with his family. Stephenson started full-time work at thirteen years old – which meant a crushing 66-hour week in the calico printing works. This intense and physical six-day week would have left anybody very little time for anything else. Presently, Stephenson's family moved to the village of Whalley in the Ribble Valley. On his first Saturday off, he climbed Pendle, which stands at 1,831 feet. The effect upon this young man, who had been brought up under the blackened skies of ceaseless industrial activity, was transfiguring. He gazed upon all the distant heights, 'sharp and clear in the frosty air. That vision started me rambling and in the next sixty years took me time and again up and down the Pennines and further afield.'

Stephenson was now a fifteen-year-old apprentice on short-time working. While this was an inconvenience in financial terms, it did at least allow him more time to pursue this fresh passion. 'I would set out before sunrise and make a round trip of up to a hundred miles,' he wrote. 'Nights I spent rolled in a groundsheet in the lee of a drystone wall, or in a barn if one were handy ... [occasionally] a village policeman would question me closely as a suspected runaway.'[1] He was also bright. He studied hard at night, and eventually won a scholarship to study geology in London at the Royal College of Science. This was quite an achievement, but his quick intelligence was also matched with a certain steely obduracy. In 1914, at the coming of the Great War, when Stephenson was 17, he was called up – at which he declared himself a conscientious objector. Even now, it's difficult to imagine the will and the bravery involved in making such a decision – especially at the start of the conflict, when jingoism was running at its highest. 'Of course I was the subject of a good deal of abuse,' he recalled, 'accused of coward-ice and all the rest of it and threatened I should be run out of the village, but I never suffered any violence there.'[2]

He was called up again in 1917, but steadfastly ignored the summons. This time he was escorted from home, under guard, into the Third East Lancashire Regiment, 'and after three weeks in the guardroom,' he recalled, 'I was court-martialled.' The result of this was a sentence of twelve months' hard labour. He was sent to Wormwood Scrubs, a notoriously tough prison in west London. 'The solitude of prison didn't bother me so much as some people,' he recalled, 'because I had been accustomed to wandering day after day by myself over the hills.' There was another unexpected upside: 'I did a lot of serious reading I wouldn't have done on the outside.'[3] It takes quite an unusually strong-willed personality to be able to see the cheerful aspects of life in Wormwood Scrubs.

After the war, Stephenson returned to the block printing trade. One night, he joined an organised reunion of conscien-tious objectors – all those who had also been jailed – and on that occasion, he fell in with a number of senior Labour politicians, such as Philip Snowden. Soon, Stephenson was working with the Party: he persuaded Bernard Shaw and Bertrand Russell to address Labour meetings. Stephenson was there doing all sorts of fixing jobs behind the scenes when Labour came briefly to power in 1924, fell back into opposition, and then formed a second government from 1929–31.

Such spheres of influence could not help but benefit this canny political fixer and it was clear to his friends and colleagues that he had a gift for writing – his accounts of the 1932 Kinder Scout trespass for the *Manchester Guardian* had been eagerly read. Not that he was supportive of the methods used by the BSWF on that occasion; like many ramblers, Stephenson was sceptical about the wisdom of using such confrontational tactics (we might also see an extra layer of scepticism here too; that felt by the solid Labour man for the more extremist Communists).

In 1933, Stephenson was encouraged by Ernest Bevin to become a full-time journalist. As such, he started out writing weekly articles for *The Daily Herald*, specialising in 'outdoor' stories. He also got the chance to indulge his deepest passion by assuming the editorship of *Hiker and Camper* magazine.

Mass trespasses aside, this was the point at which all these outdoors activities were putting down very deep roots in the cultural life of the country. Both the urban working classes, and the steadily growing numbers of the young middle classes, shared this enthusiasm for escape. Stephenson was now required to attend meetings of the National Council of Ramblers' Federations and the Co-operative Holidays Association. In 1935, he wrote the article for which he is still most famous: an essay in *The Daily Herald* about his dream of a 'long green trail' that would stretch from the Peak District to the Cheviots. While he had to wait thirty years for this dream – inspired by the Appalachian Trail in the US – to be realised, the article proved to have a more immediate resonance. In the countryside near Sheffield, the rights-to-access rallies continued. John Bunting now recalls the sight of around 3,000 walkers all gathered together, and how, as a young man, Mr Bunting mingled with the likes of Labour grandees-to-be Hugh Dalton and Barbara Castle.

In 1943, as the turning point in the Second World War at last seemed to have come, Tom Stephenson joined the Ministry of Town and Country Planning as a press officer. One might have imagined that such a Ministry would be rather sidelined at a time like that, but the shape and the nature of the land after the war were a pressing subject. Of particular interest was the nascent notion of National Parks, which Stephenson helped to publicise in 1945.

It was also at this time that the idea of a Pennine Way was itching ever stronger at Stephenson. A limited form of access to mountains and moors had been won, but what about the freedom to trek across the very spine of the nation, through some of its wildest and most unforgiving scenery? At the very idea of it, there were some in Whitehall – ministers and civil servants alike – who seemed fearful that such a thing might come to pass, contrary to the interests of property owners. To them, the idea had a sniff not merely of Socialism, but of Communism. The precedent it would set would seem to hint that no land could remain completely private. Come May 1945, there was a new Labour government, led by Clement Attlee and ushered in on the back of victory in Europe. There was also a new minister at Town and Country Planning: Lewis Silkin. Stephenson at this time insisted to him that there 'must be facilities for access to the wild, uncultivated parts of Britain, drastic revision of footpath law, and the creation of national parks and long-distance footpaths'. In 1948, Tom Stephenson became Honorary Secretary of the Ramblers' Association. Seventeen years after that, he was standing proudly in Edale, there to celebrate the inauguration of the Pennine Way.

John Boyle, a former policeman who was one of the very first to walk the Way, put his finger on the curious appeal of this rather wild and woolly route: 'On Saturday 24 April 1965, I was one of twelve Manchester City Police Cadets who set off to walk the 280 miles of the newly opened Pennine Way,' he told the Ramblers' Association website:

The group were aged between seventeen and nineteen ... and had been trained in map reading and compass work in preparation. Campsites were set up along the route but each lad would carry their own personal equipment and take a turn at leading the route.

I remember the bleakness of the moors and the fact that it appeared to rain all the time ... As the walk progressed, we were walking on autopilot due to tiredness and the conditions. The camaraderie of the group and the challenge kept us going. We were determined to finish the walk.

On Friday 5 May, we walked into Kirk Yelthom to be greeted by local dignitaries who congratulated us on being the first organised group to walk the full length of the Pennine Way. At the time, I did not fully understand what a tremendous experience and opportunity I had been given. I continue to walk with family and friends – but now at a more leisurely pace.

* * *

As well as his great achievements for the walking movement, Tom Stephenson was also an interesting example of a self-taught botanist and geologist, passions that were very much woven into his appetite for walking. In that sense, he was part of an admirable tradition that stretched back as least as far as the seventeenth century. That particular period had brought a whole new way of looking at the world. The intricacies of plant life were starting to become a source of immense intellectual fascination. There are records of a Cromwellian soldier called Thomas Willisel, who was commissioned by a society of London botanists to walk all over the country in search of fresh specimens. 'Our English itinerant presented an account of his autumnal peregrinations about England, for which we hired him,' the botanists wrote. In the eighteenth century, one Lady Bentinck also commissioned people to explore the corners of the British

Isles in order to bring back fresh species – not merely flowers and plants, but also insects and fossils – for her to study and display. But Lady Bentinck's men did not find their missions easy: because of the Enclosure Acts, any deviation from the roads on to private land, to explore hedges or even to get up on to high ground, laid them open to accusations of trespass, with landowners going further, and labelling them highwaymen.[4]

Among the first groups of urban walkers, in the early parts of the nineteenth century – those men and women who would leave the industrial towns for air on Sunday – there were many who had a lively fascination for plant species and rare flowers. There was, for instance, the Natural History Society of Newcastle and the Tyneside Naturalists Field Club and the Bristol Botanical Society. Meanwhile, one nineteenth century Sunderland newspaper urged its readers to go out into the country for long, exploratory walks: 'To the student in the science of geology, it affords a rich field for inquiry; it gives to the invalid new life and vigour; cheers the moody and depressed spirit.'[5] So it was that weavers and miners alike developed a fascination with the flora to be found on field trips. Tom Stephenson himself recalled a weaver from Burnley. Ernest Evans had risen from this occupation to become head of the Natural Science Department at Burnley College, after his botanical walks had led him to teaching the subject in night-classes in the Burnley Mechanics Institute. Stephenson acknowledged Ernest Evans as being an extraordinarily influential figure: 'Evans was a great rambler and many of his students rambled with him. He was above all a practical naturalist, making frequent field excursions, and introducing his students to geological features.' The *Burnley Express* went a little further, stating that Evans 'knew every crag and moor, every hill, valley and clough around Burnley – and he knew the home and haunt of every plant and animal in this area of Lancashire.'

Anyone who now sets out on a hike with a smartphone and Internet access, enabling them to instantly identify any unusual flower or plantlife that they come across on a ramble, should give some thought to the dedication, fervour and memory of these Victorian self-educated rambling botanists. There was a Manchester shoemaker called Richard Buxton whose zeal for studying the natural world, while out on twenty or thirty mile hikes, was intense. One who met him described his range of knowledge thus in a letter to the *Manchester Evening News*:

> In the summer of 1857 or 1858, I went on a walking tour to Cornwall, when I made a pretty large collection of plants, many of which when I got home, I could not find names for, so I went to interview Buxton and see if he could help me. He knew every one, of course, and could tell me all about them.[6]

You might be tempted to think that unlike the later Kinder Scout trespassers, and various other walking campaigners, the natural historians and the botanists formed a pretty apolitical branch of the rambling movement; that their concern was not so much with access, as with the discoveries that could be made. But this would be a simplification, for these walking groups were not separate from wider communities – they were part of them. After vigorous hikes in the hills, or through the valleys, they would go to the pub and discuss all sorts of pressing current issues. The slight difference here is that such walking groups by and large met with the approval of the grander London natural history societies and institutes, and the findings and studies of men like Ernest Evans were appreciated. Botanists like Richard Buxton were concerned with private property, as they wanted to appeal to the better natures of the big landowners in allowing men such as himself to make a study of their land. In the 1850s, Buxton made this measured – yet emotionally rather cunning plea – to such landowners, worded so as to emphasise subservience as opposed to aggression:

The lords of the soil will yet allow the pent-up dwellers in the crowded city to walk about and view the beauties of creation – yes, not only permit it, but derive much true pleasure from seeing the sons of toil rationally enjoying themselves in rambling through their domains and exploring the wonders of nature ... I therefore would venture to request the landowners, at least to preserve the old footpaths which cross their fields and woods, if they should decline to allow fresh ones to be made, like their forefathers of old.[7]

There were concerns elsewhere, however, that the labouring classes in general were losing all touch with the countryside. R. C. K. Ensor, in 1902, took some workers from Manchester out on a field trip and commented that 'none of them knew or could name forget-me-nots, daisies, dandelions, clover, pansies or lily of the valley.'

Around a hundred years later, with the establishment of the first National Parks in the 1950s, the botanical fascination became a cornerstone of the entire walking movement and the Nature Conservancy Council was founded. By then it had become glaringly apparent – in country and town alike – that years of industry had had a nightmarish effect upon a number of different species. By this time, the London reaches of the river Thames were pretty much dead. Thanks to all the industrial effluent flowing through those waters, there was not a fish to be found.

In the country, the biggest threat to wildlife – intensive farm-ing – was only just beginning. As if sensing, early on, the dangers that lay ahead, one of the purposes of the National Parks was to ensure that rare species continued to flourish. Later, the spirit of those walking botanists, from Buxton to Stephenson, also found fresh life with the creation of the Sites of Special Scientific Interest (SSSI), which gained a particular boost with the 1981 Wildlife and Countryside Act. As an acknowledgement of the importance of the environment – hitherto extremely faint on any politician's radar at that time – these Sites were very strictly administered, and gave the fullest possible protection from what were described as 'damaging agricultural operations.' Now, in some parts of the country, it is only in the Sites of Special Scientific Interest that a walker can get a sense of being somewhere that belongs to one particular regional locality – as opposed to standing on the edge of a vast brown wind-blown prairie that could be in either Cambridgeshire or Oregon.

As soon as it opened in 1965, the Pennine Way was an immediate draw for thousands. Six years later, again through the clear good influence of Stephenson, came the epic trail of Offa's Dyke, snaking along the English–Welsh border, from Chepstow through to Wrexham and to Prestatyn in North Wales. Like the Pennine Way, Offa's Dyke swiftly became something of a cult in its own right, appealing especially to hardcore long-distance walkers.

The contrast with the Pennine Way is – in many parts – highly attractive. Instead of rough brown moor and peat, the Offa's Dyke walker is faced with springy green hills, trees, rivers and deep, hypnotic valleys. It also has the charm of a certain obscurity. Far from big towns or cities, or motorways, the winding trail of Offa's Dyke can occasionally give you a glimpse directly into centuries gone. There is a clear sense of history having happened here: from the old woodland of the Wye Valley to the small market towns of Shropshire; from the ruins and glimpses of historical industrial remnants, such as the old lime kilns near Oswestry, to the blowier regions of the north of Wales as the Path at last begins to approach the sea.

The Pennine Way might have Hadrian's Wall at its furthest extremity, but Offa's Dyke is an almost continuous line of historical development, starting with the Anglo-Saxon earthworks themselves, erected by King Offa of Mercia in the eighth century as a means of keeping out the Welsh – or, to put it another way, 'aboriginal British hordes.' It ensured that the 'Men of the West would never escape from the isolation of their peninsula,' wrote historian Norman Davies, 'that their language and culture would develop in directions not shared by other insular Celts, and that far into the future, they would assume a separate national identity.'[8]

Rather like the West Highland Way – another long trail inspired directly by the success of the Pennine pioneer – the Offa's Dyke trail invites you to walk along a line of still vivid history. In the case of the Highland path, that history can be picked out in the form of the old military roads that were driven through the glens as part of the campaign to subdue the Scots. Offa's Dyke offers perhaps a more cultural sense of conflict. Though two thirds of the Path lies directly within the Welsh border, there are other parts that continue to teeter along the border between England and Wales, delicately flipping from monolingual to bilingual signs.

Tom Stephenson himself was a very firmly upland, moorland man. He confessed that the prospect of lowland walks simply could not excite him in any way. But the winding trail of Offa's Dyke offers something rather better than the occasional brown, wet monotony of the peatlands; it climbs and dives and swoops, deep down into river valleys, up sharp, unexpectedly steep hills – the rather demanding 'Switchback' section of the Shropshire hills being a firm favourite among many. For the long-distance walkers – a taste, incidentally, that seems to be growing in popularity, much like long-distance running – the prospect of 177 miles is no less a lure than the Pennine Way. Though for some, there can be outbreaks of unrealistic enthusiasm. Recently, a friend of mine found, on a stretch of Offa's Dyke near Oswestry, that after seventeen and a half miles of walking her feet suddenly failed to respond. As she put it, 'they just went on strike.' Her walking companions had no option but to call it a day and take her to the pub. 'After some wine, my feet were better,' she said cheerfully. Historian Marion Shoard said of Offa's Dyke path, a little more poetically, 'We can feel the presence of previous ways of being by retracing the steps of our ancestors along the routes which they have bequeathed to us.'[9]

Throughout the 1970s, Britain came to be crisscrossed with such routes or 'Ways': from the north Highlands to the South Downs, long-distance walkers found less in the way of hindrance. In England and Wales, there is The Cleveland Way, the Cotswold Way, the Glyndwr Way, the Hadrian's Wall (Way), Pembrokeshire Coastal Path (Way), and good old North Norfolk Way. In Scotland, they have been even more lavish in the distribution of the Ways: from Rob Roy Way to the aforementioned West Highland, from the Great Glen Way to the Arran Coastal Way (a path that circumnavigates the neat west coast island). Not forgetting the Formatine and Buchan Way and the East Highland Way. All of these long-distance trails opened up the mostly uninterrupted opportunity to ramble along for days, and on terrain that is nearly always easier than sucking bog. In one sense, walkers might view these mighty footpaths as great pulsing arteries – or, if we switch metaphors, as motorways for ramblers. And we can attribute much of this current enthusiasm for long-distance trails and indeed all other paths to the work of Tom Stephenson. Even in his old age, he was a vehement campaigner. In the 1980s, he was prominent in the protests to do with the lack of access to the Forest of Bowland in Lancashire, a vast chunk of which is owned by the Duke of Westminster. Even that late, thousands of acres were peppered with 'private' notices and signs expressly forbidding trespassing.

If we see the walking movement in Britain in terms of – yet one more metaphor – waves, then Tom Stephenson's inspiration formed a high tide through the 1960s and the 70s; the long-distance trails opened up a country to many who had previously not given much thought to hiking at all. Stephenson died in 1987, just at the point when the walking movement was making further determined pushes against the entrenched interests of landowners and local authorities, and when it was once more facing the implacable hostility of an unfriendly government. Throughout his walking life, though, Tom Stephenson had been the most perfect representative of every ideal that the walking movement stood for: a man who asked for nothing more than the chance to stride across moorland, and savour all the wildlife on it. He had no need of the Country Code; respect and love for the land was clearly hardwired into him. Although it does not count as 'uplands' in any sense, the Ridgeway, running from Bedfordshire to Dorset, also stands as a sort of legacy to his work. It is also on this path – especially on one stretch in the Chiltern Hills – that one can navigate the modern day idea of trespass, and explore its limits in the most startling way.

CHAPTER 13

Wendover to Princes Risborough: Chilterns and the History of Trespass, Via Some Very Private Property

The word 'trespass' these days has an antique quality; we perhaps associate it more with its King James Bible usage than with any sense of physical intrusion. In any case, ramblers are by no means the only people to impose themselves upon private property. In the Chilterns, just a few miles north of London, a rather larger proposed incursion is being fought furiously. It is a conflict which might have a curiously beneficial side effect for walkers.

The posters are everywhere; on every lamp post, every tree, every stretch of fence. 'Stop HS2', is their gaudily spelt out message. The people of the Chilterns are united in one great common cause, and that is to thwart the building of a new high-speed rail link across this self-consciously beautiful area. The fear that this mooted railway line has been generating is as old as the fear of all railways, stretching back to their genesis in the mid-nineteenth century. Not merely that the trains will bring noise and ugliness, but also that the line's construction will rip open the pretty landscape, almost like a scalpel opening a body. The imagery is deliberately visceral. The people of the Chilterns fear that they will have more than most to lose.

This, it is argued, is an area that is a distillation of all the beauty of England. Here there are great swathes of old woodland of oak and larch and birch, fine country parks, and cherished wildlife, such as the once rare red kites, which now swoop and circle with wide winged aristocratic languor in the skies above.

Here is an area where villages of russet coloured brick and flinty churches and little greens seem almost absurd in their Englishness. Indeed, used as the locations for the popular TV detective series *Midsomer Murders*, this preposterous Englishness became controversial when the show's producer claimed that they didn't use black or Asian actors because they would unbalance that very particular 'traditional' feel. Yet the area – which is hugely popular with walkers – has real history too. If we reach back a couple of centuries, we see conflicts about the entire subject of trespass, and about the sanctity of land ownership.

One local conflict dating back almost 300 years involved another form of land seizure. Amid all the acts of enclosure of the eighteenth century came a new term: emparkation. Land that was once there to be worked – either arable or pasture – was now adapted by the landowner for quite a different purpose: that of private enjoyment, and of leisure. Rich wet furrows and hedges of sharp entangling hawthorn were transformed into artful gardens and carefully manufactured wood and glades, with new lakes and rivers and streams. Landscape artists such as Humphry Repton even created artificial hills and valleys for their patrons. For the majority of people who lived in and around such areas, this now meant being excluded from the land that perhaps they had once toiled upon. For with emparkation came very solid, tangible walls. The borderlines between private and public property were more sharply defined than at any time since the castles and their keeps. In 1726, Daniel Defoe visited a community near Tring in Hertfordshire, where such a process was just beginning:

There was an eminent contest here, between Mr Guy, and the poor of the parish, about his enclosing part of the Common to make him a Park; Mr Guy, presuming upon his power, set up his pales, and took in a large parcel of open land, called Wiggington Common; the Cottagers and the Farmers opposed it, by their complaints a great while; but finding he went on with his work and resolved to do it, they rose upon him, pulled down his banks, and forced up his pales, and carried away the wood, or set it on a heap and burnt it; and this they did several times, until he was obliged to desist.

If the good people of Tring imagined that they had won some sort of permanent victory over this tyrannical overlord, however, they were mistaken. 'After some time,' wrote Defoe, 'he began again, offering to treat with the people, and to give them any equivalent for it. But not being satisfactory, they mobbed him again.' Clearly, though, Mr Guy had some clever emoluments up his sleeve, for even after this outbreak of protest, he gave emparkation another go. When Defoe returned to the area some time later, he noted the developments with interest. 'How they accommodated it at last I know not,' he wrote. 'But I see that Mr Guy has a Park … I mention this,' he concluded, 'as an instance of the popular Claim in England, which we call right of Commonage, which the Poor take to be as much their Property, as a Rich Man's is his own.'

Quite so, and yet the rich men tended to win through. As parks grew, and the uses and the ownership of land sharpened further into the recessionary years of the early nineteenth century, the notion of trespass as a serious transgression also seemed to grow greater. With the parks came greater suspicion on the part of the landowners – especially of vagrants, and of travelling men and women. And they mirrored, in many ways, the old Royal Forests, with their exclusive rights to game. John Clare wrote much about the 'mildew' and 'tyranny' of enclosures, and in his poem 'The Mores' he recalls being able to walk and ramble and roam in country that was once open:

> Unbounded freedom ruled the wandering scene
> Nor fence of ownership crept in between
> To hide the prospect of the following eye
> Its only bondage was the circling sky

Then, some verses later, he surveys, with cold rage, the changes that have been wrought upon this ancient walkers' landscape:

> These paths are stopt – the rude philistines thrall
> Is laid upon them and destroyed them all
> Each little tyrant with his little sign
> Shows where man claims earth glows no more divine
> On paths to freedom and to childhood dear
> A board sticks up to notice 'no road here'.

Enclosure, then, is not merely an affront to rights of way, and to the common enjoyment of a beautiful landscape; it also has the effect of trampling on precious memory, the very roots of child-hood. Today, those who campaign against paths that have been obstructed, or old woodlands that have been closed off, feel much the same sense of emotional violation – that to lose a path is to lose part of the fabric of your life. As the nineteenth century progressed, the law was still very firm on what constituted tres-pass. Even a site such as Stonehenge, then owned privately, was subject to these same rules. A Judge Farwell gave his opinions on how such a place should be regulated:

The liberality with which landowners in this country have for years past allowed visitors free access to objects of interest on their property is amply sufficient to explain the access which has undoubtedly been allowed for many years to visitors to Stone-

henge from all over the world. It would indeed be unfortunate if
the Courts were to presume novel and unheard of trusts and
statutes from acts of friendly courtesy and thus drive landowners to close their gates in order to preserve their property.[1]

Now, when you stride around in the glowingly abundant
Chilterns – specifically, upon one particular woodland path near
Wendover – you feel the occasional tremor of a trespasser's
discomfort when you reach a very particular place. It is a path
upon which the most careless walker becomes extremely attentive within the space of a few yards. Yet it is also this area that
illustrates so abundantly the strides forward made by the
rambling movement in the last thirty years or so. Take the path
up the hill from Wendover railway station, and within minutes,
you are staring at a very large sign. It is the first of very many, all
shouting the same thing: 'The Ridgeway'. This is one of the most
thoroughly reclaimed roads in Britain, and it constitutes almost
the walker's equivalent of a motorway. Stretching roughly from
Hertfordshire to Dorset, east to west, and spanning roughly 180
miles, it has in recent years become something of a national
jewel. For what track – save the North Downs running through
Kent – could boast a comparable history?

The Ridgeway has Bronze Age roots, stretching back as far as
the fourth century BC; along this grey chalkstoned road would
walk men and horses, merchants and merchandise, travellers,
soldiers, economic migrants. It is extremely easy to imagine the
soft leather of their shoes scuffed with the white dust from the
road. It is also along this track that you can easily imagine figures
from a variety of ages – including Hardyesque sufferers like Jude
the Obscure – walking forth, up and down the gentle slopes of
these ridges. Here is Jude as a young lad doing that very thing in
1896:

Not a soul was visible on the hedgeless highway, or on either side of it, and the white road seemed to ascend and diminish till it joined the sky … the whole northern semicircle between east and west, to a distance of forty or fifty miles, spread itself before him; a bluer, moister atmosphere, evidently, than that he breathed up here.[2]

The view from the top of Coombe Hill is one that seems to transcend time. Hundreds of feet beneath you, on a vast plain of contrasting greens, is the classic English patchwork: mostly fields of pasture, with some brown fields of arable, divided by thick dark green hedges, stretching off into the blur of distance. What hits you is the lack of anything obviously twenty-first century in view – until, that is, you round the corner of the monument on the hill and find yourself gazing upon the hazy, Turneresque prospect of the Didcot power station some twenty miles away. Its far distant cooling towers, flickering in the gold autumn light, look a little like ancient earthernware beakers in shape and colour. So even with modern industry, landscape is patterned with echoes.

Just before you head off into another copse of trees, there, down in the valley, snug and sheltered and secure, you get the first glimpse of a most exceptional redbrick property, about a mile or so away. A quick saunter through the silvery green of a birch wood carefully coppiced, then across a road, into a field – and suddenly the path signs are quite a different matter: these new ones are stern and stark, and designed to trigger anxiety. The walker is now piercingly aware that he must stick to the track for – as these large black notices at 100-yard intervals proclaim – trespass on this particular property would be a criminal offence. Judging by the proliferation of very heavy, large, black security cameras, you suspect it might even be a little more than that; that if you did decide cheekily to turn right and stroll through this pasture field, you would be surrounded within seconds by men with machine guns. Yet the unwary walker might have no idea – if he had not consulted a map, say – that he is now standing within the bounds of Chequers, the Prime Minister's weekend estate. Move along the narrow brown path running at the edge of the field, towards a line of beech trees and what looks like a road; except that when you are standing on it, you realise it is not a road but a driveway leading up to the house itself. To your left are some very serious, locked gates. It is now that you realise that you are actually *inside* the estate. It is a weirdly thrilling moment, simply standing there in that pleasant afternoon silence, on that grand drive. How many heat detecting devices are homing in on my rucksack, remotely checking for sinister devices? Upon how many screens is an image of my face being projected, while it is checked against images of rather more fanatical folk? You simply cannot help wondering: if you were to now turn right, on that drive pointing towards the house, and break into a quick trot – the house itself is no more than about 400 yards away – how long would it be before you were mown down by marksmen? The Prime Minister has been rather more lenient with me, though, than a great many other landowners in the past would have been. Also, I suspect, this patch of path running through the Chequers estate has not been open that long. I cannot imagine for one moment the idea of 1950s Prime Minister Harold Macmillan tolerating walkers within a mile of his business.

* * *

High above wheels a red kite. Until a few years ago, the only ones left were to be found in North Wales – there were none in England at all. Now they seem to be back in force. The one lazily circling my head, seemingly buoyed on thermal currents, has a very relaxed air. You wouldn't have thought that it was eagerly hunting carrion. They are quite wonderful to watch when they are swooping down; not far from here, in a friend's back garden,

I have seen a magnificent red kite glide insouciantly in at the suggestion of some dropped kitchen rubbish. Meanwhile, Chequers represents a nice example of late, unobtrusive emparkation. Here, in the lee of a wooded valley, a small sanctuary has been established, with geometrical ordered roads and trees and hedges; while the fields immediately around it represent the edited highlights of countryside.

We return to questions of land ownership and property rights; one of the arguments that anti-HS2 protestors – among them local farmers – have deployed has been precisely to do with walkers' rights. The new line, they have argued, will result in the abolition, or indeed the complete destruction, of dozens of local footpaths. Added to this, they say, will be the destruction of the beautiful views from the Ridgeway path. In other words, they appear to be saying, one of the grounds for stopping HS2 is the rights and aesthetic considerations of walkers. It is a rather lovely point; one that tells us much about the political position of today's ramblers, and the weight of opinion that they are perceived to carry.

Let us not forget the ground upon which we walk and, in several senses, its tremendous value as well as its attraction. 'The Country Landowners Association welcomes considerate walkers,' proclaims a yellow sign upon a five bar gate. Well that's very good of the CLA; considerate walkers are suitably grateful. But the notice seems calculated on another level to let it be known that we are just one step away from transgression; by all means use the footpath: but make sure that you remember exactly who all this belongs to. Ramblers are quite accustomed to such narrow eyed passive aggression. It is preferable to the outbreaks of aggressive aggression that we still read about from time to time.

In the 1990s, there were regular battles between ramblers and the millionaire property developer Nicholas Van Hoogstraten, who has an estate down in Uckfield, East Sussex. His house,

Hamilton Palace, was the largest private residence built in Britain, and was adorned with a copper dome. The house also had a mausoleum. Added to this, though, was a 150-year-old footpath running a little distance away, from which the house was visible. Van Hoogstraten referred to ramblers as 'the great unwashed', and 'the scum of the earth'. He blocked access to the footpath by means of concrete blocks and old refrigeration units. Locals and Ramblers' Association campaigners repeatedly petitioned the local council to take action; the council seemed powerless in the face of such an implacable and aggressive figure. In the meantime, any walkers who did contrive to get beyond these crude barriers were intimidated and harassed by security guards and contract workers. It was only really when Van Hoogstraten was wrongly jailed in 2002 (the conviction was quashed a couple of years later and he was released) that at last the council paralysis was broken, and the obstacles to access were removed.

Another blow to walkers' pride came from the reedy singer Madonna in 2004, when she and then husband Guy Ritchie succeeded in blocking access to a path across their estate, Ashcombe Park in Wiltshire. Two overriding reasons were cited. First that because there was so much game shooting, walkers would be at risk for half the year. Second, and perhaps rather more germane, Mr and Mrs Madonna felt 'their human rights would be infringed' by members of the public tramping around in sight of the house, or even just by sitting on the paths and watching them. The difficulty is that – perhaps even more than politicians – pop stars are rather vulnerable to the attentions of disturbed people. Look not only at John Lennon, but also at George Harrison, who was attacked by an intruder on his Oxfordshire estate. If I was Madonna, I'm not sure that I would be that keen on seeing perfect strangers milling around near my French windows. And in fairness to herself and Ritchie, the walking ban did not apply to Quakers; there is reportedly a

Quaker burial ground on the estate, and access to it was not blocked in any way.

It's difficult in those kinds of cases. Apparently less difficult was the recent case of a landowner in Kent, who in August 2010 was locked in bitter dispute with local walkers, and found himself receiving very unfavourable coverage in the newspapers. Walkers complained that since buying the estate, he was blocking access to a previously well-used path. His view was that the path across his land was home to many rare species, and as such should be accorded the status of a Site of Special Scientific Interest; it would be deleterious, his team argued, for the local wildlife to be disturbed by constant access.

Those ranged against him argued that the path in question was part of the ancient Pilgrim's Way, and was self-evidently a long-term key walking route. It is still not quite known how the entire dispute has been resolved, but the interesting thing is the way that the press seemed to automatically side with the ramblers, rather than with the landowner. When it came to the public inquiry on the subject, prominence was given to the voices of his local walking opponents. In this sense, times have changed, and very clearly in favour of the walker. It is actually not all that long ago when more barbarously minded landowners – using devices such as mantraps and spring-guns – were regularly favoured by local magistrates. Such savage implements themselves dated back to an even older conflict that raged on from the time of the Norman landgrab: the war between landlord and poacher.

* * *

Mantraps, now featured chiefly in reruns of vintage thrillers, had steel jaws that would clamp with lightning speed the leg of the transgressor, biting through both flesh and bone. If the trap was set in a particularly remote location, it was perfectly possibly for the poacher (or general interloper) to die in this position through blood loss. Other sorts of mantraps were held to be more humane, in that they didn't cut the flesh, merely smashed the bone. In 1821, Sydney Smith wrote:

> There is a sort of horror in thinking of a whole land filled with lurking engines of death … the lords of manors eyeing their peasantry as so many butts and marks, and panting to hear the click of the trap and to see the flash of the gun. How many human beings educated in liberal knowledge and Christian feeling, can doom to certain destruction a poor wretch, tempted by the sight of animals that naturally appear to him to belong to one person as well as another, we are at a loss to conceive.[3]

William Cobbett also found instances in the early-nineteenth century when any trespasser was eminently deserving of sympathy, especially in cases of wood-gathering, where areas of trees had been enclosed by the local landowners. In the winter, such wood was vital as fuel, and there were cases in the West Country where certain timber poachers articulated a feeling within small communities that such a resource had once been seen as common, like water, and that it was a fairly obvious moral wrong to have had it removed from them in this fashion.

Even in the Edwardian age, a walker's act of trespass could change the course of a life. In his recent book about the friendship between the poets Edward Thomas and Robert Frost, author Matthew Hollis cites a trespassing incident in 1914 that was the pivotal moment in the association between the two men. While on one of their customary walks around May Hill in Dorset, the two men were confronted by a gamekeeper with a gun. In an angry exchange, the gamekeeper told them to 'clear out'; Frost countered that he was entitled to roam where he wished. Indeed, the incident so infuriated Frost that the two poets followed the gamekeeper to his home, where they confronted him. This time, the keeper was altogether more threatening with the gun and the poets once more backed off. But Edward Thomas considered that he had behaved in a cowardly fashion, insufficiently supportive of his friend, throughout; and later, the incident played upon him, more and more – his fear, and his apparent failure to stand fully by Frost. Hollis quotes Frost as saying: 'That's why he [Thomas] went to war.'[4]

The use of guns by keepers and farmers persisted for an extraordinary amount of time. Tom Stephenson cited a case as recent as 1953 when two ramblers in Sussex were blasted in their faces by a spring gun – in essence, a shotgun hidden in the undergrowth. The men, wounded but otherwise all right, traced the gun to the bracken. Their case came to court. The gamekeeper in question claimed that he had mistakenly loaded the shotgun with cartridges rather than blanks, and that he had been using this method to warn him of poachers for the last twenty years. He claimed that in all that time, there had been no mishaps of any sort, and that this device was really merely an 'alarm gun'. He was asked, if this was the case and that it was merely the sound of the shot that was necessary, why the gun was not pointing at the ground? However, the gamekeeper was backed up by the local police, who insisted that such armed guns were legitimate. The gamekeeper was acquitted.

* * *

It might be worth swiftly hearing a word on the subject of trespass from the most famous gamekeeper in literary history. Oliver Mellors, Lady Chatterley's lover, is quite assiduous about his job. But when it comes to trespass and the law, his attitude is at best ambivalent:

'I had to go getting summonses for two poachers I caught and, oh well, I don't like people.'

He spoke cold, good English, and there was anger in his voice.

'Do you hate being a game-keeper?' Connie asked.

'Being a game-keeper, no! So long as I'm left alone. But when I have to go messing around at the police station, and various other places, and waiting for a lot of fools to attend to me … oh, well, I get mad.'

Mellors has a more personal sense of 'trespass' than that encompassing the woodland; it is very much to do with his own privacy, and his own desire to be alone. One wonders about all those real life gamekeepers, the sort whose job it partly was to chase urban scamps like John Bunting off the moors. The notion of trespass, and the sense of an unwarranted invasion of property, is felt by Mellors' employer Clifford Chatterley, much more keenly:

A jay called harshly, many little birds fluttered. But there was no game; no pheasants. They had been killed off during the war, and the wood had been left unprotected, til now Clifford had got his game-keeper again.

Clifford loved the wood; he loved the old oak trees. He felt they were his own through generations. He wanted to protect them. He wanted this place inviolate, shut off from the world.

'I want this wood perfect … untouched. I want nobody to trespass in it.'

Fiction it may be, but we hear a groundswell of the sort of emotion that many landowners really do feel; the sense of heritage, the idea of land being safeguarded and passed down through the generations. The notion, above all, of proud inheritance. To them, walking or rambling is a very clear transgression. The walkers might leave no trace of their passing, but the mere idea that they have disregarded the idea of private property, treated it as though it were nothing more than an airy abstraction, poses a very direct and emotional threat. In that sense, the walker as a figure represents pure anarchy, caring nothing for old ties, or possession. The walker stands at the head of a more destructive principle; if he can wander over private property, as though it belonged to no one and everyone simultaneously, then what about all those who might follow?

Today, even with open access and the fact that so much land seems to be owned by the National Trust, there are very particular laws about trespass. According to the Ramblers' Association, trespass is where 'a person who strays from the right of way, or uses it other than for passing and re-passing, commits trespass against the landowner.' In most cases, trespass is a civil rather than a criminal matter. A landowner may use 'reasonable force' to compel a trespasser to leave, but not more than is reasonably necessary. Unless injury to the property can be proven, a landowner could probably only recover nominal damages by suing for trespass. Of course you might have to meet a landowner's legal costs. 'A notice saying "trespassers will be prosecuted", aimed for instance at keeping you off a private drive,' the Association continues, 'is usually meaningless. Criminal prosecution could only arise if you trespass and damage property. However, under public order law, trespassing with an intention to reside may be a criminal offence under some circumstances. It is also a criminal offence to trespass on railway land and sometimes on military training land.' In the case of beleaguered celebrities, there is also such a thing as 'aggravated trespass' which is also viewed seriously. This is the sort of trespass carried out by crazed fans intent on getting close their idols.

I know it is heresy among walkers to say so, but are there not occasions when we should feel some sympathy for landowners? As a walker, I often find myself feeling rather embarrassed when a path seems to wind close to a private front door, or trails across what is obviously somebody's back garden. Yes, the path might well have been there since the sixteenth century; equally though, you don't want to make people feel uncomfortable by peering in through their kitchen windows. There is a telling thought experiment that you can carry out. If you had had some good fortune and as a result, you were to buy a house in the country, and this house had a big garden, and perhaps a field or two, and a path, how far away would the path have to be from your windows before you felt truly comfortable: 20 yards, 100 yards, 250 yards, out of sight altogether? Is it perhaps that those who hail from towns are more sensitive to intrusions on private space, given the scarcity of that space in cities? More pertinently, might it also have to do with fear of crime? No one is ever going to think that a pair of married middle-aged ramblers are career burglars. However, there are rogue elements operating in rural districts, and for many people, it is difficult not to become a little tense at the sound of unfamiliar footsteps marching close, or of fleeting glimpses of strange figures nearby.

So we raise our sunhats to the current Prime Minister, David Cameron, and all his predecessors who have been so gracious about inviting us to the edge of Chequers. Happily, it now also works both ways – that is, the grand man in the grand house hobnobbing on the rather more populated footpaths all around. Over Christmas 2010, Mr Cameron together with wife Samantha, education secretary Michael Gove, and also in their party, the actress Helena Bonham Carter, wandered out of Chequers and up Coombe Hill, with all the other Barbour jacketed, golden labrador walking ramblers. And this very upper-middle class Prime Ministerial party happily posed for photographs with other walkers. This would never happen in a city; it could only ever happen upon a popular footpath frequented by like-minded middle class people, in sensible walking shoes and warm woollies. More than this: the invincibly upper-middle class Camerons have in a curious way conferred the ultimate respectability upon rambling. Instead of sticking to privately owned ground, they instead went walking on land that is, in effect, held in trust on behalf of the State. I can't help feeling that the Kinder Scout trespassers would have regarded this warmly.

Less than a hundred miles to the west, though, and there is a great mass of land so forbidden to the casual walker, that even the Prime Minister himself would have to ask before he and his wife and guests could ramble across it. Even then, it is not completely guaranteed that permission would be granted on any particular day. That would depend very much on where the tanks were rolling.

CHAPTER 14

Warminster to Battlebury Fort, Salisbury Plain – an Effort to Reach England's Inland Atlantis

There is an attractive illusion of softness about the west of the country. It's there in the plump fecundity of the green meadows and valleys, the slow, swirling rivers, and on the breeze riffled turf of the Downs. It is of course there in the lilt of the accent. The look of the young people at the railway stations – dreadlocks, tie-dye tops, piercings, alternative hats – tells you that there is something assured and relaxed and detatched about this part of the world. The land all around here, from Stonehenge to Glastonbury Tor, from Silbury to Avebury, is rich in an unusual abundance of legends and folklore. For the rambler, this can somehow imply greater freedom to wander; that such historic rural acres must surely be thrown open to all.

I am in this part of the world to try and walk upon some territory that is the exact opposite of easygoing; a chunk of land that is roughly the same size as the Isle of Wight yet utterly forbidden. This area seems ringed with stone circles, ancient longbarrows and Neolithic mounds; but is itself entirely, straightforwardly, hard as bullets. It is Salisbury Plain. Ever since the military started appropriating chunks of it for training purposes, from the late-nineteenth century onwards (and most spectacularly during the Second World War), the Plain has been steadily cut off, quadrant by quadrant, to any form of traveller.

As a result, it is almost unspeakably tempting as a walking proposition. Exactly how far can a rambler get in to Salisbury Plain from the west side without being run over by a tank or blown up by a rocket or – perhaps slightly more pertinently – being arrested on suspicion of espionage? In this sense, the MOD's occupation of much of the Plain is thematically in keeping with all those strange old West Country legends. For when you look at these old folk tales, from Silbury to Glastonbury onwards, you realise that they all have one thing in common: a secret, underground element. Silbury Hill in Wiltshire, for instance: the legend is that this was where Arthur's knights were sleeping, awaiting the day when the Once and Future King would arise and lead his men once more to reclaim the land. It is a megalithic construction, a strikingly strange man-made cone of earth and grass rising some 300 feet above the level land around; in 1968, curiosity got too much for the BBC, which televised a dig within the hill and found nothing. In fact, this absence of anything at all – from skeletons to ceramics to jewellery to beakers – somehow seems even more baffling. Rather like Rachel Whiteread's inverted life-size 'House' sculpture in London's East End, the emptiness of Silbury Hill – combined with the artfulness of its construction – seems to give it a megalithic postmodern quality, if such a thing can be possible.

Sadly, the least mystical place in this otherwise preternatural area is Stonehenge. The A303, ceaselessly swishing with passing cars and coaches, means it is simply impossible to get any kind of a sense of atmosphere. I am old enough to remember when one was allowed to simply wander in and around the circle itself, looking for traces of blood on what they then called the Sacrificial Stone. Now one must wander in and around a Heritage Centre instead. Even though this is a World Heritage Site, the sense is that of a diminished wonder. It is even difficult to slip into a reverie about the people who transported these stones such vast distances, and the miracles of engineering they wrought with practically nothing in the way of tools. What the place lacks is that essential sense of quiet awe. This wasn't the case in the day of novelist John Cowper Powys. In his 1932 book *A Glastonbury Romance*, when swathes of the Plain were still navigable on foot, there is a passage where the character John Crow feels mysteriously impelled to walk a tremendous distance to see the ancient stones:

> As he plodded along the hedgeless white road over Salisbury Plain, John Crow became acquainted with aspects of bodily and mental suffering till that epoch totally unrevealed to him ... The difference between the pallor of the road, which was sad with a recognised human sadness and this ashen grey sky overhead was in some way disturbing to his mind.

As he goes on, light turns to twilight, and the skies of Salisbury Plain acquire a more numinous quality, suggestive of 'fleeing hosts of wounded men with broken spears and torn banners and trails of blood and neighing horses.'

I am setting off from Warminster, on the western side of Salisbury Plain. Given that pretty much a third of the Plain is currently in the hands of the army, for training purposes, I want to see exactly where the boundaries for eager ramblers lie. Surely in these days of pretty much Total Access, it seems inconceivable to me – as both a town-dweller and a civilian – that the military would not have bowed at least a little to public pressure. Are there no paths, for instance, that one might be able to use from Tuesday to Thursday, for instance, when the tanks are not rolling? The maps, understandably, will only tell you so much. As the train draws close to Warminster station, I see that the track line is bordered by vast warehouses and lines of dark green military vehicles. I always knew this was an army town, but it is rather bigger, and very much more military, than I had imagined. Unlike other parts of the country – where the walker is presented with a dazzling variety of signposts helpfully pointing at paths in all directions – it is obvious that the Warminster authorities have other priorities. As it happens, I know which direction to walk in to find the Plain. But there are no little green or brown signs to confirm this. Nor, obviously, road signs. It is almost as if the Plain simply does not exist in civilian terms. But my walker's antennae are set twitching by quite another sign. I am standing, it seems, on the Imber Road.

Imber is still the cause of small outbreaks of local bitterness. For this tiny village in the middle of Salisbury Plain was part of the Second World War army land seizure. In 1943, the village's inhabitants were evacuated, so the place could be used for training purposes. Indeed, it was put to rather effective use: the main training exercises focused upon the forthcoming Operation Overlord. British and American troops used the village and its surrounding area in tactical manoeuvres. There may have been some idea or suggestion, somewhere, that when the war was over, the village would be restored to its re-housed inhabitants. But it never was. And now it remains tantalisingly out of reach, a ghost village with weeds growing out of the pavement, and a church in which nobody prays, in the middle of a zone across which it is expressly forbidden for civilians to walk. To be fair to the army, it is not as if Imber was a bustling metropolis: strikingly, even in densely populated southern England, this village, lying in the middle of the Plain, was pretty remote and extremely small and the local rural economy, even before the war, must have been a little fragile. On top of this, the compensation given to those who were moved out was quite generous. Nevertheless, the resentment felt might be a culmination of both this and the army's steady appropriation of what was once an extraordinarily wide open region, a 'plain as free and open as the sea,' where as historian Ralph Whitlock continued in his book *Salisbury Plain* (1955), 'a man could walk where he would, shaping his course by sun and by stars if needs be.'

In recent years, the MOD has bowed a little to local feelings, and there are the occasional days when the road is opened to the public and Imber can be visited. They hold a church service there every Easter. The fact is that even if the place were to be opened up once more, it would be a little too late for its original inhabitants, or indeed anyone else who wanted to live there. Time has swallowed Imber up. For the walker, it's not just a question of a lost village, but of a lost mass of pristine, unexplored, virgin countryside; an inland Atlantis. Imagine that springy turf, stretching off on to an empty horizon, the short grass beneath the feet, the sensation of walking beneath an illimitable sky with the clouds as soft as the chalk beneath, knowing it could be a day before any sign of habitation comes into view. How many thousands of walkers must have chewed their lips with frustration just at the very idea of it?

On this wooded footpath leading out of Warminster town and up a comically stumpy hill, fringed with large untidy trees, there are the familiar pleasures. Large hares loping off in all directions, and small wagtails, flitting from bush to bush – sufficiently disturbed by my presence to keep going in front of me, yet not sufficiently disturbed to fly off altogether. This part of the country is particularly rich in hares. One might imagine they will be more plentiful on the Plain itself, given that the only real peril is that posed by vast lumbering tanks. The same goes for so many species of bird. One especially rare exotic breed was recently reintroduced, rather triumphantly, onto the Plain: the great bustard. Here is the first paradox of military occupation: the absence of humans from the landscape allows other species – and the great bustard was absent from this area for a good many decades – to flourish.

In response to frustrated walkers, the MOD does point out an unexpected upside to the quarantine of Salisbury Plain: it has afforded not merely the bustard but all manner of rare species a great deal of protection. In fact, the whole plain has been designated a Site Of Special Scientific Interest. Here – if only the walker was allowed to have a look at them – there are wildlife riches not to be found anywhere else in the country. The grassland itself is of a type judged to be of 'great antiquity' by English Nature, in the sense that unlike practically everywhere else in Western Europe, the area has not been intensively farmed. So the short grass that you would see – if you could – would most likely be very much the same as that seen in the Neolithic age.

Among the different varieties of unspoilt grass, and the herbs among it, are some of the most wonderfully poetic names: red fescue, lady's bedstraw, salad burnet, hairgrass. The SSSI is also concerned with rare flowers and plants, such as burnt orchid and purple milk vetch. There is an abundance of wild thyme on the Plain, as well as field fleawort. And flitting madly around the bright specks of flowers are similarly vulnerable and treasured butterflies, such as blue adonis and marsh fritillary. The area is popular with rarely seen birds; as well as the bustard, there are buzzards, stone curlews, long-eared owls, wheatears and Montagu's harriers.

The MOD is quite insistent on another point: that the area is extraordinarily rich in archaeological terms, and the exclusivity of the region thus protects all manner of long barrows and other prehistoric structures. This is the second paradox of military occupation; the preservation of the integrity of ancient structures. Again, the walker is presented with an almost unbearably attractive set of images – a landscape so ancient and so unspoilt that among its tombs are to be found species that would have been there when those tombs were first built. Of all the unattainable places in Britain that we – or at least, those of us in this lifetime – will never see, this one somehow seems the most perfect. Not far from here – I can see it, from the vantage point of this high field – is the curious rippled grassland at the top of a hill denoting a Neolithic fort. Will it be possible to get to it without being shot down? On the other side of the slope I am on, I see a rather surprising potential obstacle. In the big hollow down beneath, between me and that tantalizing hill fort, lies an entire modern village, a mirror to the old market town of Warminster on the other side of the hill. This is the Warminster Garrison.

Down the hill, and back on the road, you can tell immediately that you are no longer on an ordinary main road. You are in a twilight zone. There are road signs, but they point to unfamiliar things and in unfamiliar fonts. This is no longer recognisably a public highway. So where does the curious walker stand? There are rather stern MOD signs forbidding photography. I had actually brought a disposable camera with me. In this paranoid age, I daren't even take it out of my bag. There is another road sign, slightly antique in nature, redolent of Captain Mainwaring and the war: it has a burgundy background, with a very old-fashioned typeface – it proclaims that one and a half miles up this road, there will be no access owing to military firing. But this sign is so old as to make me doubt its modern relevance.

A little further on yet, the road beneath me is getting stranger and stranger still. Now it is nearly white in colour, floured with dust. I keep on expecting some military vehicle to draw up, and for me to be asked for my papers. The only transport going past consists of perfectly ordinary looking cars, and they all seem to be coming down the Imber Road. So how far can one get along it? On the brow of another hill, I see a very large red flag. Even I know that this signifies a firing range. On this road – which is now creeping ever upwards, ever more temptingly to the brow of another hill, beyond which lies that beautiful plain – there are no such flags.

No one has told me to stop, so I don't. A little way ahead, at the summit of the hill, I see a whopping great obstacle to my plans for further progress. It comes in the form of a 1960s built low-rise building, a flat grey rectangle, with an old tank parked outside its gates – and a soldier carrying an automatic weapon. He sees me approaching from about 250 yards away. It is suddenly all a little awkward. Should I shout something out? Wave? Smile? All I do is plod on. The soldier walks back and forth by those big gates. He appears to be pretending that he hasn't noticed me. I now studiously look about me as I walk, engaged in a charade of looking for a footpath sign.

This is quite a different prospect to that of walkers being confronted by a landowner. For in those circumstances, you generally know where you stand, legally and ethically. But this is land that is being paid for by me, the taxpayer. And where's the harm? It's a jumpy era we live in though: surveillance cameras, identity checks, flashing lights on GCHQ computers. When I eventually get to those gates, I am feeling a little apprehensive, almost as though military police are going to swoop from nowhere and arrest me. The soldier continues to pretend not to have seen me. I look along the road and see the giant red flag. The only thing now is politeness. I ask the soldier if I have inadvertently walked into a dead end. Perfectly friendly, he tells me that if I were to continue along that road, I'd be dodging bullets. He asks where I want to get to? I reply – rather wispily – that all I want to do is see some of Salisbury Plain. At first, he seems to find this rather too wispy. He frowns, and looks set to start asking some more questions about my intentions. Then, as I bleat about trying to find a peripheral footpath, the soldier grins and we are on the same side. He tells me that he once tried to organise a cycling event with friends through parts of Salisbury Plain, but it was no go, even for those in the army. He explains that there are always a few walkers who seem to want to hurl themselves straight into training areas. He also explains that getting any kind of access, even after pleading with the MOD, is incredibly difficult. If I come back at Easter, he says, I can go and see Imber on one of those special annual Open Days.

The soldier now points towards the Imber Ranges Perimeter Path, the one that I was initially less keen to explore – the word 'perimeter' alone suggesting being on the outside looking in.

This path, which stretches for thirty miles and is in itself a sort of concession from the MOD, will lead on to the hill fort, and in the absence of any other options, I make my way on to it. Instantly, my low expectations are dissipated. Here is a path that leads right on to the fort itself. Before that, a moment of rather baffling ambiguity at a wooden pedestrian gate. There is a big red sign warning of 'Danger!' It is all about unexploded ordnance and 'staying away', and suggestions of no access. Does that mean that I am not allowed any further, or is it simply a warning of what lies ahead? Doubly confusingly, and by means of complete contrast, the MOD has also stuck up one of those colourful weatherproof laminated tourist boards, loving illustrated with examples of the rare birds and fragile plant species one might expect to see beyond the big red danger sign.

Through the gate I go and instantly down the track in front of me comes a dark green military vehicle. I stand to the side. The soldier in the cab nods his acknowledgement. Clearly I am allowed. A little further towards the fort and several more military Landrovers and trucks come down the track, and I receive polite acknowledgements from them all.

This is now terrific fun. The fort I am now standing on is a thing of weird wonder. A path runs along the top of the perimeter bank of earth; there are other such banks, together with occasional trees growing out of the fuzzy grass. This is Battlesbury Fort, and it dates back to the Iron Age. Upon this ancient man-made plateau is an old tomb. When the sound of the military vehicles dies away in the distance, you are left listening to the gentlest of breezes whispering through the grass. You imagine the work it must have taken to create this mighty earthern structure. From the start of this path, you gaze out across the valley of the River Wyle, and across to even larger hills, a sombre blue-green in the afternoon sun.

Then you turn and follow this thin path, which is beige with chalkiness, and supple, like Plasticine. From this high ripple, you see a very beautiful vista. Aside from the white of the military road, which winds and snakes away into the distance, there is the grassy plain that looks like pale green, faintly yellow Fuzzy-Felt. The air is punctuated with the sharp cracks of far away guns being fired; oddly, the noise is not remotely intrusive. A couple of hundred feet or so directly beneath me, in a vast rectangle of darker, scrubbier green, there are some geometrical structures that are coloured like copper targets.

As this path ziggers round the perimeter of the old earth fort, more of this Salisbury Plain landscape is opened up to the eye at least; you imagine these beautiful soft Downs stretching for mile after mile. The terrible question presents itself: has this vast tract of land actually benefited by being off-limits to daytrippers and dedicated hikers alike? One other side effect of an entire area being turned into a State secret would appear to be some very colourful local legends of a science-fictional nature. One of the most fondly remembered came in the 1960s: it was the story of 'The Warminster Thing'. This phenomenon started off as a mystery noise, a weird clattering and crashing that induced a sense of oppression in those who heard it. Then it acquired a visual dimension, and the eager interest of the press, when strange light displays – from which further uncanny noises seem to emanate – were reported. It became a brief national craze, and also kicked off a rather longer lasting local tradition. Later that decade, the town became the focus of a combination of old school flying saucer enthusiasts, and West Country hippies. On summer nights, they would walk up the hills just west of Salisbury Plain – in particular, Cradle Hill – armed with binoculars and cameras.

The alien enthusiasts are still with us today. The area around Salisbury Plain continues to get an unusually high number of reported sightings. In a sense, both spotters and aliens have become woven into the cultural landscape of the West Country. And in a slightly wider, more philosophical sense: is there a curious mirroring correspondence with all the longbarrows and roundbarrows in the area, and these dreams of futuristic space craft? There was certainly that old hippy theory that ancient sites held a sort of interstellar significance, that UFOs used them as markers; that Stonehenge was some sort of age old marker beacon for gods from the skies. The idea, whatever you may think of it, has at least a poetic consistency and resonance: the notion that what lies buried far beneath has a direct relationship to the wonders in the skies above; and in the middle, we humans mill about, stuck between these two sublime extremes. There are those who are not impressed by this kind of thing. In the 1970s, many local bed and breakfasts hung up signs proclaiming: 'No hippies'. What appears to have happened is that the hippies moved in full time, anyway. Their descendants are the young people I saw on the platform of Salisbury station.

I spend a good ten minutes standing very still, at the top of Battlesbury, on that thin ridge looking down across the almost featureless plain, with its dips and hollows and ridges – the land-scape that has now inspired several generations of hippies, making their votive walks to sacred sites all around. But some mysteries perhaps are better kept mysterious.

In 1793, when Wordsworth wrote his poem 'Salisbury Plain', his walking narrator, travelling over 'Sarum's Plain' with a sigh as the 'troubled west was red with storm fire', saw the place as an eerie and harsh wilderness. But on a fine, keen spring day, it doesn't feel like that at all. We might all be better off not being able to swarm over it, though. Despite the philosophical import-ance of granting walkers access to all corners of the isles, it is paradoxically nice to feel that there is one wodge that we cannot know at all. Taking a final look across that haunting landscape, it now seems clear why this place and the areas just west of it have picked up such a mystical reputation, especially in the post-war years: while intensive agriculture destroyed thousands of miles of hedgerow and green pastureland, and turned once familiar countryside into bleak, bitter prairies, this part of the world has maintained an unusually strong link with the past, perhaps more so than any other place in Britain, save the Hebrides. When we look out over this Plain, we are looking directly into a parallel history, a view of what the land might have been. It is only natural that it should evoke a stab of yearning.

CHAPTER 15

A Diversionary Walk on the Weird Side: A Brief Flit from Ley Lines to Stone Circles to Pan

Rambling can sometimes have a metaphysical dimension. The very word is used to denote stream-of-consciousness discourse; the rambling walk is, in some senses, the free-floating physical equivalent. You can stroll along as though in a trance. This aspect of rambling – the walk with an unconscious impulse – has found echoes in some curious corners of history and culture, from ecclesiastical art to cult television. In the 1979 television drama *Quatermass*, the eponymous Professor in a dystopian future Britain is attempting to trace his missing teenage grand-daughter. It transpires that she has joined The Planet People – a hippyish cult, spread across the world, that is convinced that benevolent aliens are going to transport them to a new planet. As the Planet People process across the English countryside towards the ancient stone circles that they think are the alien launch pads, their leader navigates using not a compass, but a simple plumb-bob. As these young people walk in groups through fields and across bright, summery meadows, they all repeat just one word, hypnotically, 'Ley, ley, ley …'

Walking and mysticism have always been the most natural companions. In this modern age, a walk with a numinous dimension – either to sites such as Wayland's Smithy (a Neolithic

burial site) in Berkshire, or the Rollright Stones in Oxfordshire
– is a secular rambler's guilty pleasure. Why would anyone ever
visit the otherwise undramatic countryside that surrounds the
Rollright Stones? How much sharper is one's appreciation of a
field, or a copse, if such a place is considered to be steeped in the
spooky atmosphere of an ancient, unknowable past? In the
1970s, it was the ramblers' craze involving ley lines that was
picked up – with characteristic satirical energy – by Nigel
Kneale, the writer of that *Quatermass* series. Kneale was
responding to a combination of a rise in ecological awareness
and the fashionable lure of pre-Christian religious beliefs.
According to this fresh branch of mysticism, you could only
truly 'find' yourself by rejecting science and technology, instead
seeking wisdom from the land itself. It was not uncommon to
see walkers with dowsing rods; either searching out hidden
streams, or following the so called 'leys'. What exactly were –
indeed, are – these supposed to be? Ley lines have come to be
defined by enthusiasts as hidden lines of 'earth energy', that glow
through the ground in distinct geometric patterns across the
country. The points at which these lines meet are marked with
sacred places, from Salisbury Cathedral to Lindisfarne, from
longbarrows to ancient wells, from prominent hills to secluded
chapels. Apart from apparently giving visiting UFOs a form of
supernatural sat nav (though quite why a floating craft from
space, viewing the ground from high up above, would need such
navigational aids is unclear), they are also there to guide walkers
who are sufficiently tuned in to the telluric currents. Clearly, the
entire idea has somehow got completely out of hand. It was all
much simpler – and relatively rational – when first proposed
and popularised by photographer and amateur topographer
Alfred Watkins in 1925 in his book *The Old Straight Track*.

While Watkins's conception of 'ley lines' connected up sacred
sites, they noticeably lacked an inherent mysterious energy.
These hypothetical lines, present only in the human eye and

imagination, were there for the much more straightforward and practical purpose of guiding Neolithic man on his various journeys on foot. The idea of ley came to Watkins with something of the force of revelation. After years photographing beauty spots across the county of Herefordshire, in that late Victorian efflorescence of the art of photography, he was one day sitting studying a map and suddenly he saw it: various sites – from stone circles to Neolithic earthworks, to prominent churches – appeared to be aligned along straight lines. This was a different thing from established roads like the Ridgeway or the Icknield Way. This was something very much older, and pointed to a past that seemed much more harmonious than the present day. These ancient lines pointed through a land well before the Enclosure Acts; a land without hedges or fences, and across which men could walk with impunity. The lines would not only ease trade, but also ease travel and migration. How did impossibly old longbarrows mesh in along these lines with relatively new churches? The explanation was that those churches had themselves been built on the sites of previous churches; and before those churches, the sites were associated with a religion very much older. The walker could apparently guide himself across the land by following these lines.

It has been noted that the idea found an immediately enthusiastic response from the public because first, around the 1920s, there had been a surge of interest in landscape art. Secondly, ley lines gave a seductive suggestion of what the land had looked like in a simpler, happier age. The book rode a wave of sentimentality about the countryside itself; the reason it was such an underground hit was that it came just at the point when city dwellers began to regard the countryside as being threatened.

In 1925, and in the years beyond, there was a building boom which saw towns and cities encroach ever further into what had once been quiet land. Architect Clough Williams Ellis wrote of urban sprawl in *England and the Octopus* in 1928. He and his admirers had a particular loathing for speculative suburban property developers, and for the arterial roads which stretched out from the capital, with residential schemes popping up around them. Williams Ellis appealed to the virtues of traditional ruralism.

Another reason for the book's success is that there was a contemporaneous passion for archaeology, helped by the 1920s British expeditions in Egypt. Ley lines gave the notion of an ancient wisdom embedded in the land, like Saxon treasure or Roman remains. To the middle classes of the 1920s and the 1930s, who were escaping from the cities at the weekend in their new motorcars, and then exploring hitherto remote areas on foot, this opened up an England which they thought must have been lost forever. It echoed with their concomitant discoveries of tucked away villages, and still rustic farmsteads.

We are reminded of a haunting scene in the Kent-set, Powell and Pressburger wartime drama *A Canterbury Tale* (1945). Landgirl Alison has come walking up the hill outside Chilham to join the old Pilgrim's Road. She has a deep emotional connection with the place; this is where she and her archaeologist fiancé had shared a perfect caravanning holiday excavating the old road. Now her fiancé – an RAF pilot – is missing, presumed dead. Alison walks along the old Pilgrim's Road searching for a moment of solace on a perfectly quiet, sunny, summer's day. Then, from somewhere behind her, there is the sound of a lute, jingling bells, and high spirited laughter. Yet as she whirls around, there is no one there. She is entirely alone. In that moment, we think what she is thinking: that she heard a group of medieval pilgrims, on the final stage of their journey to Canterbury. The old road, with its old purpose, clearly holds the memories of centuries. They are there for anyone who is attuned to the benign atmosphere of the place. There are walkers now who come to places like the Rollright Stones – a circle of seventy-seven small megalithic oolitic limestone standing stones – with at the very least a subconscious wish to hear such echoes. Certainly, you will find many visitors to this field are rather quieter and somehow more respectful than those secular tourists who visit cathedrals.

* * *

The superstitious walker is one thing; the religious walker is another. In the Middle Ages, some churches adapted an old Pagan symbol to turn walking into a symbol for the journey of life itself. The labyrinth – that is, the single pathed labyrinth, as opposed to mazes, with all their trick dead ends – is an ancient design that can be found all over the world. Its most familiar incarnation is the maze beneath the Palace of Knossos in which, according to mythology, dwelt the deadly Minotaur. The labyrinth crops up, ploughed into the earth and stony ground, all over Europe, and is attributed to 'the Celts', whoever they were.

The medieval Catholic church in some places acquired this design: a unicursal path, weaving and winding through twelve concentric circles, divided in four by a cross – for worshippers to process around. The exasperating turns and reverses, the unexpected changes in direction, were all supposed to mirror one's mortal progress; the destination was fixed and certain. There is a meditative quality about walking a labyrinth; since it is a single path, there is no need for any conscious decision making about direction, and so one wanders with part of the mind dreamily disengaged. This kind of disengagement makes one more receptive to the symbolism.

The extreme opposite end of this lack of decision making is the hedge maze designed by Greg Bright at Longleat, in Wiltshire – perhaps the ultimate expression of a form that found particular fame with Hampton Court's eighteenth-century example. Bright's furiously complex design has paths that stretch to a mile and a half, and which potentially could be wandered for about three times that length. The exercise is explicitly to disorientate the walker, not merely in topographical terms, but also meta-phorically. A further diabolical complication of the Bright design is that there are no dead ends – rather, paths that simply loop back on to other paths, in vast swirling vortices, meaning that the walker could conceivably end up going around and around in circles without necessarily even knowing it. Frustration and exasperation grow. There might occasionally be just a flash of irrational panic; how long could one be forced to walk around and around in these recursive patterns?

For Greg Bright – a Glastonbury man – the maze was not just a puzzle for Bank Holiday daytrippers to solve. His mazes, rather, were about throwing the mind, and the body, open to new possibilities. He wrote once of how he had been attracted to the idea of 'the strangeness of routing'.[1] And he had a point: the entire purpose of a maze for the walker is the thrill of getting lost. It is the relinquishing of control.

There is another curious echo here. In 1971, before he found fame, Bright dug out a maze in a field at Pilton, in the West Country. This was like the swirling Longleat version, but this time rendered with deep trenches. Surely the artistic compulsion here sprang from something even more ancient than the maze itself; the cursus.

The cursus was a Neolithic earthwork – essentially, two paral-lel ditches dug out, and stretching sometimes as far as five miles, in the period 3,600–3,000 BC. There is evidence of such struc-tures near the Thames, punctuated with barrows and longbar-rows, and in which have been found fragments of pottery. It is believed by some archaeologists that these trenches were used for the purposes of ritual walks, or processions. We think of these structures, and then we think of the earthwork maze that Bright created, again for the purposes of processing and, in a sense, losing yourself.

In the cases of mazes and labyrinths, it is never difficult to detect a mystical or metaphysical dimension to such a walk.

There are some Christians who are extremely distrustful of labyrinths. The sort of revelation and disclosure that they can conjure is not, they think, the type that is good for the soul. In other words, by disengaging to such a degree, by falling into a sort of semi-trance, one is vulnerable to the influence of darker powers, even to the occult. That some Christians voice this is a striking echo particularly of Edmund Spenser: the wild woods that formed his maze in *The Faerie Queene* were bad for the soul as well as the body.

* * *

There will always be pilgrims, making their way to sacred sites. During the seismic upheaval of the Reformation in the sixteenth century, the Protestant aim was to rid the English landscape of any signs of idolatry. These included crosses and shrines by the roadside. Even then, there were certain sites – which, themselves, had been adopted by the early Christians centuries beforehand – that proved a little more resilient. People simply continued to walk to them. Such sites included ancient holy wells and healing springs that had themselves been recalibrated from an older faith. There was St Winifriede's Well in Wales; medieval Catholics went there believing it to have healing qualities. The Reformation in theory should have put paid to such pilgrimages; but in fact, a little later, Protestants started going there too. Indeed, there were sites in rural Wales and northern Scotland right into the twentieth century where such healing wells continued to be visited by those eager for miraculous cures. In Wales, there were 'rag wells', springs where strips of clothing would be left tied to hazel trees by those hoping for a cure for skin diseases. Similarly, in the eighteenth century, all those monasteries and abbeys that had been left in ruins by the Reformation became themselves holy places of pilgrimage for Catholics.

We also see a curious parallel between the places that modern walkers are drawn to, and the places our ancestors went. It is not just the stone circles that continue to attract people who otherwise would have no time for anything preternatural. There are the curious shaped hills, like Pendle in Cumbria, with its witchy legends, and Pecked Hill in Wiltshire. Springs, too, still attract visitors. It might now be rare to find occurrences of walkers leaving little strips of clothing; but before we chuckle at the quaintness of such an idea, consider just how many people still throw coins into wells. The impulse – the appeal to some nameless power present in the water itself – is exactly the same. Though according to a weirdly thriving strain of English literature and art, from the medieval period onwards, we ought perhaps to make sure we understand exactly what we are worshipping in the countryside as we make our way through those bosky groves. Some of us might have an attachment to the idea of Gaia theory; the notion that the earth itself is a living organism. Certainly there is a tendency among many of us to personify nature.

Think of all those centuries old churches adorned with Green Men; these grimacing uncanny stone carvings of men who seem to be composed of leaves. It always seems so strikingly strange that this alarming character – precise origin mistily unknown – features within as well as without the churches in question. The old Pagan gods of the British countryside are not always benevolent; quite the reverse. In legends and stories, they are indeed more often malignant, malicious and vengeful to anyone who even unknowingly crosses their paths.

There is the Greek God Pan, who pops up many times. He is benevolent both in Keats's *Endymion*, and in *The Wind in the Willows*. The version of Pan who, at least for our age, seems to have much more abrupt and recognisable resonance is that portrayed in the creepy Saki short story *The Music on the Hill*. In this, a rather unsympathetic woman bags herself an apparently meek husband; she insists that they move to his estate in the country where she might better mould him, and indeed the lands of his estate. On her first walk out into that country, it seems as though the land will not be quite so yielding as she imagines. She is disturbed by the laughter of an unseen boy – 'golden and equivocal' – and subsequently not much impressed by a statue of Pan in a wooded arbour, about which she complains to her husband. It seems to the wife that in these parts, the country folk seem almost to worship Pan. He answers that only a fool would not do so. On another solo walking expedition, the woman transgresses further by taking some grapes that have been left by the statue of Pan. She is almost immediately terrified by the face of a 'gypsy boy' grimacing through a hedge at her. Later, her husband calmly assures her that there are no gypsies in this part of the world. The final walk brings the final terrifying confrontation with this sinister, unknowable form of Paganism: a hunted stag, which fatally charges the woman as the air around is filled with the sound of pipes and once more, the noise of a boy's laughter, 'golden and equivocal.'[2]

On one level, this is a nightmare shared (still) by a great many urban dwellers: that the people who live in deep country are in the thrall of gods and beliefs more ancient and more malicious than anyone can know. But the curious thing about the Saki story is that even in the mounting unease, we also perfectly understand the cruel justice of the narrative. The country is there to be taken seriously, frivolous interlopers who seek to impose themselves upon it cannot be allowed to prevail; it is as if they are trying to change the laws of nature. Perhaps the sinister god Pan can relax in the company of modern day walkers. Far from being despoilers, we are almost supernaturally keen, in eco terms, to give something back to the land, and to keep our carbon footprints to a doll-like minimum. Even if there are moments in wooded glades when we find ourselves jumping at a half seen movement, or oddly aware that there is someone else nearby, it is all part of the pleasure of being in a place where man's influence is more limited.

Fundamentally, what Alfred Watkins was doing with his ley lines back in 1925 – and without quite realising it – was grabbing the land back from centuries of Protestant and Catholic appropriation. By seeing that churches stood on old sacred sites that could be linked, he was essentially uncovering a hidden history. The point is not that the lines are all straight, or form patterns; if there is any such thing as a ley line at all, it is a Neolithic navigation aid, using the most obvious beacons dotted throughout the country. In allowing for some degree of mysticism, Watkins was reminding us that there was religion here long before Christianity arrived.

In the *Quatermass* serial, the Planet People cannot be stopped in their relentless, hypnotic walk through the leafy English countryside. But the final, horrible irony at the climax is that the guiding alien intelligence bids the young people to return, and to gather in the concrete ugliness of Wembley Stadium. In the end, they have simply been drawn back to the city from which they sought to escape; now they face annihilation. A great many unhappy city dwellers might know the feeling only too well. There are those who, when they escape, catapult themselves as far away from any hint of civilisation as they can. Like the hermits of old, or wise men in the Himalayas, there are those who seek the complete contrast of utter solitude. But pure solitude is not quite as easy to find as one might think.

CHAPTER 16

Exploring the Lures of Solitude and Dodging The Grey Man of Ben Macdhui

This dark green ocean of spruce trees, blowing under the wind with a soughing that sounds like anger, and the sharp grey hills behind rising into the sombre sky, present an irresistible prospect to the solitary walker. The authorities and the rescue services might well wish that this was not so.

The Cairngorms, in the Highlands of Scotland, are these days presented to the world through sunny tourist marketing as some form of gigantic adventure playground. Yet this region also continues to draw in those who wish simply to listen to the sound of their own breathing as they wander alone. These hills and their paths have always seemed especially attractive to the more philosophical kind of rambler.

While the physicality of the climbs, and the harshness of the weather, have a kind of extremity, there is the accompanying extreme of being so far away from anyone else. While in the city, solitude is considered an undesirable, even unsettling state – the word 'loner' is only ever used in a pejorative sense – out on jagged, scree-strewn paths, loneliness seems more natural and also much more attractive. In this respect, we have all been preconditioned by the Romantic movement. In the Cairngorms, this freedom to clamber, and to find oneself the sole figure in a wild, high landscape where the clouds skim low over the ground, was hard won. Although all Scots will tell you that, unlike in England, there was never any real law of trespass there, this is simply not true. In the nineteenth century, landowners were if anything more zealous than their English counterparts. In the 1880s, there were some 3.5 million acres of deer forest in the Highlands, and those acres were implacably patrolled by armies of gamekeepers, or ghillies. Since the economy of the north had been fading fast in that period, there was little that could have stopped such a transformation. Yet as that era progressed, another opposing craze took hold: the passion for hillwalking. This found its full voice in the Cairngorm Club, which was founded in 1893. The campaigning MP James Bryce, who had been fighting to push his Access to Mountains Bill through Parliament, was a central figure. In a speech, Bryce said:

> I have climbed mountains in almost every country – I have travelled in almost every country where mountains are found, and I have made enquiries but I have never heard of a single instance in which the pedestrian, the artist or the man of science has been prevented from freely walking where he wished, not even in those countries where the pursuit of game is most actively followed.

He went on, blisteringly:

> The scenery of our country has been filched away from us just when we have begun to prize it more than ever before ... the Creator speaks to his creatures through his works, and appointed the grandeur and loveliness of the mountains and glens and silence of the moorlands lying open under the eye of Heaven to have their fitting influence on the thoughts of men, stirring their nature and touching their imaginations, chasing away cares and the dull monotony of everyday life.

Elsewhere, Bryce evoked a long vanished golden age of freedom: 'eighty years ago, everybody could go freely where he desired over the mountains and moors of Scotland,' he said. 'I am informed by friends familiar with Scottish law that there is no case in our law books of an attempt to interdict any person from walking over open moors and mountain – except of recent date.' Bryce had been opposed in the House of Commons by the MP for Argyllshire, Colonel Malcolm, who argued that 'access' meant that the walker would have freedom to trample wherever he wished. There was a particular Scottish term for what he was against: 'stravaiging', which means wandering at will. Another opponent of access was Lord Elcho, who hailed from a Scottish landowning family – Elcho Castle is just three miles outside of Perth. In 1892, Lord Elcho had this to say of the prospect of tourism opening up the hills and the glens: 'They [the tourists] would bring nothing with them and they would leave nothing behind them. The family paper and broken ginger beer bottles are the only traces left behind them.'[1] If only he could see the litter-free swarms of tourists clambering around those family lands now.

Members of the Cairngorm Club were determined, and they were never afraid of confrontations with ghillies and landowners, which would always be written up enthusiastically in the Club's house journal. They faced apparently unyielding opposition: it is reckoned that by the end of the nineteenth century, the majority of Scotland's Munros – the peaks that rise 3,000 feet or more above sea level, and so named after Sir Hugh Munro, who in 1891 listed them – were closed off to ramblers. The open countryside was planted with fierce signs and notices warning of the hazard of being shot at. Some old roads were shut altogether. However, by the opening decades of the twentieth century, thanks in part to the intellectual pressure and unfriendly publicity from the Cairngorm Club, those old roads were gradually, if reluctantly, opened up.

Despite all these formidable discouragements, Aviemore, right in the centre of the Scottish Highlands, has been a potent lure for hearty types across the decades. While Edwardian climbers beetled up these hills in tweed and stout shoes, there was, in the 1960s, a burst of startlingly sophisticated modernity as Aviemore

sought to reinvent itself as a swish international ski resort. The
celebrity factor did not quite match Val d'Isere. Nevertheless, in
the winter, the skiing at Aviemore is still huge. Now the town has
also learned how to pull people in for the summer months too:
angling itself deliberately towards walkers.

In recent years, the Scots – with their fresh new devolutionary
assembly – have been taking quite a dramatic stance. Whereas the
pro-rambling Labour MPs in England have long faced a formidable establishment of country interests, the Scots MSPs, almost
as soon as they had the chance from the year 2000 onwards, have
been stentorian about the absolute rights of anyone to walk
where they will; especially out in the gusty wild of the Cairngorms.
Though the war has long been won, they continue to find fresh
skirmishes and battles to fight: there will always be estate owners
who seek to block access somewhere (a recent case involved a
footpath near a secluded castle just outside Perth). The vast
tamed wilderness of the Highlands also presents us with one of
those exquisite walking paradoxes. While it is certainly pleasant
to have a landscape that is open, rather than shut, to ramblers – a
landscape where walkers' needs are anticipated and catered for
– there is also a residual spark of frustration, almost unconscious.
And the source of this frustration? It is to do with that desire for
complete solitude. It is not so much that the wild places are
vanishing; it is more that the opportunities to be fully, genuinely
alone are disappearing. The greater the numbers who seek solitude, the harder it is to find; for it is the remotest spots that are
now the strongest lure for so many ramblers.

The views from those mountaintop cairns must be shared,
and sometimes with a surprisingly large crowd. We might imagine that the Cairngorms is one of the few remaining parts of the
country where solitude might be celebrated. It isn't. In fact, the
area has its very own ghostly legend that seems to be a sinister
parable about the perils of being on one's own. 'The Grey Man
of Ben Macdhui' has the distinction of being a spectral story

tailored to walkers. The first to give the tale real legs was Professor Norman Collie of the University of London, in 1925. In keeping with the tradition of the Sunday Tramps and other energetic men of learning, he was extremely enthusiastic about hill climbing. But on one wintry day in 1891, as he was scrambling around near the top of Ben Macdhui and beginning his descent, his view of the hills was changed, as he told the Cairngorm Club: 'I began to hear the sound of noises in the loose rock behind me coming down from the natural cairn on the high plateau,' he said. 'Every few steps I took, I heard a crunch, and then another crunch, as if someone was walking after me but taking steps three or four times the length of my own.'[2] Professor Collie, who was alone, tried to reason with himself that he was experiencing some form of natural, aural hallucination. But despite trying to assure himself this, he now began to be seized with an extraordinary irrational fear. As he descended faster, so the footsteps behind him grew deeper and longer. At that point, it became too much, and Professor Collie now ran down that hill, and did not stop until about four miles later.

The story so impressed the members of the Cairngorm Club that it made the press, and there was a mini Grey Man brouhaha. It seemed that there had long been tales of a suffocating, brooding presence being felt on the hill, and a sense among solitary walkers that they were no longer alone. To be on that hill when the clouds are low, or when the heavy mist has set in, you might see how one might suffer the apprehension that something else was out there. But many others have experienced the same phenomenon in perfectly fine atmospheric conditions, which has led to speculation that there might be something about the hill itself. Other walkers came forward with their stories: of a curious noise almost beyond hearing; of an increasing sense of oppressiveness, no matter how fine the day. There are solitary walkers who have heard voices near the summit, even though there was no one else to be seen.

There are stories of some other walkers seeing a large, indistinct figure in the distance on the hill's summit, giving the idea of this presence a distinctly yeti like feel. These tales seem slightly out of keeping with the rest. Chiefly, the Grey Man is an aural rather than visual phenomenon. Some stories culminate in eminently reasonable walkers being seized not merely with fear, but also with profound depression. Ben Macdhui seems to have a particularly special atmosphere. Those who knew the hills of this region intimately sometimes suggested that there was more to them than anyone knew. In the 1940s, the leader of the Cairngorms Rescue Team, Peter Densham, acknowledged that there was something strange about Ben Macdhui and the hills around it, too. Not just disconcerting footsteps, but also a high-pitched noise that could not be explained, and which left whoever heard it in a profound state of nerves. 'Tell me that the whine was but the result of relaxed eardrums, and the Presence was only the creation of a mind that was accustomed to take too great an interest in such things,' he said. 'I shall not be convinced. Come, rather, with me at the mysterious dusk-time,' he continued, 'when day and night struggle upon the mountains. Feel the night wind on your faces, and hear it crying amid rocks. See the desert uplands consumed before the racing storms. Though your nerves be of steel, and your mind says it cannot be, you will be acquainted with that fear without name, that intense dread of the unknown that has pursued mankind from the very dawn of time.'

Possible scientific explanations for the Ben Macdhui tales include the effect of creaking, melting ice around old snowy footprints somehow recreating a noise similar to footsteps. In terms of seeing spectral figures, there is the Brocken spectre effect – a hilltop optical illusion caused by a particular angle of sunshine that can throw one's shadow into the air. The Ben Macdhui legend suggests a force that is not human, a presence that is generated by the very mountains themselves. We can actually discern something else at the pleasurable heart of such eerie tales: the challenge that stark solitude poses. Those who sense the Grey Man are alone. Their fear, even though it seems to consist of that solitude being invaded, sounds actually as though it might be the fear of being alone itself.

Ever since those soaringly Romantic paintings by Caspar David Friedrich, of solitary men, their backs to us, standing atop mountains and gazing out over richly detailed cloud capped peaks, the idea of walking to find solitude has also had a dimension of therapy, that a temporary removal from society might act as a form of psychic balm. It is not difficult to understand why, especially when the walkers concerned are city-dwellers. To leave the rush and tear of the streets, and to find perfect silence away from all humanity on top of a vast hill miles even from the nearest village, seems soothing, refreshing, natural. There is also an element of temporary misanthropy, which comes to us all from time to time. 'One of the pleasantest things in the world is going on a journey; but I like to go by myself,' wrote William Hazlitt in 1821. He felt it was better to dispense with the nuisance of companions because 'you cannot read the book of nature without being perpetually put to the trouble of translating it for others.'[3]

The rather less grumpy thoughts of novelist Robert Louis Stevenson nonetheless run in a similar vein on the matter, although we might also see that he was bringing a tremendous amount of energy to the subject, in his essay 'Walking Tours':

> A walking tour should be gone on alone, because freedom is of the essence; because you should be able to stop and go on, and follow this way or that, as the freak takes you; and because you must have your own pace, and neither trot alongside a champion walker, nor mince in time with a girl. And then you must be open to all impressions and let your thoughts take colour from what you see. You should be as a pipe for any wind to play upon.[4]

Surely this depends on what sort of country one is passing though. Certainly if one is ambling through the meadows of East Sussex, or dawdling along high banked Devon lanes, then certainly one's mood will be lifted like a swallow on a warm breeze. Out here in the Cairngorms, the solitary walker is not so much absorbing the landscape, as defining himself against it. Moods are not quite so osmotic, nor tranquil. In solitude, a walker develops a distinct relationship with the landscape around him; one that tends to intensify the sense of a spirit of the place. But just because a place has a distinct feel to it does not mean that one will feel at one with it.

In the first half hour of Werner Herzog's otherwise uneven remake of *Nosferatu* (1979), the brilliantly authentic Roma villagers in the shadow of the Carpathians will not let estate agent Jonathan Harker take one of their horses for his journey up the mountain. It is their way of trying to stop him going. It is not just their fear of nameless phantoms; it also seems to be the very landscape itself that inspires a sense of terrified awe. So, without horses, Harker is forced to continue on foot all day long if he is to meet the Count at the Borgo Pass. The sequence that follows blends the art of Caspar David Friedrich with the music of Wagner; climbing ever higher up the track into the desolate peaks, Harker takes rests, sitting on rocks, watching clouds skim with uncanny speed over the hill tops, and watching the movement of the pale orange sun as it starts to set behind the highest mountain. He is a man alone in a vast landscape of flitting, fleeting shadows, a landscape that seems, somehow, to be brooding and to be watching him.

In prolonged periods of solitude, the walker will sometimes naturally start to ascribe such attributes to the hills and valleys around him. They cannot simply remain neutral. There is something that runs deeper than that too. Perhaps there is even some sort of geological resonance in these harsh places, maybe even some sort of odd aural effect caused by wind on rocks, that suddenly turns complete solitude into the sense that one is not alone, that the hills are indeed alive. Jean Jacques Rousseau used his solitary walks to concentrate his thoughts on his feelings of separation from society, which he then articulated in a series of essays. A. H. Sidgwick, in his Edwardian walking essays, was having none of it: with cheerful, comical bluster, he set out all that he considered thoroughly unnatural about those who walk alone. 'Walking alone is, of course, on a much lower moral plane than walking in company,' he wrote. 'It falls under the general ban on individual as opposed to communal pursuits. The solitary walker, like the golfer, or sculler, is a selfish and limited being.' He added: 'Walking alone … is an abnormal function of life, a subject for pathology rather than physiology.'[5]

A similar paradox of walking is that walkers are perpetually in search of the unspoilt; yet by their very presence, and by their numbers, they are changing the areas they seek out. The north-east of Scotland, beyond the shadow of the Cairngorms, is one such region. Formerly a land of small farms, with a coast dotted with tiny harbours and fishing villages, it was both sparsely populated and considered remote and poor. Unlike the rugged, romantic west coast, with its great mountains and dreamy islands, the flat, gorsey prospects to the east of Inverness seemed nondescript. Even the vast beaches, looking out on to the stern and flinty North Sea, seemed colourless. In Lewis Crassic Gibbons' 1933 novel *Sunset Song*, set in this region, the heroine Chris Guthrie is listening to singing in the barn on the occasion of her wedding. Even though the various folk songs start off being high spirited, they soon become more melancholy, each streaked through with intimations of mortality:

> It came on Chris how strange was the sadness of Scotland's sing-
> ing, made for the sadness of the land and the sky in dark autumn
> evenings, the crying of men and women of the land who had
> seen their lives and loves sink away in the years, things wept for

247

beside the sheep-ouchts, remembered at night and in twilight. The gladness and kindness had passed, lived and forgotten, it was Scotland of the mist and rain and the crying sea that made the songs.[6]

Of course, the mist and the rain and the crying sea now have their own attractions. Thanks in large part to the business of walking, this once neglected area has now perked up beyond recognition. In doing so, however, it has inevitably lost a little of its old austere, melancholy flavour. Go down to the harbour at Lossiemouth on the remote Moray coast, for instance – it is there as the prelude to a fantastic sandy beach walk that stretches for miles up the coast. Instead of rusting old fishing boats and pungent gutting sheds, you will find instead a rather jaunty and chic waterside restaurant; the very idea of such a thing would have seemed science-fictional in the 1950s. Elsewhere, old railway bridges spanning salmon-flashing rivers are buffed up and pressed into service as properly surfaced walking paths. Rambling among the boulders and twisted branches washed up on the coast at Speymouth, the solitary walker can not only savour the sounds of the sucking waves attempting to pull the stones back off the beach, but also know that his very presence is encouraged. My relatives in the area rather revel in this new walking economy, which has brought with it swanky organic ice cream shops, and walking boot emporiums. What the region loses in unique identity, it surely gains in this evolution of quality of life.

Some areas in England, by contrast, have cunningly sought to trap their essences, even magnify them. The landscape of the Brontës, for instance, is one that the authorities in Yorkshire have worked very hard not merely to maintain, but also to intensify. There, walkers are openly invited to consider that they are rambling into the pages of their favourite fiction.

CHAPTER 17

A Day Out in Brontë Country – What Happens When Much-Treasured Walking Landscapes Become Theme Parks

Some of the Ramblers' Association's bitterest and most exhausting and yet most tediously miniature struggles have involved signposting. These footpath signs – planted next to hedgerows or stiles, by red telephone boxes or simply at the gates to fields – are not merely practical; they have symbolic weight. For when such signposts have been quietly removed, by farmers or anti-rambling landowners, as they so frequently have been, this has been the signal that battle has been joined. It is a sneaky semiotic trick that the landowners play: if there is no sign indicating a path, then the path therefore cannot exist. In huge numbers of cases, in every single county, ramblers have then had to carry the burden of proving that the path *does* exist; the restoration of the signpost is the unfurling of the victory banner.

Happily, in Haworth, Yorkshire, the authorities have gone to the rather mad opposite extreme. The wooden signposts are not merely plentiful; they are also carved in Japanese. For here we are in 'Brontë Country' and this part of the world has a particular cult appeal to visitors from Japan. What makes 'Brontë Country' unusual is that it seems specifically angled at walkers, as opposed to just coach-inhabiting snappers. We are being invited to sample a flavour of what Kate Bush winningly described in her 1978 hit 'Wuthering Heights' as 'the wily, windy moor.' And you can't really help getting sucked into the spirit of all of it: after all, this particular chunk of landscape is merely the logical conclusion to a process that has been evolving in more subtle ways right the way across the country.

It is the opposite of the thrilling trespass on to unknown, untasted land. It is, instead, land being thrown open to as many people as possible, and marketed like any other commodity. From the wilds of Wales to the Cornish coastal path to the Pennine Way itself; from Ben Nevis to Snowdon, there is a growing element of Disneyfication creeping in to a number of areas; the sense that the land has been pre-packaged for ramblers, and projected with a pre-determined identity. If that sounds a little disapproving – perhaps even the protest of an authentic walker searching after authentic experience – then I should apologise. I do not disapprove in the slightest. For one finds in Haworth and on these moors something that is paradoxically every bit as healthy as a walk on virgin paths. Veteran ramblers may snort with disdain but there is sometimes virtue to be found in the most sugary of theme parks.

That tasteful theme starts not too far out of Leeds, on the vintage railway line that runs from Keighley to Haworth in the summer months. Here, steam engines toot, the tea shop till tinkles, and extravagantly moustached guides shout 'all aboard!' As the engine splutters under a bridge, an open window admits a dense cloud of tasty vapour into the carriage. In this non-smoking age, the very idea is met with horror by several passengers, who rush to close the windows as though an entire nest of wasps had got in. Just a few minutes later, you are at Haworth station, which has been lovingly titivated to remind you of every black and white film you have ever seen. So we walkers – and there are many of us on this train, admiring the frowsy old fittings – are thoroughly primed through this welter of imagery. It is not enough to walk in these parts, you must step into a larger narrative. Ideally you should, from the point of view of the local tourist board, buy into it. The village itself sits dourly aloof from its neighbouring town atop a steep hill, facing out over the Pennine moors. This faux village is a vortex of genteel tearooms and little museums with attractions along the lines of 'The Very Desk At Which The Brontës Wrote!'; a forbidding church and quaint second hand book dealers; and a pub, The Black Bull, that proudly and rather tastelessly makes known the fact that it was here that Branwell Brontë drank (omitting the detail that his fatal alcohol dependency was fuelled here). Here is the very post office from which the Brontë sisters posted off their manuscripts to their London publishers. If Haworth did not have the Brontë connection, one wonders if that post office would have survived the closures programme.

We are not here for museums; we are here for the paths that lead out to great Brontë landmarks, such as the house that suggested Charlotte's Thrushcross Grange and more import- antly, Top Withens – the old ruin that is said to have inspired Emily's *Wuthering Heights* itself. This is where those rather wonderful signposts come in. One can leave the village by several means but the path that leads out by the side of the church – through the 'kissing gate' – seems as good a one to follow as any. The churchyard seems to be filled with mad escaped hens; perhaps this is some Brontë novel detail that I have missed. After just a few minutes on a paved path pointing upwards, you are suddenly out in the open. For anyone who has a taste for the bounce of heathland, or the knee-deep struggle of peat, this walk will seem somehow a little deodorised. The path is perfectly ordered, neatly levelled and in some places paved. Great care has been taken with steps and stiles. There are some slopes, to be sure, but nothing that requires any huge effort. The point is that you are now out in 'Brontë Country'. You are invited to imagine that you are seeing this world through the eyes of Heathcliff or Cathy or Jane Eyre or Rochester. Even in the summer months, you should be able to summon the sensation of icy exposure, the bitter knuckle-throbbing brutality of the cold and the wind. Even if you consciously resist, it is still difficult to avoid doing it: after all, the entire narrative of *Wuthering Heights* is set into motion by a walk. Heathcliff's tenant Lockwood, having already once visited the Heights, claims to be spurred into a return visit by his own house being filled with the 'infernal dust' of a servant girl cleaning the fireplace.

> I took my hat, and after a four miles walk, arrived at Heathcliff's garden gate just in time to escape the first feathery flakes of a snow shower. On that bleak hill the earth was hard with a black frost, and the air made me shiver through every limb.

Lockwood has only intended his visit to be a brief one; the snow puts paid to that. And his notions of walking back home provoke Heathcliff's heavy mockery:

> I wonder you should select the thick of a snow-storm to ramble about in. Do you know that you run a risk of being lost in the marshes? People familiar with these moors often miss their roads on such evenings.

Obviously, for the summer daytripper, such bloodcurdling warnings are not necessary. And even in the most outlandish conditions, there would be precious little opportunity now for a walker to lose the road. In the far distance loom several remote hillside farmhouses, any one of which might serve as Top Withens. Yet despite the sunshine and the mild air, you still can't help imagining Lockwood approaching such a bleak prospect; or indeed imagining a night spent in such a place, with the tempest howling across the moor, and the knocks at the casement window as spectral Cathy plaintively tries to get in.

Actually, I have judged the day for my walk nicely; that point just after mid-summer when the first pinky dots are showing on the heather and the whole moor is about to explode into purple. Unfortunately, thanks to scattered dung, there is also an orgy of horseflies, dancing and capering. Anyone who has ever been stung by a horsefly will know to be wary of them. Even a town-dweller like myself knows better than to attempt to provoke them. Thankfully, there are a great many other walkers here other than myself, so their attentions are diluted. And as we pick our way in the direction of the 'Brontë Waterfall' – just exactly how far will the local council take this Brontë theme? – there is an empty dilapidated cottage, the dark windows glowering reproachfully at those seeking to peer in. For dedicated ramblers as opposed to casual visitors, there is another, competing narrative in this landscape, not two miles off on Haworth Moor. It is a rather more recent narrative but – to walking enthusiasts – no less intense. Because access to a particular stretch of land not far from here has only been permitted for the last few years or so. Even as late as 1995, the Ramblers' Association was compelled to hold a rally there – attended by the then shadow environment secretary, Frank Dobson, and by Ramblers' president Janet Street-Porter – both there to demand that walkers be allowed to set foot on this turf.

The land was owned by Yorkshire Water. And in fact on the day of that Rally in the mid 1990s, it graciously permitted access to walkers. But it is an illustration of how, in the 1980s and the 1990s, the final great battle between ramblers and landowners reached a new peak of rancour. We shall return to these venomous disputes in the next chapter. Suffice it to say here that the disparity between the use of permissible and non-permissible walking routes can be comically great. From the determinedly commercial Brontë paths – what tourist, having seen these moors, is not going to return to Haworth and ransack the gift shops? – to the unbranded swathes of moorland seemingly there for the purposes of harbouring great reservoirs alone. It's not that the personal is political; it's that the personal is now commercial. Every form of leisure activity is now a form of economic transaction. That goes for walking as much as anything else; from the money spent on train fares to the amount laid out for specialised anoraks and boots. So why then do we flinch from the more openly commercial side of walking? Many walkers do so not out of snobbery, but more to do with a sense of aesthetics. There are those, for instance, who argue that some beautiful rambling landscapes have been deformed by the demands of mass tourism.

There is the instance of Mount Cairngorm in the Highlands, with its mountaintop Ptarmigan restaurant (these rare birds can sometimes be spotted on this peak). There is also the extremely distinctive purple funicular railway that helpfully runs up the side of this mountain, delivering visitors efficiently to the lavishly stocked gift boutique in the Blofeld-style bunker at the top. At the time this funicular railway was built, about ten years ago, the protests were banshee shrill. The train was considered a desecration of the pure white and grey mountain, an indigo excrescence that would also disfigure much of the untainted landscape around.

Ranged against these were the practical facts: for about four months of the year, these trains would be bearing skiers, rather than hoisting them aloft on chairlifts, which were more vulnerable to the extremes of weather. No one would deny the town of Aviemore that fundamental wellspring of funding. And the remaining months? The trains would be carrying the walkers – for this was the way that the town would be paying for itself out of season. The tougher walkers, of course, would hoot at the idea of taking a ride on such a thing – and they are still free to hoot, since there is no bar to walking up the mountain from its base. In fact, there is a perfectly helpful path, carved right into the side of that pure, untainted granite.

The key point about this new railway was that it made it possible for less mobile walkers to enjoy the summit. Walkers, in fact, like my grandmother. She was always not merely keen, but almost compulsive about walking. Even in her nineties, her appetite for getting out into the country never diminished. Obviously, a 3,000-foot climb up to the peak of Mount Cairngorm would not really have been practical. The funicular railway, however, made such a trip to the top possible. Once up there, you can of course give the gift bazaar the slip and instead wander around outside, supping in those sumptuous views, gasping at the way the frozen wind snatches the oxygen straight from your lungs. My grandmother absolutely adored it, as I am sure countless thousands of other visitors have done in the years that it has been in operation. Added to this, the sheer scale of Scotland's hills and moors means that such a contrivance on just one mountain is really not too much of a loss to the more purist walkers.

There have been similar controversies surrounding Mount Snowdon in North Wales. First concerning the little railway that gamely chuffs up the hill, and then about the café-restaurant at its summit. The railway has been there for over 100 years, a thing of wonder in its own modest right, so any initial controversy has rather died down a little there. The café is a different matter; its first incarnation appeared some sixty years ago. Then the unlovely concrete structure began to disintegrate under the force of so much wild weather. The Prince of Wales – normally so exquisitely wrong about anything architectural – eventually declared it 'the highest slum in Britain.' Just several years ago, the café was rebuilt, this time in rather dignified and austere granite. Now the train had somewhere a little swankier to deposit its passengers. When it first opened, it was not recommended to delicate bon viveurs; among the menu choices was Knorr's Cup-a-Soup – having said that, there are those for whom, upon reaching the summit of such a mountain, the very idea of this instant steaming soup would be absolutely wonderful. In a rather wider sense though, the wail has continually gone up about the mountain's very integrity having been snatched away from it. But there is another way of approaching this: whatever integrity Snowdon had was pretty much starting to crumble as soon as the eighteenth-century walker and chronicler Reverend Gilpin set eyes upon it and added it to the growing list of picturesque treasures to be sought out by visitors from all over. Whether a cafeteria or an unadorned summit which is still none the less milling with brightly clothed walkers, it's difficult to see the difference if you are talking about distractions.

Over in Derbyshire, many were concerned about the recent paving operation that took place over the opening stages of the Pennine Way. For this, in its own way, seems every bit as blatant as a funicular railway. You walk with almost absurd ease and speed over vast smooth slabs, glancing at the mulchy peat on either side of this supremely helpful walkway. There are now two issues here: one, again, is the question of opening up a difficult – though hugely popular – piece of land to as many walkers as possible, at whatever stages of ability. The second is the preservation of the land itself. The paving has been necessary not just for access, but also to avoid further erosion of the peat. With so many thousands of walkers trailing along this route, there was a real possibility of the hills being worn away into the ground. So with the paving, you lose authenticity. Without it, however, you are in danger of losing the path altogether, authentic or not.

In Haworth, though, authenticity occasionally comes off the rails completely; for instance, you can't help frowning a little at such contrivances as the 'Brontë Bridge', a modest little stone effort crossing a mere gurgle of a stream deep in a little valley. Even if the spot seems to be popular with families and picnics on a refreshing summer's day such as this, it seems somehow a slice of cheese too far. It is only when one starts clambering up the other side of this valley that the old 'Wuthering' sense returns; for just a mile away from here is the wreck of Top

Withens. For the walker, then, there is this dilemma: you become peeved if some Brontë landmarks seem insufficiently austere, then doubly peeved if you are coshed into seeing this area through that one prism alone. The solution is to take a deep breath and simply enjoy it for what it is: an exhilarating prospect of deep green, with the immanence of rich heathery purple. The Brontë connection might be what brings you here, but it could have been worse. They might have lived in Croydon.

The other slight difficulty for this part of the world – in the eyes of a purist rambler at least – is the way that this once wild, rugged county has been so ruthlessly domesticated by competing works of popular fiction and memoir, and by television. *Wuthering Heights* at least painted this area in Gothic brushstrokes of wild freezing tempests. But in the twentieth century, when the country vet James Herriot began publishing his wry diaries, the Yorkshire moors started to take on what looked like an element of caricature. Like the people, the land was perceived as having the qualities of 'gruffness', a certain sort of 'no-nonsense' feel. When the 1970s BBC TV series *All Creatures Great and Small*, based on Herriot's books, came along, the harsher edges of this landscape were smoothed and moulded into a sort of souvenir teapot heritage vision. Admittedly, these good-hearted memoirs and fables were set a little further north in the county. But the Yorkshire image was all of a piece. Now the moors and the dales came to mean something quite different: vintage cars, fairisle sweaters, bathos-laden farmers with obstinate cows, hearty open spaces. The glowering menace summoned by Emily Brontë became a Sunday evening property advertisement.

The serious, hardcore walker will always scoff at such examples. None the less, it cannot be denied that these popular books and television shows have inspired vast numbers of people to leave their cars and explore the Dales. Who can really argue with their inspiration for doing so? Whether they admit it or not, even the most hardcore walkers pick their cues from art and literature – their defence will be that the art in question will be slightly more highbrow than TV sitcoms. To an extent, art still has the power to claim ownership of certain vistas and views. We have only to point to Constable: how many times has 'The Haywain' been used not only as an example of landscape art, but also as a template to measure the same area against today? Vast numbers of walkers in Suffolk eager to see that exact spot cannot deny that they are pulled in by a perfectly reasonable curiosity. Moreover, there is something to be said for artistic and literary connections opening up areas of Britain that might otherwise be withering economically. An example in the north of the country is that of the Borders area, which follows the course of the River Tweed. There is a new, relatively long-distance path, called the Sir Walter Scott Way. Many of his novels were either set in, or inspired by, this region, and the trail itself features many Scott-themed souvenir opportunities – houses lived in, taverns visited, Woollen Mills selling his tartan.

Meanwhile, the Suffolk coast – and the genteel seaside towns of Southwold and Aldeburgh – have benefited enormously from the dual draw of Benjamin Britten and the annual Aldeburgh music festival. This is the upper-middle class walking equivalent of *Last of the Summer Wine* Yorkshire expeditions. Here we have a landscape – both the shingly beaches, and the flat, gorsey heathlands and boggy marshes that stretch inland – that seems calculated to appeal to those sorts of walkers who either have their own weekend places, or who rent properties off the Landmark Trust. The Disney flavour is still there, but because of the rarefied class aspect, it somehow seems just a little less vulgar, a little less 'mass appeal'. The totemic walking figure of this class is the late W. G. Sebald, whose exquisite and ghostly prose flitted through this region in *The Rings of Saturn*. His account of one such walk from Southwold to Dunwich is a powerful evocation of eerie alienation – a cross between Britten and M. R. James. Having done the same walk – about three miles, if that – I'm pleased to say that my own impressions were a little more cheerful, not least because of the sharp clear light on that particular day. Even the tricky-to-negotiate banks of shingle, over which you have to walk at a constant cambered angle, could not detract from the mood; every footstep sounded like the crunching of crisps, while above, the marsh birds circled and sang their idiosyncratic rising songs.

*   *   *

Back up on the highlands of 'Brontë Country', we can see that these areas, no matter how they are labelled, attract subtly differ-ent types of walkers, and that Brontë Country is at the more determinedly populist end of the scale. But places like Haworth illustrate the terrific importance of the outdoors, and of walk-ing, to the modern rural economy. In the last few decades, the notion of leisure in the country has been led firmly by ramblers. What are the protests of water boards now when walkers can keep entire villages and communities afloat?

It's time to weave back, past happy hordes of various ramblers – some in huge family groups – back down the slopes to Haworth to get in a pot of tea before the train home. Brontë Country has thrown up an interesting paradox for the rambling movement generally. The more the land has been brilliantly opened up, the more the land has been carefully – even chum-mily – signposted. But the rambler, by tradition, chafes at the very notion of being instructed which direction to head in. Instead, he or she prefers either to rely on finely detailed maps, or to vault over a stile and extemporise his explorations. The very notion of 'Brontë Country' – or indeed 'Sir Walter Scott Country', or 'Jane Austen Country' in Hampshire – wraps all of these beautiful paths up in quite another form of ownership: an ownership of imagination. The walker may wander about with an unprecedented amount of freedom, but the price is that quite a few of these territories now come with tags and labels hanging off them. As a result, the walker's own imagination and thought processes as they wander up and down can potentially be quite dramatically impeded. There are two options: either shake the head firmly, increase the pace, draw deep breaths into the lungs and ignore those footpath signs. Or you might simply abandon your natural snobbery about such things, and revel in it. After all, a good blustery Wuthering walk is hardly going to detract from your enjoyment of the Brontë sisters' works. It is altogether more likely to deepen your reading. So what the walker sacrifices in terms of freshness of impressions, the reader gains by being able to see a landscape through the eyes of such authors.

As a postscript that should make most Brontë fans feel rather better about any sense of commercialisation, I nipped into the Haworth tourist office to see if I could pick up leaflets to do with other local walks. As I did so, I saw a family standing at the information desk. The father was asking: 'Can you tell us where it is they film *Emmerdale*? We want to visit *Emmerdale*.' The speed – and the sheer detail – of the information officer's answer suggested that he had been asked this same question concerning the venerable ITV soap opera a great many times before. You might even be interested to learn that *Emmerdale* is now filmed on a closed set to which there is no access; but the original village that the serial used as a location is still very much there, and open, and nearby. Where? I forget. Ask the information officer yourselves. And take heart: there are worse reasons to be drawn to a footpath than the footsteps of literature's greatest lovers. You might instead be drawn by a desire to be close to the shade of Annie Sugden.

CHAPTER 18

Recent Furious Countryside Battles: The Patches of Forbidden Land that Remain and an Unsuccessful Attempt on the River Path at Windsor

Given that there is such a thing as the 'Thames River Path', and given that it is advertised noisily by means of big signposts up from the Estuary, it is a matter of some surprise to find that even now, there are sections that one is not even allowed within 500 yards of. This necessitates confusing and maddening detours. I don't mind quite so much when the path might happen to trail across the Berkshire gardens of former TV celebrities such as Michael Parkinson or Paul Daniels. But near Datchet, in Berkshire, the annoyance takes quite a different turn. This otherwise blameless and pretty little satellite of Windsor stands as a sort of metonym not only for everything that ramblers have been striving to achieve; but also for how, despite everything, they are still, occasionally, thwarted. All it really comes down to is a matter of three quarters of a mile; a trifling bagatelle in an otherwise magisterial 177-mile stretch. The immoveable obstacle that forces the walker off the river here has a wider symbolism in a battle that is still being fought.

The 1980s and the 1990s saw a great, final push towards the establishment of a 'right to roam'. This was a period in the walkers' movement where the anger and bitterness on both sides – walkers versus landowners – boiled even higher than before.

The ramblers triumphed in a philosophical sense; but they could not claim complete victory. For by unfortunate coincidence, this was also a period when farmers and country people were hit by a succession of heartbreaking crises – combined with what seemed to them like ill will from Westminster. It was looking to many in the rural community as though it was no longer possible to make a living from farming; the big supermarkets were starting to exert unbearable pressure on small producers.

Then came the nightmarish outbreaks of cattle disease, wave after wave. All this at a time when the government was preparing to outlaw hunting with hounds, which to many country folk was a signal of bigoted class based hostility. This friction between farmers – who had already been forced to change the face of the landscape into that of blank zombie prairies in order to allow for industrial scales of growing – and the politicians had started burning again in the 1980s. This was exactly the time that the walking movement started to exert its own increased pressure. The Ramblers' Association, seeing the need for further progress, put an heroic effort into changing views on wider access to paths. Walkers started to meet opposition that seemed almost as bad as that of the 1930s. While they grabbed some notable prizes – in terms of hearts and minds as well as opening up previously private land – there are some barriers that seem to be impassable, even today.

Outside Datchet, we find one of them. In my innocence, several years back, I had taken a quiet spring Saturday to wander along the Thames river path from Shepperton, at the far south west frontier of London, near the ceaseless roar of Heathrow. Initial impressions – brick suburban terraces, endless screaming jumbo engines – were not promising. Almost immediately, though, once actually at the banks of the Thames itself, this river path began to disclose an entire unsuspected watery world of hidden marinas, obscured boatyards, teeming weirs, and, most attractively, small islands on which sat houses; homes that could only be reached by means of a drawbridge.

This seems to me the *ne plus ultra* of the English domestic dream; safe and secure on one's own tiny island, cutting the world off at will. It feels a little like a small child building a den with sofa cushions. This is a place that only walkers could ever see. The path threads along the water, and the road is far enough back not to get a glimpse, so that you are in a separate, slightly secretive realm. The walker looks at these lagoon dwellers, out on their balconies, and they look back at the walker. The river path winds on, and becomes more sylvan, more languorously willow trailed. After the austerity of the estuary, this section seems instead to have a silky decadence about it; even the wildlife feels richer, more luxuriant. It trails through to Runnymede, and it is here that one is supposed to feel the currents of history. But actually, it is rather difficult to imagine King John and Magna Carta in this place. It instead seems a shade too Pre-Raphaelite; you expect to see Ophelia under the water, rippling and pale.

At this point, you are aware that just a few miles off lies the ruritanian pomp of Windsor, and the idea of this path sneaking and snaking around the base of that biscuity fortress puts some pep in the pace. It is immediately deflated about a mile or so before reaching Datchet. For it is at this point that the Crown decides that walkers should not be permitted any sort of proximity to certain Royal acres. You are instead required to cross the Albert Bridge and start marching crossly along a road towards Datchet, now seethingly aware that you are not only separated from the river; but also on the wrong side of it. This is not merely a matter of private land and trespass, this is land paid for by the taxpayer, combined with the perfectly reasonable assumption that a river path is by its nature unobtrusive, and should be more open than any other kind.

Those on a careful lookout, and forearmed with local knowledge, can eventually pick the river path up again. It might be on the wrong side of the river, and it might not always seem as if the walker is completely welcome on it, but it is there.

However, that Saturday some years ago, I was not to know this. Without a map – why ever would I have needed a map to follow a river path? – I went wrong.

I doubled back over the Albert Bridge, perplexed, looking for some way to rejoin the river on the side that I had been walking – perhaps there were signs that I missed. The outcome was the same. I ended up slogging the entire perimeter of Windsor Home Park on an uncomfortably busy road, until I reached the town of Windsor from the other side in a towering rage. All for the sake of about three quarters of a mile of restricted path. I should have consoled myself with a wider view. For the mere fact that there is a dedicated Thames river path at all – finally made official in 1996 – is itself a tribute to ceaseless campaigning, throughout a period of implacable opposition. This was partly to do, in the 1980s and early 1990s, with a substantial Conservative parliamentary majority. It is the party that has always traditionally represented the interests of the property owner; yet during that period, the interests of the property owner became almost fetishistic. With strength in numbers that could out-roar most other parliamentary voices, Conservative MPs became increasingly vocally hostile to the demands of the Ramblers' Association.

It didn't help that the Association's demands were somehow conflated, in political minds, with the advent of the New Age Traveller. In the 1980s, there was growing rural anger about increasing instances of trespass, with such travellers installing themselves on private land, caravans festooned with anarchic symbolism. New Agers had also fought with police at the so-called 'Battle of the Beanfield' in 1985 when, on the dawn of the Summer Solstice, they sought to get unfettered access to Stonehenge. The image in the popular press was that of 'crusties' – unsettling anti-establishmentarians smelling of cannabis and patchouli oil, with mangy dogs on strings, and a maddening dependency on welfare benefits. As a grouping, they also had a most unfortunate ricochet effect on ramblers. For in 1986, in an attempt to curb the Travellers, the government passed an enhanced Public Order Act with new clauses to do with trespass. Such a Public Order Act applied to walkers too. Although it was generally intended to be aimed at those who were occupying land, or holding all-night raves, the Act could in theory also encompass those who were perceived to be causing a nuisance in other ways; for instance, if a landowner insisted that ramblers were damaging rare wildlife.

It encompassed the more unusual cases, too, such as those involving naked walkers. Every now and then, there will always be a militant naturist group that protests that it has the right to stage nude walks. Such a walk took place a few years ago in Dorset, raising money for a marine charity. The walkers concerned – all pretty old and all men – were escorted along the route by police who did not know where to look. The nakedness itself is apparently not illegal *per se*; the difficulty arises when said nudity causes alarm in others. Given that these walkers had on only rucksacks and boots suggests that the spectacle they presented was probably more comically revolting than alarming. Still, it was against people such as this that the new Public Order Act could be invoked. Also in 1986, Paul Tyler, the Tory MP for north Cornwall, made a speech to the Country Landowners Association concerning the very idea of a 'right to roam.' He stated:

> The claim of a 'right to roam' is fatally flawed. Nobody has the 'right' to intrude into another's property, be it in the towns or the countryside … an unrestricted 'right to roam' will cause untold damage to the more fragile ecosystems and possibly ruin the finer qualities of our rural environment. The object has to be an agreement on access.[1]

Now, while such a speech sounds like excuses for keeping people off land, it must also be said that the argument against such a roaming right is quite legitimate. For when a right is conferred, it is much more than simply allowing something to happen. It also suggests that there will be consequences and redress if that something is not allowed to happen. In the case of private land, and of walkers, the anxiety was clear to hear: what if invading armies of rambling yobs took this as a charter to maraud across fields and through gardens as they chose? What if landowners were sued by walkers who wished to gain access to the bottom of their back gardens? Would this mean that the rights of walkers had more weight in court than the rights of farmers and country dwellers?

There is an echo here of that old antipathy: country folk disliking the idea of urban daytrippers turning their meadows into picnicking grounds, strewn with debris. In the recent US TV series *Mad Men*, set in the politically incorrect early 1960s, one of the more shocking scenes involves ad man Don Draper on a picnic with his family. At the end, they shake the rubbish and leftovers from the rug on to the grass, and simply drive off, leaving it there. This is exactly what farmers and landowners over here thought that walkers did. This fear went deeper. Even as late as 1996, Prime Minister John Major was referring to a putative 'right to roam' as 'a charter for rural crime.' We have only to think of the later case of reclusive Norfolk dweller Tony Martin, opening fire upon one of the young men who sought to burgle his house in the middle of the night. Major was tapping into an idea of walkers as transgressors; as interlopers from the towns whose intentions were sometimes malign.

In the mid-1980s, just as the heat of the landowners' rhetoric was intensifying, so too was the zeal of the Ramblers' Association. In 1985, it launched its 'Forbidden Britain' campaign, aimed at opening up great swathes of the landscape, such as the Forest of Bowland in Lancashire. For the first time since the 1930s, there were mass rallies held in places such as Yorkshire's Thurlstone Moor attended by many rambling veterans and pioneers, as well as contemporary politicians. This was also a measure of the continuing bi-polarity of British politics. On the whole, the walking movement tended to be a Labour issue; generally, it was opposed by the Conservatives. It is interesting, for instance, that that Public Order Act was toughened up further in order to take account of increasing numbers of Hunt saboteurs, who are also, of course, overwhelmingly Labour supporters.

Ramblers were at pains to point out that Britain was pretty much alone in Europe when it came to questions of access. Sweden, for instance, had *allemansratt* – in essence, everyone had the right to go everywhere, except directly across crops or into private homes. The same is true for Norway. In the 1960s, West Germany enacted Forest Laws, opening up vast tracts of the north Rhine and Westphalia. This open access was eventually brought in across the whole of the country in 1975. Elsewhere, Spain, Portugal and France could be walked with ease. What exactly was it in the British character that made politicians and activists, landowners and walkers, take up such rigid and unyielding positions?

On the left, there was a great deal of romanticism attached to the issue, too. In the early 1990s, Labour leader John Smith was a passionate enthusiast for clambering over the Munros. His parliamentary colleague, Chris Smith, often accompanied him on these trips. After John Smith's sadly premature death, Chris Smith was instrumental in proposing the idea of a 'John Smith Memorial Act'. He told the 1994 Labour conference:

> People have fought for hundreds of years for the right to roam where there is still fresh air and beauty to be enjoyed. We [the Labour Party] will enshrine that right in law – so that this land can be our land – and not just the Duke of Westminster's. I stood with John at the top of a mountain. The snow was hard under-

foot. The cloud was blowing across. We could see for miles and John looked and felt on top of the world. He would have wanted everyone to know the exhilaration of such moments.

But ramblers were associated with a sort of urban counterculture. For people who lived and worked in the country – for whom economic decline and changing working practices were causing increasing amounts of stress – the townie in all forms generated a new degree of irritation. Ramblers were perceived to have an urban arrogance about them; they gave the impression of behaving as they pleased without giving any recognition to farmers or tenants. They were perceived as being the enemy of the true countryman, in all their objections to hunting and other field sports. They were perceived as being fathomlessly ignorant when it came to farming methods, and the reasons why there had to be fences and hedges.

In this sense, things have hardly changed over the last 100 years. But in the 1990s – a time of great crisis for food producers, with scares about Mad Cow Disease, salmonella and listeria sweeping farms across the land – ever louder demands for access from walking groups met with a coalescing hostility. New Labour's victory under Tony Blair in 1997 meant that ramblers finally had the purposeful heavyweight political backing from Westminster that they had craved. This support was met with increasingly bitter opposition, from bodies such as the Game Conservancy Trust, as well as the House of Lords.

By 1999, the government was ready to present a new Countryside Bill to the House that would incorporate, for the first time, the principle of a right to roam. For Blair's ministers, this was a tribute to their late leader, John Smith. To the Conservatives, and various bodies in the countryside, it was an outrageous new burden – placing further weight upon the shoulders of already hard done by farmers and landowners. There were those on the anti-roaming side who argued that if walkers and their dogs had unlimited access to every moor, then the nesting periods of some of Britain's rarest bird species would be irretrievably disrupted, and the very birds themselves would be in danger of disappearing altogether. Added to this was the argument that an enforced opening up of tracts of land would lead to extra levels of insupportable bureaucracy for landowners who were already making significant concessions to the walking movement as it was.

The largely unspoken source of tension at this time was a sense throughout the countryside that this new Labour government – perceived to be formed of smart Islington cliques – was imposing the views and values of urban dwellers upon the country, and was doing so maliciously. For there was not only a question of access for walkers, this Labour government was also explicitly committed to banning hunting with hounds. In other words, there were large numbers of people in the country who regarded Labour as a party determined to wipe out their way of life, a quasi-Stalinist regime that sought to dismantle every tradition. These dissenting country folk may have had a point; it was certainly the case that a number of Labour MPs did indeed have a scarlet faced visceral dislike of the Tory shires. The high emotions raised by the hunting issue – on both sides of the argument – were barely rational and more often quite simply hysterical. Those on the anti-hunting side saw posh people in red coats galloping across the country at will, for the sake of tearing innocent foxes to pieces. Those on the pro-hunting side saw sanctimonious left-wing city dwellers getting themselves worked up into a class war frenzy.

The issue of rambling got caught up in that battle, in the sense that the most prominent figures in the walking movement also happened to have close ties with the Labour Party. For newspapers such as the *Daily Telegraph* at that time, ramblers were Trotskyists. Conversely, for a great many ramblers, newspapers such as the *Daily Telegraph*, and its landowning readers, were advocating a sort of pre-1832 world, where property conferred absolute right and power.

For many country people, it seemed as though economic difficulties in towns and cities always galvanised the government into action; while similar difficulties in the countryside were ignored. It was perhaps inevitable that walkers would act as lightning rods for this new, ugly mood. Country commentators such as R. W. F. Poole advocated marches, where farmers and other country folk would exercise 'their right to roam in the cities'. As he tartly went on to state, they would not leave the streets littered with crisp packets and lager cans and broken fences, as walkers in the countryside did. There were other flash-points. Around that time, an ominous outbreak of swine fever, leading to the slaughter of thousands of pigs, was attributed by furious farmers not to overly intensive pig farming, but to one careless walker who had, it was believed, dropped a half-eaten, infected sandwich which was subsequently eaten by a pig.

In late 2000, Parliament voted through the Countryside Rights of Way Act (widely known as CRoW); it was an extraordinary moment. From that point, there was now such a thing as a 'right to roam', even if it carried restrictions. You had the freedom to walk over mountain, moorland, heath and downland. Such rights were still to be negotiated in some regions, such as the South East, but the legislation carried both the weight of symbolism and also what seemed like an irreversible philosophical position: that walkers and ramblers were not trespassers. However, any jubilation that walkers' groups felt was swiftly, horribly extinguished. For early in 2001 came the epidemic of Foot and Mouth; and it was at this point that, despite Parliament, walkers became a focus for rural anger. For it was believed by a great many farmers that walkers were carrying the virus on the soles of their walking boots. The abiding images of that time are of dead cattle burning on pyres; stark illustrations of just how heartbreaking and devastating this outbreak was to those who had farmed all their lives. When the outbreak began, apparently in Northumberland, it appeared to catch the quintessentially urban government unawares. Then as the highly-contagious disease spread from farm to farm, from parish to parish, and then county to county, all the way across England and Wales, with terrible speed, fierce measures were enacted.

Farm tracks were awash with disinfectants; motorists were told to avoid certain of the smaller roads (for fear of the virus being picked up by tyres); and most pressingly to ramblers, thousands upon thousands of footpaths were closed. The paths ran too close to livestock; walkers could conceivably come from anywhere and, according to farmers, walkers were in any case notoriously careless and indeed uncaring about the countryside.

So it was that for a period of months, the countryside in effect closed down. For walkers, this meant not merely the footpaths that ran through fields with animals; but also the picturesque trails, from the Lake District to the South Downs. Meanwhile, to farmers and other rural dwellers alike, the effect was apocalyptic. Not only was there the dread, then the trauma, when livestock showed symptoms of Foot and Mouth; there was also the economic impact, which was nuclear.

Many farmers – through the National Farmers Union – campaigned for footpaths to remain strictly barred throughout the crisis (there were occasional indications of rogue walkers breaking embargos). But those farmers soon found themselves coming under pressure not only from local walking groups, but also the Department for the Environment and indeed local tourist boards. For it was found that the absence of walkers was having a doubly catastrophic effect upon rural economies: bed and breakfasts had no business; little villages found that visitor numbers had dwindled to a trickle. Ironically, then, this was also a crucial moment for the walking movement; for it was at this point that it became abundantly clear just how vital ramblers were now to the rural economy. No matter how much distaste there might have been in certain quarters for people with sticks and cagoules, it was now blazingly apparent that the country needed them.

After about a year, when the raging epidemic had burnt itself out, and after countless thousands of cattle had been slaughtered right the way across the country, the footpaths began to re-open. At first, the process was very cautious, almost polite and hushed, as though a national funeral was taking place; walkers were still advised to avoid, if they could, following routes that led them alongside livestock. Though it was merely coincidence that the right to roam and the ravages of foot and mouth came at the same time, it seemed to some that both things were pointing in the same direction: industrial-scale agriculture was no longer enough to sustain farms or small communities or even entire rural regions. The thought here was: let the walkers walk – why not? Far greater damage had been inflicted upon the land by forces rather larger than rambling enthusiasts. There was a silent capitulation from a great many landowners – and indeed it seemed to some that the future now lay in encouraging as many revenue bearing visitors and walkers as possible. Long sought after walkers' destinations – such as the previously forbidden Chrome Hill in Derbyshire – were now, theoretically, available to all.

Glitches remain of course. Some along the Thames Path, with a few irritating forced diversions. Datchet and Windsor are not the only offending areas; there is a staggeringly vast and ugly Thames Path digression that you must take around the River Darent just outside Dartford in Kent. Meanwhile, the picturesque urban river stroll between Greenwich and Tower Bridge still has several infuriating sections where you are not only obliged to leave the river, but also to walk through some of the most formidably gloomy streets in Europe in order to re-join it. The obstacle to the river in that particular case comes in the form of old naval wharfs that successive governments have taken literally decades to decommission. No offence to the people of Deptford but the Pepys Estate – through which you have to walk instead – does not fill the soul with elation.

Much as you might think, then, that the major battles have all been fought and won, this is still not quite the case. Just as the very notion of a right to roam coalesces and settles in, are there some final fences and barriers that we will never be able to cross? Are we ever going to be able to find any kind of accommodation with those – from motorists to jealous woodland owning landlords – who seek to keep us away from their own dominions? What sort of future can we imagine for the pursuit of rambling?

CHAPTER 19

From Chilham to Canterbury along the North Downs Way: The Future of Walking and of the Countryside Rolled into one Ancient Pilgrimage

> And specially, from every shires ende
> Of Engelond, to Caunterbury they wend,
> The hooly blisful martir for to seke.

That, at least, was the case in 1387 when Chaucer began to compose the General Prologue for his *Canterbury Tales*. Now, standing in the wilfully quaint village square of Chilham in Kent – with its half-timbered buildings, white weatherboarded houses, eighteenth-century manor house at one end and old church at the other – I can see visitors from shires further than Chaucer would have imagined. These pilgrims from around the world may be broadly secular and their goal may simply be the chalking up of another sight. Even so, the nature of their journey takes on a deeper dimension when they leave the car and set off on foot.

There are some walks that seem to us so familiar that we are in danger of overlooking them altogether. The North Downs way – or, as it becomes at some stages, the old Pilgrims Road – is one that anyone who lives in the south will think that they know already. Orchards, hops, woods, spires: is there more? So instead, people go haring off in other directions, in search of greater novelty and more unusual sights. Yet this particular seven-mile section of pathway not only perfectly illustrates how landowners and walkers have found some sort of new understanding; it also, slyly, offers a vision of the future and of the past conjoined. It is a future in which walkers have a far greater part to play than they might ever have thought.

At the time of writing, there is a great deal of disquiet in rural Kent, and across the whole of the South East, concerning the government's plans for new homes. The coalition is seeking to make it easier for houses to be built on greenfield sites. Those who live in villages near these mooted 'extensions' are not merely nervous that their views are going to be ruined, or that their tranquillity is going to be destroyed or that their property values are going to slump. They are also furious that precious land is going to be 'concreted' over. The very idea of taking a rich green meadow, and filling it with semi-detached homes, roads, and pavements, is akin to sacrilege.

This reaction – which seems universal – tells us that the land is no longer seen as a resource to be worked; rather, it is regarded as heritage, needing protection in the way that listed buildings receive it. You will hear the argument with increasing frequency: the land is our legacy. And now, extraordinarily, walkers might be viewed as guardians of that legacy. Imagine the 1932 Kinder Scout trespassers not being pushed back, but instead being invited to open up as many ancient tracks as they can. Imagine then their rights to walk those tracks being absolutely insisted upon by landowners and councils alike. Those trespassers would not have believed it. Yet this is where we are going; ramblers are certain to be co-opted into a new battle for the soul of the countryside. Our walking rights will soon be labelled 'inalienable'. For the more that we appreciate local beauty spots, and elevate them to attractions, abundant with rare species, the harder it will be for property developers to move into such places.

Chilham, with its tempting proximity to high-speed railway lines, is exactly the sort of place that housing ministers must have in mind as they contemplate their housebuilding schemes. Yet the deliberately quaint historical atmosphere – one can almost hear harpsichords in the air in the village square – also seems fragile. It wouldn't take much to snap it. I head down the hill out of Chilham churchyard, along the North Downs Way, and almost immediately straight up another hill towards Old Wives Lees. The mules of Chaucer's day must have found this weary clip-clopping territory. The pale sky above is crisscrossed with white vapour trails. Just over seventy years ago, also in the month of August, those trails had rather more dramatic significance, as those below in the fields of Kent watched the war being fought above their heads. Even now, climbing past the first of many orchards, I find myself wondering how much shrapnel still lies in the soil all around. Recent history always has the sharper edge of emotional resonance.

Even on this most famous of trails, the walker is not entirely at liberty to stray; for some local farmers, barbed wire has clearly been seen as a necessity to guard those rich orchards, the trees of which are now filled with ripening dusty pink and golden apples – the strongest association is that of 1930s schoolchildren scrumping. Walkers, clearly, are just as prone to temptation. For all the historical resonance of this route – all that proud heritage of pilgrims and merchants – the pathway itself only became an official entity in 1978. The Ramblers' Association pushed hard for its creation, and it was eventually officially opened by Dr Donald Coggan, then Archbishop of Canterbury. It was worth it. While it may lack the wild drama that so many walkers from the cities seek, it has an atmosphere that encourages quiet reflection; surely the more prized quality in a path. It is a route that can wholly take one out of oneself. It is exactly this quality that rural campaigners right across the country are bracing themselves to protect. Walkers were once the invaders; now the invaders are bulldozers.

The new fight over the land will be intriguing, as most areas will frantically point to some unique aspect of beauty that would result in it being spared. This path, for instance: I head off down another hill and find myself strolling through a tight pergola formed of lime trees, on either side of which are more of those juicy red orchards. This is where the entire 'Garden of England' cliché comes back to startle the complacent. There is a vast difference between thinking of a Kentish orchard, and actually seeing the thing in all of its mouthwatering beauty before you. As a means of discouraging the scrumper, the pergola is a good idea; I find myself staring through a matrix of twigs and leaves at all those richly laden branches beyond, sagging under the weight of Bramley, Cox, and Empire, and all on a hill overlooking a verdant valley juicy with promise.

There are already many new houses in this area, by which I mean houses dating back to the 1950s. They cling to the slopes of the Downs, dotted along the roads. The housing ministers of Harold Macmillan's day presumably thought that there was nothing especially sacrosanct about this area, so they built extra homes in villages such as Chartham. That presumably means that there could be room for even more houses. Perhaps in that very orchard I have been drooling at.

Even to me, the most committed of town-dwellers, just the idea reverberates with a dull clang of horror. It gives a sudden fresh gravity to that phrase 'Garden of England'. I have never before considered myself much of a rural conservationist. But in none of the many walks I have taken around the country could I have pointed to a place and said: 'Yes. Build here.' Not even on the Thames estuary.

* * *

Now the path continues, ramrod straight, along a valley floor, scything through an insect-buzzing field of pale barley; it gives the impression it has done so for many centuries. The further you go on, the more the real weight of this path's history begins to bear down. There is the tug that Chaucer's assorted knights and millers and pardoners must have felt; that over the crest of the next hill must surely be the towers of Canterbury cathedral?

Even for the most secular walker, it is difficult not to feel it; the thrilling expectation of what lies over the horizon. They might not be motivated by the religious piety of the pilgrims, but nonetheless, the feeling is in its own small way spiritual. On this or any one of thousands of other walks across the country, the rambler will find with each step that his or her frame of mind has been changed, if only minutely. As a church service imposes its own peace and rhythm, so a good walk lifts the mind above the quotidian.

You are walking an impossibly old road. Even if you can't hear the ghosts of pilgrims, you still find yourself staring as though in a trance at those rosy, gold-burnished apples, at the hills upon which so many thousands of these trees are growing, and down into the valley far below, along which runs the River Stour. What would be the point of being here if you did not feel Zephyr's breath and allow your own veins to become bathed in such liquor? This is as much a road for lovers of literature as it is for those of a religious frame. The climax of seeing the cathedral spires is deferred, continually; the ridge of one horizon commands a view of another valley of apples. Even the most anti-religious walker cannot help but be struck by the subliminal associations: Canterbury, and the Eden-like orchards surrounding it. At this time of year, the pickers are poised. The hills around are filled with workers' caravans, a modern day version of the cockney shanty towns that sprang up for the hop picking. This particular farmer is clearly rather more relaxed about us walkers, for I am now insouciantly strolling down the side of an entire forest of apples, trees as short as Shetland ponies, stretching for acres. One can imagine that one is a giant, towering over woodland.

It's difficult for the town-dwelling walker not to stare at all those richly laden branches and try to work out how the business works. How many apples are there here, and how many supermarkets will they be shipped to, and how many people will they be sold to? More: how much will the farmer make, and – even on this great scale – is it really that profitable a concern?

In the latter stages of the twentieth century, farmers were viewed by many urban dwellers as cosseted; producing unnecessary crops in return for vast European subsidies. They were engaged in pretend agriculture; growing things that nobody wanted. Yet these were the same landowners who were aggressively ploughing up footpaths, and building fences across rights of way.

For any walker of my generation – brought up in the 1970s – the whole question of the purpose of countryside like this has been coloured deeply with the nostalgia of old films, and of elderly relatives harking back to a golden age of hedgerows. In this part of Kent, even as late as the 1950s, there would have been carts drawn by horses. In a curious way, this draws us round to the anxieties of today's Council for the Protection of Rural England. It is beset by a terror of loss. Yet this sense of loss has been there since before the start of the twentieth century – all generations since then have fretted in some form about the countryside. Thomas Hardy was in a perpetual depression about the mechanisation of farming, and about the impact it was having on the land.

Now the vulnerability of farmers is more glaringly apparent; rather than being seen as irascible trespass fetishists, they are instead struggling figures working extraordinarily hard simply to keep farms afloat. As a result, the walker treads with more consideration.

The modern pilgrim is close to reaching the end of his road. There is the brief diversion of a DEFRA-supported patch called 'No Man's Orchard' – wrinkly sixty-year old trees, bearing not only Bramley apples, but also the responsibility for harbouring all manner of biodiversity, including moths like the four dotted footman and the satin lutestring, as well as butterflies such as the peacock and the orange tip. Aside from this, the path into Canterbury is tugging the walker back into an all too modern age. It crosses over a dual carriageway; descends past electricity substations, scrubby fields and unfussy suburbs; and at last! As I walk around the edge of a vast roundabout, the spires of the cathedral suddenly materialise into view, about one mile off down a long, tree framed avenue, the perspective and the proportion rather startling.

The structure – from this angle, and with the busy wide road leading up to it – seems gigantic. Yet while the walker is corralled beneath a subway and pops up on the other side in a street of pleasant Victorian terraces, the cathedral disappears again. Indeed, it does not rematerialise in the walker's eyeline until one has beetled the mile into town, and started weaving around the little lanes that surround its precincts.

We are lucky to be in an age where the walker at last has the moral high ground. Our enthusiastic activity brings health and happiness without side-effects. Our carbon footprints are dainty. Where we walk, innkeepers prosper. The clearest indication of the standing of walkers comes when one reads newspaper coverage of fresh disputes involving landowners. All the papers – from the right-wing *Daily Mail* to the left-wing *Guardian* – instantly take the side of the walker. The very notion of trespass – which of course always had a rather wobbly legal footing – now appears a quaint throwback, like smoking on tube trains.

The countryside is richly threaded with loudly proclaimed routes, clamouring for our favour. Here, in Kent, the Garden of England has thrown itself open to us all. How can a walk in these parts not have a temporarily transfiguring effect? It is places like this that make one realise, with a jolt, just how extraordinary the commonplace is.

However, if I were a religious man, and I had been making my way to Canterbury with a serious heart, I would be extremely upset at what I found in the city centre itself. A town that is given over to the pursuit of milking the cathedral crowds; crowds that have already been charged £9 to gain entrance to a once-sombre place of worship and pilgrimage. A place which is now, in essence, less a cathedral and more an over-lit, noisy, sub-Harry Potter theme park with a distended gift shop attached. As a walker, the aesthetic considerations are the same; but there are at least a couple of consolations.

Pilgrims to Canterbury were expected either to do penance or receive a blessing. After seven and a half odd miles, you are entitled at the very least to the blessing of a cup of tea. If not a pint. Both forms of refreshment are almost absurdly well represented in the lanes around the cathedral.

In a more figurative sense, for many dedicated walkers now, the level of access to land all around the country has created countless pilgrimage possibilities; not to shrines or temples, but to previously forbidden areas. There are woodland glades, previously the fiefdom of a privileged few, that can now be tiptoed through by all. There are fresh perspectives to be had from hills that were once closed to climbing. Of course, there are still large stumbling blocks. The creation of a round Britain coastal path – announced in 2009 – will take a number of years, and will be strewn with all manner of obstacles, not least from those who own property by the sea. Then there are the paranoid energy companies, turning land around power stations into Orwellian panopticons, viewed on CCTV from every conceivable angle. This is the modern equivalent of snobbish water boards; now walkers near power stations are presumed to be saboteurs and terrorists. In political terms, the new Conservative-led coalition does not seem to share Labour's enthusiasm for the entire issue of walking, and of free access. But the Ramblers' Association – recently re-branded as 'the

Ramblers' – has all the traction; in the case of the coastal path, it is not if, but when.

Extraordinarily, Britain will be among the first countries where full access to the coast in its entirety will be possible. It is already pretty much the case in Wales. The idea is eye-rubbingly astonishing. Contrast this with the United States, where so much of the coastline is privately owned and fiercely guarded. This will be the really dramatic climax of the Ramblers' work. It is not merely a question of a pressure group winning an argument; it is getting the rest of society to the point where no one could understand how anyone could be opposed to their aims.

Walking has assuredly changed my view of the entire country, and certainly the way that I engage with new landscapes. By which I also mean that I am no longer afraid of cows. As a Londoner, I rarely ventured out beyond the M25. Doing so, to different corners of the country, has deepened my understanding of different regions. I know that I have only dipped a toe in. As a walker, I have not explored either the most secret or most hidden byways; I have tended towards the more popular because, as I say, there is no point in being familiar with a place purely on someone else's terms. Before going there, I had formed a strong image of Kinder Scout, because of the countless accounts from keen fans of the area. Yet not one of these accounts could fully match what I saw and heard for myself. One person's familiar is another person's strange and beguiling.

When you get way from the maddening uniformity of high streets and edge-of-town retail warehouse lands, there is still much to startle, and to jolt one out of clichéd preconceptions. This is also why I increasingly dispense with maps. We currently live in a sat nav superstate; rare is the journey these days that isn't plotted out by some silky voiced android on a tiny screen. But walking is different; it is about freedom, and about the thrill of random choices. Now that we have the opportunity to place our feet on so much land that was previously cut off, why do so through the nagging exactitude of maps? Isn't there more fun doing it the Alfred Watkins way – that is, scrambling to the top of a hill, and taking in all the landmarks for miles around, and trying (and failing) to orientate yourself by them? If, after all, you are walking in ordinary English farmed countryside, then what really are the consequences of getting lost? Starvation? Lunacy? Your crow-pecked bones eventually found in a hedge? This is simply one man's opinion. There are many who rightly adore maps, and can spend hours poring over them, their eyes and their imaginations flickering over all those contour lines.

Walkers now have a moral duty to roam as much, and as widely, as they can. We live in an age of multiple anxieties, but one remarkably constant fear, stretching back decades, is that we are in danger of losing the countryside that we love. That by aggressive speculation, or neglect, or simple ignorance, or by buying cheap food, we are contributing to the destruction of fields, of precious habitats, of rare, almost extinct species. The encouraging side of this terror, however, is that we have para-doxically entered a golden age of conservation. For every batch of those unwelcome new-build properties on greenfield sites, there are now meadows set aside by farmers especially to encour-age the return of wildflowers, and delicate little known insect species. Meanwhile, impregnable Sites of Special Scientific Interest are now dotted all over the map of the British Isles. Old woodlands in many areas are protected with a ferocity that borders on the medieval. Into the middle of this new covenant with the countryside – a relationship where the town-dwelling visitors show a new and proper level of consideration to those who work and protect the land – strides the walker. They yearn to see rare wildflowers, and listen to the songs of birds thought long gone. They know that in many areas, their feet are there on the soil on condition of good behaviour – whether it is a ripen-ing cornfield or a stretch of protected downland. You will find that walkers treading the edges of bio-diverse marshes show more quiet reverence, and more lightfooted delicacy and respect, than any of the noisy visitors who throng modern day Canterbury Cathedral.

The fear that we are losing our native natural wonders is having the effect of propelling large numbers of walkers out into all corners of the countryside. The beneficial result is that they bring with them revenue that, in a virtuous circle, helps provide further protection for those wonders. We modern walkers are also unconsciously honouring the rambling pioneers; those nineteenth-century working class men and women who headed out on Sundays into the open, noting as they did all the botanical and geological splendour. Not to mention the 1932 Kinder Scout trespassers, who were not afraid to face prison sentences in their struggle to establish natural justice: that the open acres of the country should be free to all.

Generations have fought very hard, and with amazing persistence, to throw open those fields and meadows and river paths and coastal walks and great long moorland yomps. The best we can do is to get out there, enjoy them to the hilt, and ensure that the generations to come enjoy them too.

ENDNOTES

CHAPTER 1

1. Daniel Defoe, *A Tour of The Whole Island of Great Britain* (published in several volumes from 1724–1727)
2. Tom Stephenson, *Forbidden Land: The Struggle for Access to Mountain and Moorland* (Manchester University Press, 1989)
3. —, ibid.
4. Marion Shoard, *This Land is Our Land* (Paladin, 1987)
5. *The Journeys of Celia Fiennes* (Cresset Press, 1947)

CHAPTER 2

1. William Wordsworth, *A Guide Through The Districts of the Lakes in the North of England* (first published 1810, supplementary essays in later edns; (R. Hart Davis, 1951)
2. Celeste Langan, *Romantic Vagrancy – Wordsworth and the Simulation of Freedom* (Cambridge University Press, 1985)
3. Marion Shoard, op. cit.
4. Lord Pearson of Rannoch, interviewed in *The Herald* newspaper (30 September 2002)
5. Timothy Brownlow, *John Clare and the Picturesque Landscape* (Oxford University Press, 1983)

CHAPTER 3

1. Harvey Taylor, *A Claim on the Countryside* (Keele University Press, 1997)

2. Sir Leslie Stephen *Men, Books and Mountains* (Hogarth Press, 1956 edn)
3. A. N. Wilson, *The Victorians* (Random House, 2002)
4. A. H. Sidgwick, *Walking Essays* (Edward Arnold, 1912)
5. Harvey Taylor, op. cit.

CHAPTER 4
1. Celeste Langan, op. cit.

CHAPTER 5
1. William Crossing, *A Guide To Dartmoor* (A. Wheaton and Co, 1914)
2. Sabine Baring Gould, *A Book of Dartmoor* (Methuen, 1923)
3. J. B. Priestley, *English Journey* (Victor Gollancz, 1934)
4. Tom Stephenson, op. cit.
5. Stephen Sedley, 'Plimsoll's Story' in *London Review of Books* (28 April 2011)
6. As quoted by Tom Stephenson in *Forbidden Land*

CHAPTER 6
1. Alfred Wainwright, *Fell-Wanderer* (Frances Lincoln, 1966, with subsequent adumbrated edns)
2. As quoted in Hunter Davies, *Wainwright – The Biography* (Michael Joseph, 1995)
3. William Wordsworth, *A Guide Through the Districts of the Lakes* (1951 edn, with supplementary essays)
4. ——, ibid.

CHAPTER 7
1. Dylan Thomas as quoted by Jonathan Mulland in *Gower* (Collins, 2006)
2. ——, ibid.
3. A. H. Sidgwick, op. cit.

CHAPTER 8
1. Timothy Brownlow, op. cit.
2. As quoted by Patrick Wright in *The Thames* (BBC Books, 1999)
3. Joseph Conrad, *The Mirror of the Sea*, collected essays (first published 1906)

CHAPTER 10
1. Dennis Potter, *The Changing Forest – Life in the Forest of Dean* (Secker and Warburg, 1962)
2. W. G. Hoskins, *The Making of the British Landscape* (Hodder and Stoughton, 1955)
3. Oliver Rackham, *Ancient Woodland – History, Vegetation and Uses in England* (Edward Arnold, 1980)
4. G. M. Trevelyan, foreword to *Walking Tours and Hostels in England* (Country Life, 1936)
5. ——, *An Autobiography, and Other Essays* (Longman, 1949)
6. ——, foreword to *Walking Tours*, op. cit.

CHAPTER 12
1. Tom Stephenson, op. cit.
2. Ibid.
3. Ibid.
4. Harvey Taylor, op. cit.
5. Ibid.
6. Ibid.
7. Ibid.
8. Norman Davies, *The Isles* (Macmillan, 1999)
9. Marion Shoard, op. cit.

CHAPTER 13
1. Marion Shoard, *The Theft of the Countryside* (Paladin, 1980)
2. Thomas Hardy, *Jude the Obscure*, book I, chapter 3 (first published 1895, Penguin edition 1984)

3. Celeste Langan, op. cit.

4. Matthew Hollis, *Now All Roads Lead To France* (Faber and Faber, 2011)

CHAPTER 15

1. Greg Bright, *The Great Hole Maze*, introduction (Fontana, 1975)

2. H. H. Munro, *The Music on the Hill* (first published in 1911)

CHAPTER 16

1. Marion Shoard, *Right To Roam* (Oxford University Press, 1999)

2. Affleck Gray, *The Big Grey Man of Ben McDhui* (Impulse Publications, 1970)

3. William Hazlitt, *Selected Essays* (Unworth Press, 1956)

4. Robert Louis Stevenson, *Across the Plains: With Other Memories and Essays* (Chatto and Windus, 1892 edn)

5. A. H. Sidgwick, op. cit.

6. Lewis Crassic Gibbon, *Sunset Song* (first published 1933)

CHAPTER 18

1. As quoted by Marion Shoard in *Right to Roam*, op. cit.

FURTHER READING

Belloc, Hilaire *The Old Road* (Constable, 1910)

Clare, John *The Journey From Essex*, ed. Ann Tibble (Carcanet New Press, 1980)

Cobbett, William *Rural Rides* (Penguin Classics reprint)

Davies, Hunter *Wainwright – The Biography* (Michael Joseph, 1995)

Davies, Norman *The Isles* (Macmillan, 1999)

Deakin, Roger *Wildwood: A Journey Through Trees* (Hamish Hamilton, 2007)

Defoe, Daniel *A Tour of the Whole Island of Great Britain* (Penguin Classics reprint)

Gray, Thomas *Thomas Gray's Journal Of His Visit to the Lake District in October 1769* (Liverpool University Press, 2001)

Hoskins, W. G. *The Making of the English Landscape* (Hodder and Stoughton, 1955)

Jarvis, Robin *Romantic Writing and Pedestrian Travel* (Macmillan, 1997)

Landry, Donna *The Invention of the Countryside: Hunting, Walking and Ecology in English Literature 1671–1831* (Palgrave, 2001)

Mabey, Richard *The Unofficial Countryside* (Collins, 1973)

Macfarlane, Robert *The Wild Places* (Granta, 2007)

Orwell, George *The Road To Wigan Pier* (Victor Gollancz, 1937)

Priestley, J. B. *English Journey* (Victor Gollancz, 1934)

Pryor, Francis *The Making of the British Landscape – How We Have Transformed The Land From Prehistory to Today* (Allen Lane, 2010)

Rackham, Oliver *Trees and Woodland in the British Landscape* (Dent, 1976)

Reed, Michael *The Landscape of Britain – From Beginning to 1914* (Routledge, 1990)

Robinson, Jeffrey Cane *The Walk: Notes on a Romantic Image* (Dalkey Archive Press, 2006)

Sebald, W. G. *The Rings of Saturn* (The Harvill Press, 1998)

Shoard, Marion *This Land is Our Land* (Paladin, 1987)

Stephenson, Tom *Forbidden Land: The Struggle For Access To Mountain and Moorland* (Manchester University Press, 1989)

Wainwright, Alfred *Wainwright's Coast to Coast Walk* (Michael Joseph, 1987)

Wainwright, Alfred *Wainwright On the Pennine Way* (Michael Joseph, 1985)

Wallace, Anne D. *Walking, Literature and English Culture: The Origins and Uses of The Peripatetic in the 19th Century* (Clarendon, 1993)

Watkins, Alfred *The Old Straight Track: Its Mounds, Beacons, Moats, Sites and Mark Stones* (Methuen, 1925)

Williams, Raymond *The Country and the City* (Hogarth Press, 1985)

Williams-Ellis, Clough *England and the Octopus* (1928, Portmeirion Bles reprint 1975)

Wu, Duncan *Wordsworth: An Inner Life* (Blackwell, 2002)

ACKNOWLEDGEMENTS

With many thanks for everything – wise judgements, shrewd thoughts and all – to Mark Richards and Louise Haines at 4th Estate; Robin Harvie, for the same; Katharine Reeve for her excellent editing; to Robin Price and Michele Cefai for the happy Ivinghoe strolls; to veteran rambler John Bunting, for inviting me to Sheffield to share his fascinating memories of a past long gone, and to Kate Ashbrook, rambling campaigner extraordinaire; to Ivo Dawnay of the National Trust for putting me in touch with rural wildlife enthusiasts; to Mark Spencer, botanical expert, for some sound advice; to Rachel Simhon, for the extraordinary Rannoch coincidence; and to Ben Mason, top literary agent, whose idea this was in the first place.